Welcome, Madam!

To Holly
on your 21st
birthday. May all
your dreams come
true.

E. Charlese Spencer

Love,
Aunt Donna
&
Uncle Dana

Welcome, Madam!

Published by Iceni Books™.
610 East Delano Street, Suite 104
Tucson, Arizona 85705, U.S.A.
www.icenibooks.com

ISBN: 1-58736-552-9
LCCN: 2005909429

This book is lovingly dedicated to Rev. and Mrs Raymond Hudson, who took me in as a daughter more times than I can count. They deserve my reward in heaven for all the cars they've loaned me on furloughs.

ACKNOWLEDGEMENTS

FOR PERUSAL OF CHAPTERS to make them more authentic I am grateful to Franklin McCorkle and the late Harold Lehmann, (two former Mission Committee chairmen) and their wives; my nurse co-worker, Helen Kopp; David M. Nabegmado and Susan P. Adam, who read for African facts and spelling; many Africans completed forms I sent by way of John and Amonna Sue Goodwin.

TABLE OF CONTENTS

FOREWORD

April 2003 Albuquerque, New Mexico: Rev. and Mrs. R. Kenneth George, Superintendent of the New Mexico District Council of the Assemblies of God, Inc. 1993 to present:

I<small>T WAS A TYPICAL</small> West African day, hot and dry. We were making our way from the coast toward the northern part of Ghana. A missionary was driving the British-made SUV, which was loaded with people and supplies. The road was unpaved and rough, so the pace was slow.

As we rounded a corner, I saw a road block; this was not uncommon in West Africa. It seemed that every few miles we faced an "official" roadblock. As the vehicle slowed to a stop, the dust boiled up from the dry road. It rose up into the car and the passengers held their breath or covered their face with a cloth, waiting for the dust cloud to settle.

Out of the guard house came a tall, thin African officer. He was dressed in a uniform and he certainly looked official. As he prepared to inspect our papers, he stooped over and looked into the vehicle. At that moment, he spotted Missionary Charlese Spencer. All at once, he forgot why he had stopped us as he ran to the other side of the car shouting, "Madam Spencer, Madam Spencer, Madam Spencer!" A big smile broke across his handsome face; tears began to flow from his eyes. It was obvious that he was thrilled to see the nurse who had delivered him when he was born and who had brought the Gospel message to his family and tribe. I later learned that this young policeman had even legally changed his first name to Spence.

Yes, Missionary "Madam" Spencer had returned home! I quickly realized that this entire trip was going to be a big celebration.

Many years before, God had called a wonderful young woman out of the hills of New Mexico and had brought her to Ghana, West Africa. She had prepared herself; she had become a minister of the Gospel, as well as an expert health care practitioner. Ghana! The land of her calling! This is the land that God opened to Missionary Spencer and her missionary colleagues to bring about a mighty move of God.

It was my privilege to bring her back to Ghana for a visit, as she once again brought courage and love to the national Church. At the time of this trip, I was her pastor at Albuquerque's First Family Church, as well as the Assistant District Superintendent. Moreover, as her health became more fragile, I could see that she was about to give up the notion of ever returning to the land of her calling. One day as I visited her in an Albuquerque hospital, I promised that I would personally take her back to Ghana.

The people of First Family Church, especially Mr. and Mrs. Richard C. Bonney, gave the money so that I could keep my promise. I will never forget the way we were received by the beautiful West African people. Each place we went godly Christians, many of who had become high government and tribal officials, met us. All of them were hoping and praying for Madam Spencer to stay with them and never leave again.

There were many tears as we explained that this great missionary could not stay, even though she dearly longed to do so. I know, when we get to Heaven, Sister Charlese Spencer will be difficult for most of us to reach because an army of beautiful black brothers and sisters will surround her. That will be the day that their prayers are answered. They will never again be separated from their beloved 'Madam

Spencer' nor from their Lord and Savior, Jesus Christ. They will live forever throughout eternity, together praising their Lord.

As you read this account of the life and ministry of Sister Charlese Spencer, I know you will be blessed, just as I was blessed as I read it.

Sincerely,
R. Kenneth George,
District Superintendent, NMDC, Inc.

Introduction

People in Africa, America, and England encouraged me to write. If my efforts make you laugh or cry, I will have succeeded; that seemed to be the constant norm for the twenty-five years I was involved in Africa. My childhood had a lot of the unusual, as I grew up in the "American wild, wild, West." It prepared me for West Africa. Many Americans and others are just now discovering both, and seem to like what they have found!

I supported chiefs, fathers, pastors, and young men to rescue a young girl from a fetish group who buys or trades for girls when they are born. The girls have no choices or rights for education, occupation, or marriage their entire life! Many people heard about one of these; few know I helped with a second rescue. Readers may laugh, cry, agree, disagree, be surprised, or even be shocked! So, fact or fiction, this is how I remember it!

Chapter One

Big Palaver

On October 7, 1954 my nurse co-worker, Helen Kopp, and I awoke in the geographical location that we had dreamed of, fulfilling years of preparation. She from Pennsylvania and I from New Mexico had just completed fourteen months of midwifery training in England. Our ship was anchored in the Gulf of Guinea, just offshore at the Gold Coast, our destination! Other ships had the small dock crowded. We were told that a larger harbor was being built at Tema, nearer to their industry and capitol city of Accra. We could see Takoradi, a town sprawled among the coastal hills covered by flowers, palm trees, and other tropical greenery. Later that morning, our ship was allowed to dock. Africans came aboard to help us down a precarious ramp to solid ground. One took Helen's hand; then another reached for my hand and said, "Welcome, Madam." Several Africans brought our bicycles and other freight down the same way. They had done this hundreds of times before. Helen never let me forget that she got to Africa before me; she was first down the ramp.

In a huge metal customs shed, much like an airplane hanger, the contents of our cartons were examined. I paid ten shillings to bring in the army surplus, wind-up record player, a last-minute gift from my nephew, Jim, as I left the United States of America. No missionary was there to meet us, but African customs officials knew what to do. One said, "No *big palaver*, Madam." He helped us phone the mission residence in Takoradi. When we got no answer, he said, "Madam, this may be one big palaver; I heard the missionary was going to America." The phrase *big palaver* was becoming a problem to me. Did it refer to all unusual happenings or just the negative ones? The customs men discussed the train schedule to Kumasi, the next nearest large town; there should be a missionary there. In checking our freight, one of the customs officials saw a tatting shuttle and asked about it. Helen said, "I'll show you." We had just learned it in England. She and the man were sitting on one of her trunks in the midst of a tatting session when two missionary wives arrived. Mrs. Wood and a visiting Mrs. Peterson said their husbands had gone north to Kumasi on business. The customs official said, "Palaver finish!" The missionary men had anticipated being back in time to meet us, but our ship had departed Amsterdam one day early. We were so anxious to get to the Saboba Clinic! We had been assured that would be our home for the next three years. It was best we did not know how long that would be!

The Woods and their children, Kitty and Jimmy, were truly leaving on furlough immediately. We learned that Paul and Virginia Weidman and their daughter, Faith, would replace the Woods family. Their son, John, would stay for school in the United States. African words flew at me; my brain ached! Names of people left my mind within minutes. Saltpond, Accra, Kumasi, Yeji, and Tamale were towns; the last one sounded like the food I ate in New Mexico!

Our first night in Takoradi could hardly be called a good night's sleep. The excitement, strangeness of sounds such as the crashing waves on a nearby beach, smells, and our talking kept us wide-eyed. Then a wake-up bell rang and we scrambled into our clothes. At breakfast, we were introduced to paw-paw (papaya), a fruit new to us. Helen's one-liner was, "Paw-paw, a good name; tastes just like Paw-paw's dirty feet smell."

It was truly difficult for the Woods family to have *strangers*, as the Africans called us, because they were indeed packed to go to America. We needed to move on! Helen said she had promised her mother she would not fly, but no train ran from Takoradi to Accra, the capitol city. We were booked to fly east to Accra on a freight plane. They prepared seats only for the passengers expected; we were the only two that day. The *flying elephant*, as it was locally called, rattled and trembled until it left the ground. Helen grasped my arm so hard it pinched me and she said, "To be absent from the body is to be present with the Lord." We heard what sounded like freight tumbling until we got to an elevation where the plane leveled off. I am not too keen on flying, so this was surely one *big palaver*! We had just gotten settled when the fifty-five miles were behind us and we descended into Accra; freight rolled the opposite direction.

The Elvis Davis family met us at the airport in Accra. His father, F.D. Davis, had signed my Bible School Diploma at Southwest Assembly of God College in Texas; I did not know he had a son in Africa. Elvis, as business manager, taxied us for days to register as aliens, nurses, and midwives, and each of us got a driver's license. One day we saw a baby floating face down in a lagoon; people were watching it. Now surely this was one *big palaver*! Elvis reported it to the nearest police station and we continued our errands.

On Sunday, we attended our first church service in the Gold Coast. The African pastor, Rev. Martin, preached in the morning service. An African man asked for prayer about putting away his wife because they had no child. A lady wanted prayer, as she had borne eight children and only two were living. These kinds of prayer requests were new to me; my heart ached and I felt God really cared. Elvis spoke in the evening service. It was a farewell for the Woods family;

they had followed us the next day by that same freight plane from Takoradi.

An African man brought his wife to the mission house for us nurses to examine. It seems he also wanted to ask us for a job at Saboba. He wanted seven pounds per month (about twenty dollars) salary. We were advised that was too much. We knew very little about hiring, except that we better get to Saboba and discover what was needed before we hired anyone. For an outing one evening, the Davis family drove us to the airport and we watched a Pan American plane take off for New York. What a feeling of ambivalence! My natural self longed to be on that plane, but no amount of money could have persuaded me to go. I felt at peace where I was. After registering at the U.S. Embassy, we boarded a train to Kumasi. It was mostly uphill and the coal smoke poured into the open windows; we became sooty-black. I thought, "All visitors should travel by train through this beautiful, lush Ashanti Forest where it stops at every little village." People in colorful clothing were talking loudly while bringing their wares onto the train or taking them off. The Ziemann family, Edwin, Bernice and two daughters, Marilyn and Patty, met us in Kumasi. There was a small African boy with them. They called him Baba (Old Man) and seemed to be very fond of him. We learned that the people, forest, and language could all be loosely called Ashanti. However, the trade language was Twi (Chuee). Each sub-tribe in the Ashanti Forest has its own language dialect and chief.

On Saturday, Helen and I walked into town and shopped at Indian stores and the outdoor market. Food, food! There were bananas, pineapples, coconuts, avocados, grain, and tubers. We were in Kumasi eight days. This allowed us to attend services in the huge new Central Church; it had not yet been dedicated. An African minister gave a sermon in English and it was interpreted into two dialects. They sang in English and several dialects. I noticed Helen singing along with them, yet I could not understand a word. I listened. She was singing, "Charley stomped on Paw-paw's toe; Charley stomped on Paw-paw's toe." It fit very well into the tune of *We Shall Reach Jerusalem!*

Two missionary men, Franklin McCorkle and Bronnie Stroud, came through Kumasi while we were there. I had met Franklin McCorkle and his wife, Aniece, at Southwestern in Texas in the mid-1940s when they were first itinerating to raise money to go to Africa. At that time, I had no idea we would someday be in the same part of Africa. Franklin was the Chairman of the Missionary Field Fellowship Committee and Bronnie Stroud, Secretary-Treasurer. The African Church was young, so these men served as officials of the Gold Coast Assemblies of God. I had not met Bronnie Stroud. Franklin and Bronnie had been to the port at Takoradi to receive mission freight since the Woods had gone on furlough. It may have been our freight; we did not know where it was at the moment. It had been crated and stored over a year. The two men kept calling unfamiliar names of people and towns like Bawku, Walewale, Gambaga, and Kumbungu, on and on. When I heard, "Vivan and Dorothy Smith at Nakpanduri," that sounded familiar! (I was first asked to go to Africa with Dorothy Buck, but she married Vivan Smith about that time so the mission called me to come meet Helen.) McCorkle and Stroud tried to continue north to Tamale that same evening, but could not find a plane, bus, or market lorry with space available, so they stayed the night with the Ziemanns. We were learning that missionaries had to be ready for any eventuality. The next morning, the men went north by government transport, a bus. That evening, Edwin Ziemann phoned Franklin McCorkle in Tamale to be sure the men got there and to tell them that Helen and I would follow the very next day by the same mode of travel.

Now that mode of travel was *big palaver* for me. We were packed into a bus so tightly that we were sweating profusely and we could not be sure whose sweat was running down our legs, nor indeed, if it were truly sweat, as there were babies everywhere. The bus made a rest stop only once before we got to the Volta River. All exited the bus, but we saw no restroom. We observed that as the people walked a short way from the bus, the women squatted, their long flowing skirts providing privacy. The men turned their backs and emptied their bladders. We took one look at this palaver and decided to brave the pythons among the lush forest. The Africans were amazed at our stupidity, but we came back alive. At the Volta River, we got out again. The bus had to wait for a ferryboat to come back to the south side of the river, so we had time to let the air dry our bodies and clothing. The children became friendly and teased us. We saw food cooking in large black pots, so we bought some that looked familiar like rice, beans, and plantain. The bus was driven onto the flat barge along with other vehicles. We walked on with the other passengers. Our bodies cooled off a bit as the barge reached mid-river. The Volta River was not very wide in 1954; it only took about thirty minutes to cross. There was one more rest stop before we got to Tamale but no more lush forest. We found an anthill taller than our heads and went to investigate while all others were squatting and turning their backs. We lost several pounds that day, as our water ran out about noon. *And did we learn anything?*

In Tamale, we met the McCorkle family: Franklin, Aneice, and three-year-old Amonna Sue. We met young Nimboo, an efficient African man who worked for the McCorkles and other missionaries for many years. Our anticipated mail was not in Tamale! We had received none since leaving England, over forty days. It was being sent to Saboba Clinic. Dewey Hale, the present Saboba resident, had come to Tamale recently, but forgot to bring our mail. I was chewing nails and spitting rivets, as I needed to know whether my sister's new baby, in California, was a boy or girl. I was sure it was born while we were aboard ship.

To lower my frustration about not getting to Saboba, I made an entire dress for Aneice. We were told that Dewey,

Naomi, and little Stevie were living in the house that we were to occupy in Saboba. Naomi Hale was a nurse, but not a midwife. She had filled in until we completed our midwifery training in England and could get to Saboba. While they were being moved forty miles to Yendi, we would get to know other areas and missionaries. That made sense, so *palaver finish*. Well, not quite! The next day the McCorkles drove us sixty miles north to Walewale, a town in the Mamprusi Tribe; the people spoke Mampruli. Two single ladies, Adeline Wichman and Pauline Smith, were stationed there, but were in the United States on furlough; they would return soon. We drove another sixty miles through Gambaga, the county seat of the East Mamprusi District, to Nakpanduri Clinic where the Bimoba Tribe spoke Muar. Vivan and Dorothy (Buck) Smith supervised that clinic. Vivan spoke Mori, the language of the Mosi Tribe in Upper Volta, where he had lived many years before marrying Dorothy. That was another country less than one hundred miles north of Nakpanduri village, so Bimobas could understand his Mori language. People and towns were gradually meaning more than just words to me. Helen and I were told that whatever the Africans said to us when we first met them, we should answer, "Naa." The intonation curves down. They seldom say anything to you until they have completed the polite greetings. Your answer to each question in the greeting can be, "Naa." It loosely means, "Fine," or "Okay," an acknowledgment of their greeting.

The McCorkles, Helen, and I stayed overnight in Nakpanduri and the next morning they took us forty miles north to Bawku. Bronnie Stroud, whom we had met in Kumasi, Annabelle, his wife, and their two children, Judy and John, lived there. The residents of Bawku were of the Kusasi Tribe and spoke Kusal. We visited, ate lunch in Bawku, and returned to Nakpanduri. The next day was Sunday. Franklin McCorkle spoke in the morning worship. He preached in Dagbani, the Tamale trade language; many of the northern tribes understand it. It was interpreted into English for us. He asked a question of the congregation, "How many of you accepted Christ as your Savior over five years ago?" No hands were raised. The Nakpanduri Clinic first opened March 21, 1951. The mission officials had staffed it with Nurse Betty June Shackleton and Nurse-midwife Hilda Eichen, both Americans. When they returned to America, two British nurse-midwives, Ann Symonds and Rebecca Davison, were placed in Nakpanduri. They had transferred to the Assemblies of God from another mission. At the time of our arrival, the British nurses were on furlough in England, so Vivan and midwife Dorothy were at the Nakpanduri Clinic; they were almost newlyweds! McCorkles returned to Tamale Sunday afternoon and left us to learn about African clinics from Dorothy Smith.

On the following Monday morning, we helped treat one hundred sixty-five people at the general clinic. Nyankpen, a Bimoba worker, was the Muar interpreter. On Tuesday morning, twenty-one women came for the antenatal clinic. They called it *conception day*, a misnomer and they knew it. Some of the women came clad in one or two tufts of leaves attached, in front and/or back, to a circle of braided grass around the hips. If only one tuft, then it was in the back for modesty when they worked on the farm or did other chores that require stooping. The chlorophyll in the leaves was beneficial as we checked for height of the fundus, fetal heartbeat, and did other procedures. I heard Dorothy tell one woman to get fresh leaves.

My diary reads, "On Wednesday after general clinic we went looking for the crocodile we had seen near a small bridge when the McCorkles brought us into Nakpanduri." An African told us the crocodile was *sweet chop*; that meant good for food. For five days, my diary said we looked for the crocodile, but came back with one or more rabbits. On the sixth day, we saw two crocodiles. Vivan shot, but somehow missed. We went home and all four of us were in their front room. As Vivan cleaned his gun, he related stories of hunting many years for meat for the Mosi people up north. As he talked, his gun discharged and a bullet went through their roof; he thought the gun was empty! He felt shaken about the incident and said he was going to get rid of his guns. At that moment, a visitor at the front door clapped his hands and called, "Agoo!" They do not knock; their houses are mud and the doors are straw. The visitor had a message from the local chief, "Do not shoot those particular crocodiles, as they are sacred." They represented his ancestors. We were grateful that Vivan had missed and the Bimobas were grateful for the rabbits we had brought them to eat. One possibly *big palaver* had become *finish palaver*!

One day, the Smiths drove us about twenty miles to the Gambaga Police Station. We made radio contact with the Tamale police. They could contact Franklin McCorkle about our return to Tamale. We were impatiently waiting to get to our own station and our mail. That major question still existed; did I have a new niece or nephew in San Diego? Franklin said we were to come to Tamale on November 16; that was ten more days. He also told us our freight had arrived in Takoradi from New York, but my gun was confiscated and kept in Custom's storage until my import license was found; I wondered who lost it. After that, when anyone mentioned our missing post (mail), I would jump to my feet and pace the floor in mock furor. I told them as long as they talked about post, it would affect me that way. We did want our mail, but we allowed it to become humor for everyone. When I would start the pacing, someone would say, "Poor thing, she has been in the tropics only a month. What will she be like in three years? Maybe we should request an immediate furlough!"

We continued to help at Nakpanduri clinics: general outpatient, prenatal, deliveries, leprosy treatment, snakebites, and other emergencies. One of the emergencies involved about twenty-five young men who had gone to a neighboring village to retrieve a girl whom they said had been stolen from their village. I understood this was quite common. They got the girl, but the clinic workers had the job of sewing them up. The man who stole the girl already had four wives. He went to jail, was tried, and sentenced by an English District Commissioner. Self-government was coming to the Gold Coast in less than three years; I wondered how similar situations would be resolved then. It made me think about my gun. I had applied for an import license for my 0.22 rifle three months prior. I would feel sad to lose the gun provided for me in New Mexico. It was perfect for meat like rabbit and guinea fowl.

Some missionaries used mosquito nets over their beds; the Smiths did not. One morning I counted over fifty mosquito bites on my legs below my knees. I wished for a tub of ice water to stand in for relief. We pledged to sleep under nets in Saboba! Now that we knew our freight was in the country, we were more anxious than ever to get to our own house. A surveyor, a single man from England, had been eating his meals with the Smiths and us. Dorothy teased us by saying the government doctor who would periodically check on our Saboba Clinic operation was also a single man. We decided that life might not be so dull in Africa after all. When the day arrived that we were told to go to Tamale, a local woman in labor was having difficulty. Dorothy had Vivan transport her forty miles north to the Bawku hospital and return, before we four went one hundred twenty miles to Tamale. There our mail was waiting for us! It was two months from the day we left England. My hands were shaking as I opened my sister's letter. My new nephew, David Edward III, had been born September 22. In retrospect, on that date, we had been in the basement of a church in Bordeaux, France "diagnosing mummies for cause of death." Nobody but nurses!

I wrote home, "Just think, David was almost two months old before I knew he had arrived. We knew there would be times like this. My mission would find me for such as a death message. We mailed Christmas cards to America in November while we had the time. Mail was now *"finish palaver."* Well, not quite! The McCorkles said we should stay with them for two celebrations and then they would take us to Saboba. November 23 was graduation day at the Northern Ghana Bible College in Kumbungu, eleven miles north of Tamale. American Thanksgiving Day would be two days later. Two American families lived in Kumbungu to teach in the Bible School. Wheeler and Eilene Anderson, with their children, Alice and Paul, lived in the old bungalow; it had been there many years. Floyd and Grace Thomas with their three daughters, Diana, Ruth, and Judy, lived in what was called the new bungalow. As we ate a meal with the Thomas family, we talked about meeting them in London just eight months prior, when they were passing through. In addition, I had long known Grace's bother and family, the Rev. Everett Smiths, pastoring in New Mexico.

Later that day, we were at the Anderson's home in Kumbungu when Dewey Hale appeared from Saboba. He had flown his plane to Tamale Airport and taken a taxi to Kumbungu. He said there was a woman at the Saboba Clinic having difficulty delivering and that Charles Greenaway's son was very ill in (French) Dahomey, east of British and French Togoland. He needed two nurses STAT! Helen and I got in the taxi with a man we had known for less than fifteen minutes. I thought, "Why is all this happening so fast when we have been in limbo so long?" It felt a bit like being kidnapped, as Helen and I seemed to have had little part in the decision. In Tamale, the taxi stopped at the mission house just long enough to get our suitcases, and we were off to the airport. To see Africa from a small low-flying plane was awesome! I had seen pictures, but the short trees, sparse bush, and dry creek beds looked as though no human could survive there. The clusters of thatch-roofed, round, mud houses reminded me of toadstools. As we flew along in this one engine, three-passenger plane, Dewey said he would drop one of us off in Saboba to help his wife deliver the woman in difficult labor, and he would fly the other one to French Dahomey. It seems they feared the Greenaway child could have polio. We three agreed that Helen should go to Dahomey. Poor Helen, she was being forced to fly again; I was glad her mother did not know!

When the small plane landed on the dusty runway in Saboba, I saw an aluminum-roofed airplane hanger, an unfinished house, and an open Jeep with a woman driver. My suitcase and I exited the plane and entered the Jeep. Naomi Hale, Dewey's wife, introduced herself as we sped a mile up the dusty road to the clinic. We heard the plane fly away. At the Saboba Clinic, I met Gylima, the head clinic worker, and the woman I was to help deliver. She was a walk-in, with little history available and no prenatal care. This was her seventh pregnancy; two had died as newborn infants. She had a cystocele large enough to prevent the head from descending. I was using an interpreter for the first time in my life to deliver a baby. My diary says, "We emptied her bladder and after some swelling subsided, we delivered the baby one hour after I got to Saboba. Mother and baby were exhausted but alive."

The family asked me to give the baby a name, along with her African name. I called her Lois after Timothy's Grandmother in the Bible. The baby's father clapped his hands while stooping slightly, a common gesture of *thank you*, and said, "A ni le tuln, paa." Literally, "Thank you for your hard work." He left and then returned to *dash* us a chicken and some eggs to complete the act of gratitude. The term *dash* was used to mean a tip, handfuls on purpose, or the thirteenth item in a baker's dozen. It was his way of doing what he could. I was emotional.

When the mother and baby were stabilized, Naomi and I walked about one-half a city block to the Saboba mission bungalow. She introduced me to her two-year-old son, Stevie, and his black nanny, Mama Sarah. What a precious little boy, and Mama Sarah was a delight. I was directed to a three-quarter bed on a screened-in porch where I would sleep. I wondered where Helen was going to sleep. The next morning, I went with Naomi to the clinic. I felt alone and nostalgic in a crowd of Konkombas as I treated and wrapped ninety tropical ulcers. This was not how I had planned to start my life in Africa. After two days, Dewey and Helen arrived from Dahomey on Thanksgiving Day, my youngest brother's birthday. The Greenaway child had broken out with measles, but was still very ill. We learned that the Hales did not plan to move forty miles to Yendi! They planned to move into the unfinished house I had seen near the airplane hanger. The Konkombas were helping to build it; they wanted the Hales *and the airplane* to stay.

The Saboba house was rustic and picturesque, but we could not think of making it home until we were in charge. Our freight would remain in storage until the Hales moved out. We missed our British teatime, but agreed to say nothing; the kitchen would soon be ours. In the meantime, we were living out of our suitcases on the northeast veranda. Yeah! We had a mosquito net like a square tent over one three-quarter bed where we both slept. At night, we tucked the loose edge of the net under the mattress all around. The top of the tent was a sheet that caught lizards if they fell off the rafters. It also caught their droppings and the stones they took up and dropped onto it. The geckoes, with their suction feet, climbed the walls and clicked loudly one to another. One morning at the breakfast table, I saw something go *plunk, plunk* into my coffee. I looked up and there on a rafter was a lizard. That triggered a vow to put ceilings in that house!

One side of our room was the outside rock wall of the house. The rest was a half circle of screen wire; thank God it was not the rainy season. December was well into the dry season, so the dust blew in one side and out the other. It was hot to us, coming from wet London. The temperature on our porch each morning was near eighty degrees Fahrenheit; in the afternoons, it was over one hundred. The only exit from our porch was a window into the Hales' bedroom. We went through their bedroom to the bathroom day or night. The bathroom suite had two rooms. One room was only as wide as the entrance door, but six feet deep. Pushed against the far wall sat a backless wooden box about eighteen inches square, with a round hole in the top, and under the box was a tin bucket. Behind that square box was a little hinged door that opened to the outside. Each morning before dawn, a sanitary engineer came quietly and removed the ten-gallon can through the hinged door, buried the contents, and replaced the tin can. Beside the box was a bucket of ashes containing a shovel. We put sand or ashes in the bottom of the tin can as a deodorant and because we hated the tinkle at our house or when we visited other people's tin cans. However, it was much better than going to the bush. The second room in our bathroom suite was a little bigger, with a cement hand basin and a cement bathtub, which had a hole in the bottom to drain the water onto the ground outside. We stood in the tub, soaped all over, and poured a pan of water over us. We replaced a plug into the drain so a snake would not be in there with us the next time.

Helen and I took more and more responsibility at the clinic so Naomi could pack. We got so extremely busy that I quit writing in my diary. I told many people to save my letters, as they would be my diary; they did and *I am grateful*. Our post office was in Yendi, forty miles away. Our mail came on a market lorry from Yendi every sixth day, in a padlocked eighteen-inch-square wooden box; only Dewey had a key. He removed the mail and sent the locked box back to the Yendi postman on the market lorry. One night our mail came after 9 P.M. We took it to bed, tucked in our net and read by flashlight for over an hour. Only the gnats were small enough to sneak in. Helen made a speech about our great tent cathedral seating ten thousand bugs.

It gave us some comfort to know there was a hospital forty miles away in Yendi, but we flew in and had no proof there was a Yendi. We were told the Yambeteu River, between Saboba and Yendi, often flooded in the rainy season and nothing could cross. The single Dr. Frank Ashworth was located at the Yendi Hospital. He was the District Medical Officer who would visit the Saboba Clinic and evaluate our operation as nurse practitioners. The British Government Administrative Agent in Yendi was also a single man. The major African tribe in Yendi, same as in Tamale, was Dagomba and their language was Dagbani. In fact, the Palace of the Yaa Naa, the Dagomba Paramount Chief, is located in Yendi; it is an important town.

One day, Gylima, the senior orderly-interpreter at the clinic, told me about his tribe. Although he was a Konkomba, his name was the word for *respect or praise* in Dagbani, so they spelled it Dzilma. He was the son of Akonsi, the first Christian in the entire Konkomba Tribe. Before Akonsi moved back to Saboba in his old age, he farmed near Yendi, so his son Gylima was given a Dagomba name. People like the Shirers and Garlocks came south into the Gold Coast from Upper Volta or west from upper Nigeria via Yendi with the Christian message. Gylima said, "Saboba is the main area of the Konkomba people in British Togo, west of the Oti River, but there are many more on the east side of the river in French Togo. Together it is the Betchabob area. The ruling Dagomba tribe on the British side shortened the word Betchabob to Saboba. Our language is called Lekpakpaln. We Konkombas call ourselves Bekpakpam. There are other tribes related to the Konkombas. Some are as far southwest as Demon and filtering south past Yendi. Some are at Yankazia, about sixteen miles northwest of Saboba, two miles west of Wapuli. U Na Febor Jayom is Yankazia Chief, a Christian. He accepted Christ as his blood Sacrifice through the George Andersons at Yendi when Teacher Samson Mankrom was in teacher's training in Yendi. Konkombas are scattered north almost forty miles, interrupted by the Tchakosi tribe at Chereponi, and then infiltrate the Mamprusi tribal area as Kombas. Some live in Gushiago and on up the road almost to the Nakpanduri Clinic area. Anywhere there are Konkombas on the east side of the Oti River in French country, they have infiltrated west across the Oti River into British Togo. Many farm as far south as Salaga, south of Tamale. Africans will tell you, "Salaga is where black men kept captured northern people and sold them to Ashanti Forest tribes. They, in turn, sold them to white men at the coast, so everyone made money." (In the 2000s, TV reporters tragically report that Africans are still enslaving Africans; some are defenseless children!)

Gylima continued his history lesson, "My father, Akonsi, farmed fifty miles south of here, just west of Yendi. During those years, a white government agent in Saboba boasted that the Gospel of Jesus Christ would never be brought to the Konkombas as long as he lived there. The Gold Coast Government built him the house you are now sleeping in; the mission bought it. Konkombas did not understand some of the Government Agent's pressures to collect taxes for roads and schools. For emphasis, one of the Konkomba arrows lodged in his shoulder. Florence Blossom, a missionary in Yendi, helped remove the arrow. My family heard the Good News about Jesus, the Son of God, giving his blood so we do not have to sacrifice the blood of goats and chickens any more. We heard it from the Shirers, Garlocks, Goodwins, and others. My father accepted this good news, moved back to Saboba and helped persuade the Konkombas to ask the Assemblies of God for medical and health providers for the area." Suddenly, Gylima laughed his loud guffaw and went on, "Until we saw the Garlock children, we thought white people came out of the ocean like the fish."

In early 1948, a World War II pre-fab army building was hauled from Accra, the Capitol, almost five hundred miles to Saboba. Mel and Marita McNutt and their children were sent to Saboba to get the building ready to be used as a clinic. The McNutts and the first nurses, Ruby Johnson and Ozella Read, lived in the bungalow previously occupied by that white government agent. For early church services, the nurses used the shade of a kapok tree, the clinic, their garage, and finally a zontamat (thatched) shelter. Gylima, with no formal education, was the only person available in Saboba to help translate the Bible, sermons, and songs from English to Lekpakpaln.

Saboba Town included Chief Quadin's village of Kpata-paab, the mission clinic and bungalow, the market area of Zango and a few other compounds. At that time, many of the first Christians lived down the road about a mile in Toma and Nalongni. Their elders were Akonsi, Beso, Maja, Chief Oden, and their families. Ruby and Ozella planned to build the first church building halfway between Saboba Market and Toma. They asked the people to start carrying head-pans of sand from the Oti River, a mile away. The nurses never saw that church completed. However, they sent a young Konkomba named Salah to Bible School; he felt that God wanted him to become a pastor. After three years of hard work and difficult living conditions, Ruby and Ozella left on furlough to America. Hal and Naomi Lehmann traveled from Tamale to Saboba to help them pack and leave. A bridge over the Yambeteu River between Saboba and Wapuli had washed away. Hal made a pontoon of canoes and metal drums on which the nurses and their luggage crossed safely. They were the Marines! Subsequent nurses to Saboba owe them a debt of gratitude. There were no nurses to replace them; the Konkomba people were without medical aid for a time.

Helen and I were the second nurse-midwives to be assigned to Saboba for a full three-year term. Besides being *kidnapped* to get to Saboba in November 1954, Helen and I were almost prisoners once we got there. We had no vehicle. We never flew in Dewey's plane again, as he charged over two dollars an hour. The Hales were not anxious to lose us again, so they never offered to take us anywhere. They knew we were not hungry; our mail was brought to us and we had a congenial, working friendship with them. On December 8, 1954, Rev. F. W. McCorkle, our Field Chairman, and Rev. J.O. Savell, the Assistant Superintendent at our headquarters in Springfield, Missouri, drove the one hundred miles from Tamale to Saboba. Rev. Savell wanted to see the Saboba Clinic in operation. In addition, they wanted to tell us there was a West African Conference at the Central Church in Kumasi, December 10-16. They wanted the two of us to have services for the children of missionaries during that conference. We agreed and returned to Tamale with them next day, so we finally had a quick view of Yendi Post Office as we passed through. We rode the other two hundred sixty miles from Tamale to Kumasi with Vivan and Dorothy Smith and their helper, Sedjab, from Nakpanduri Clinic. Names of people and places were finally familiar! Edward and Bernice Ziemann in Kumasi were leaving on furlough in the near future. As we were their guests for the conference, their daughters, Marilyn and Patty, introduced us to their parrot, which refused to talk. Each time they passed the parrot, they said, "Stupid Polly." Finally, as they passed, it said, "Stupid Polly."

Burdette and Doris Wiles, and Dick and Cheryl, would be stationed at Kumasi when the Ziemanns left on furlough. The mammoth Kumasi Central Church had been the project of Burdette Wiles during a previous term. It was to be dedicated at this conference, so he had arrived from America. West African names of countries, towns, missionaries, African pastors, and laymen were again tossed around: Jos, Nigeria; Ouagadougou, Upper Volta; Darko, Apeki, Akurugu, Dokurugu, and Amponsah. I had brain-strain from listening so hard! What fun we had with the missionary kids (M.K.s) from twenty-five families. We decided this could be a full-time assignment for someone. To our surprise, some Executive Committee at the conference decided to loan us a little 1951 British Standard Vanguard. We were elated! The car seemed to have once belonged to Betty June and Hilda, the first two nurses at Nakpanduri Clinic. It was a very light tan in color and reminded me of *Casper*, the car from my student-nurse days. We started calling it "Casper's Cousin," or "CC." With a vehicle of our own, we rushed downtown in Kumasi and bought a spare tire, two inner tubes, jack, pump, lug wrench, and a patch kit. We bought a fifty-pound sack of flour, some sugar, and other staples. We found a head of cabbage at the local outdoor market! We bought three, ten-foot-square linoleum rugs for our Saboba dining room, front room, and bedroom and two gallons of brick red cement paint for edges around the rugs. Ashanti carvers produced beautiful items of ivory, ebony, and other wood for gifts; Christmas was rushing at us! I bought Dad an ivory crocodile and Mom the Gold Coast Icon, an elephant with the palm tree beside it.

On December 17, we started our two hundred fifty-mile trek north. In the Ashanti Forest, sometimes we could not see the tops of the huge, tall mahogany trees. At the roadside, we bought oranges, avocados, and paw-paws. What a sight we must have been with a whole stalk of bananas, piled and secured, on top of the three rugs we had tied on top of the car! Along some narrow, hilly roads, we could not even see the bottom of deep canyons beside us. Both hills and vegetation got smaller as we left the Brong Ahafo Region. Halfway from Kumasi to Yeji, we found a Government Rest House at Atebubu. It had a place to spread lunch in the shade and an inside guzunder, (British) for the wooden box. In Yeji, near the Volta River ferry, we paid at the tollgate, and then walked around to see what the women were cooking to sell. We had to wait for the ferry to come back from the north bank. We tasted some kingki, plantains, beans, peanut soup, and rice. They dropped dough in hot oil and produced snacks similar to doughnut holes or hushpuppies. They were delicious! The playful children thronged us again and ran their hands along our arms to see if the white came off. After the big lorries were positioned on the ferry, they directed our little car into the small space remaining. That was our first experience of crossing the Volta River with our own vehicle. Last of all, the people walked on.

In the northern region, the vegetation got shorter and the air got hotter and dryer. The little car had seen better days; the dust boiled in around the doors. With no air conditioner, we were hot and wet with sweat and the red dust stuck; Helen was redheaded! Wet handkerchiefs tied over our noses helped us breathe. We learned to cover our heads with a thin scarf and use wet surgical masks to breathe through. We slept in Tamale that night and bought gasoline the next morning from a pump I had not seen in operation since childhood; I had forgotten. A gallon of gasoline was pumped from a fifty-five-gallon metal drum into a glass container overhead. A valve was opened and that gas ran into the tank of our car. This was repeated and we paid for the number of gallons we all counted. It cost five shillings, about seventy cents, per gallon. That was three times the price I paid in America. We drove sixty miles to Yendi and found the post office closed; it was late Saturday. Some mail would be in Saboba. As tired as we were, we asked questions in Yendi and were able to locate the graves of Guy Hickock, who died in 1933, and Beulah Buckwalter, who died in 1942. She was kin, by marriage, to the Boltons we bought our bicycles from in Ipswitch, England. As we drove on toward Saboba, Helen told me the story again, "Beulah and her family were from my home town of Lancaster. I felt that maybe I was to take Beulah's place when she died, but I told the Mission Committee I would go anywhere needed. To my surprise, they placed me here, forty miles from Beulah's grave." We were two blocks from our house in Saboba when a tie rod came loose and CC went into a cornfield. We were grateful this had not happened on the high Ashanti Forest roads or while driving onto the Volta River Ferry. Dewey Hale helped us get the car to the mission house, but we were without a vehicle again. Africans said, "Now you are *footing* it again, like us."

While we were gone, the Hales had moved out of the mission bungalow and into their unfinished house in Toma! We were so tired and darkness overtook us, yet we were forced to unload the car. Gylima, Binambil, and Biyimba, our clinic and house helpers, came running. Even Mahama, the Hales' helper, and his wife, Mary, came to help. They were still living in the quarters with our helpers until the Hales had time to build quarters for them. We tried not to look at the house that night. We washed off part of the red dust from our bodies and crawled, exhausted, into our narrow bed and under our mosquito net.

The next day was Sunday. We were just ready to go to church when we heard hands clapping and Gylima, the clinic orderly, called, "Ago-o-. Madam, a very sick baby is at the clinic." The baby had a rigid abdomen. We treated it and asked permission to pray for it. We made a mixture of salt and sugar water from a formula. We assigned someone to spoon-feed the baby nonstop. During the week, the baby was so much better that the family wanted us to give him a name. We named him Paul. The parents asked if they could come to church and give God thanks for healing their son. This happened many times through the years and the people involved sometimes became Christians, so the church grew.

We learned from Naomi that, in Yankazia, a young mother who had given birth November 28 had died two weeks later while we were in Kumasi. The Hales were planning to have a clinic in Yankazia as soon as a satisfactory runway was made for the plane, but they were still using their Jeep to visit Yankazia when the young woman died. U Na Febor Jayom, the Yankazia chief, and his people were working on the runway. Naomi brought the baby boy, David, and an elderly woman, Benimpom Mankrom, to Toma in her Jeep. The woman was the mother of Teacher Samson Mankrom, who was also filling in as Pastor in Yankazia. Since then, Benimpom had been *sitting* (living) in a house near the church in Toma with the newborn. Naomi Hale had been mixing American surplus skim milk daily for the woman to feed the baby while we were gone. On Monday, December 20, Benimpom Mankrom walked a mile, one-way, to bring that baby to our clinic. Helen and I followed the same routine Naomi had started. We boiled water and let it cool, then mixed the American surplus powdered skim milk into it. We observed Benimpom as she fed the baby. There was no refrigeration, so we sent enough of the dry powdered milk with Benimpom for the night and advised her to boil the water. She walked the mile daily to get fresh milk for David. The name Benimpom means *new creation*; Mankrom means *who is my protector*. With the good care of Benimpom, David survived; but because of the skim milk, his growth was stunted similar to the way American television actor Gary Coleman's was. His nanny, Benimpom, became his foster mother. (As I write in the 2000s, Rev. David Mankrom Nabegmado, a minister with degrees, just phoned me from Israel. He is pastor of a church in Tema, the industrial port city near Accra, the West African Capitol. He has two services on Sunday in a building that seats four thousand. I heard he requires board members to "start an outstation.")

Early on the morning of December 21, 1954, I delivered my second baby in Africa. The mother, Piger, from the village of Namaab, asked me to give the baby a name. I called her Edna, after my mother. That very afternoon, a huge truck drove into our yard. The African driver got out and came slowly walking toward our door with the largest pineapple I had ever seen; it was over a foot long. He said, "I am *Think Twice* and I have brought your freight. This fruit is for you; up here you get very few." We took pictures of it before we ate it. Helpers came from every direction to unload our freight. On the front of the truck cab, at the top, was written in big letters, "THINK TWICE."

Helen delivered more of the babies than I did at first, as

I was working on the *old* car, and cleaning and repairing the *old* house! I had learned both from my parents; now I was doing it in Africa! For instance, our drums had been stored almost two years; every item inside smelled of mildew and had to be washed before we could use them. Our gasoline washing machine, added to our freight by a church in New Mexico, was caked with red dust. The engine would not start. I cleaned the whole thing, including the spark plugs, while Helen was busy at the clinic. After two whole days of working on it, the engine sparked! The young man, Biyimba, had worked for Ruby and Ozella when they were in Saboba. We hired him full-time. After a few times of helping me operate the gasoline washing machine with wringer, he did it alone. As if we were not busy enough, the stovepipe started letting water and smoke inside the kitchen. Biyimba up-ended an empty barrel, climbed up on it and put in a new section of pipe. The drum tilted and he almost fell off. He grabbed something to steady himself and said, "Oh, Madam, left small, my chop palaver go finish." It took me a moment to know that he had said, "A bit more and I would not be here to eat another meal." The African's ability to get their message across amazed me; so much revolved around food, because it was often scant.

On Christmas Eve, Dr. Ashworth, our Government Medical Officer, ate dinner with us. Our menu was fruit cocktail for appetizer, guinea fowl someone had dashed us, hot rolls, peas, cranberry sauce, and cole slaw from our precious cabbage purchased in Kumasi. We never saw cabbage again in the remaining three years. We whipped a can of milk and topped the chocolate cake. A little coconut decorated it. It seems we asked the doctor to offer thanks to God for the food. He prayed, "For food, friends, and fellowship, Lord we thank Thee. Amen." I have used that prayer since then. The doctor was kind, helpful, and professional. After we ate, he went out to check the battery in our car and pumped air into two tires.

Christmas was on Saturday; it was also market day. Helen and I were getting ready to go to the little mud church with the grass roof for a service. Dewey and Naomi had flown to Liberia to let Mama Sarah, Stevie's nanny, have Christmas with her family. The driver of a market lorry from Yendi brought the locked box with our mail inside. He said, "We took the box to Mr. Hale's house, but *met his absence.*" We knew in a flash that we had also *met the absence of the key;* Dewey had taken it to Liberia! We put the box containing all our Christmas mail in our locked storeroom and went on to church. Pastor Salah, the first Konkomba pastor to graduate from Bible School, had recently returned from Kumbungu to assume pastorate of the local church. He had asked me earlier to speak Christmas morning. He interpreted my American English into Lekpakpaln. I did not understand what he said to the people. However, when we finished, five people came forward to accept Christ. We went home, happy to be a part of this. We became restless and writing letters made us nostalgic. Our Christmas mail was about twelve feet from us and we could not touch it! This was our second Christmas away from America and there would be at least two more. We decided to put down one of the three linoleum rugs in the dining room. We turned on my Roberts radio. Shortwave from Liberia and the Voice of America from Europe was all we could get. It waved in and out and suddenly settled clearly on *I'm Dreaming of a White Christmas.* We stopped, sat on the linoleum, and burst into tears. We got up, called our clinic and house helpers, the Hale's helpers and their wives and children, made tea, and served them refreshments. We could neither talk with them nor understand very much, but we learned how much they loved and appreciated the missionaries before us; they *named them!*

The next day was Sunday and we went to the regular services. That afternoon, we asked Gylima, our clinic worker, to take us to his father's house. We drove two miles to Toma and then walked another mile from our car to Nalongni.

Akonsi's round houses were in a circle like a wagon train at night. A four-foot mud wall making a complete circle and having only one break for a gate joined the houses. The large yard was swept so clean it looked like a table rather than a yard. There were only two items in the yard, a small mud fireplace and a broom leaning against it. The broom was long grass tied near one end; there was no handle. Gylima's father came to greet us with his wife, Mayen, and a younger woman, Majen, whom Gylima called his aunt. Akonsi was a picture of dignity. His smile showed his delight at our coming. As far as we knew, we were looking into the face of the *first Konkomba Christian.* We presented him with a woolen patchwork quilt from the Women's Ministries in New Mexico. At his advanced age, he needed warmth at night. He beamed with pleasure.

Language lessons had to fit into our busy schedule. Our first lesson was December 27, at 5 P.M. We learned, "Upi funi u nan lu n nyun." It means, "A woman came to draw water." Each previous missionary had written a little more of the language. We used what we found; an unwritten language is difficult. We were trying to keep busy and forget our elusive mail.

Gylima, Bileti, Biyimba, Kodjo, Binambil, and Njonabi, our clinic, house and yard helpers were all involved with getting our house livable. First, we put up our two beds in the one bedroom; they almost touched. I sawed and nailed lumber into a canopy frame for my bed. I sewed between clinic emergencies. Eight yards of netting was sewed around a piece of a sheet cut just the size of the top of the bed. I looked it up; the dictionary said a mosquito net over a bed could be called a canopy. No queen ever had a canopy bed like that! Helen used the frame and net from our faithful three-quarter bed on the porch until we got her canopy made. The first night we got into our individual beds and tucked ourselves in with Bible and flashlight, we *felt like royalty.* We considered communicating by smoke signals or Morse code by flashlight. We slept quickly, but our night was cut short. Just before dawn, we heard loud, blood-chilling wails coming from the clinic. We suspected that someone had died. We had been trying to help a fourteen-year-old girl, possibly poisoned. When someone clapped their hands at our door, we were glad we were together in one room! We wondered, "Will they harm us?" In trepidation and with just enough time to call the name of Jesus, we went to the door. It was Gylima and the brother of the girl. He calmly told us she had died and they wanted to take her home for burial. We learned the parents had lost four daughters that same way.

On December 31, Dewey and Naomi flew into Saboba. They brought the key and we got our Christmas mail. It brought my unanswered letters to seventy; some dated back to August. We had no duplicator, so all would be answered by hand or typewriter. December's report of our first full month at the clinic read: General medical treatments: eight hundred and eight; Surgical dressings: three hundred fifty-one; Antenatal visits: ninety-three; Lepers treated: three hundred twelve; Deliveries: four; Total treated: one thousand five hundred sixty-eight.

1. Veendam: from U.S. to England. 2-4. Helen and Charlese. 5. Midwifery classmates from many countries. 6. Our school and dorm room (see arrow). On a clear day we could see Big Ben and Houses of Parliament from our widow. 7. Floyd and Grace Thomas and three daughters at lodge where we were at mid-term test time. 8. QEMaternity Home where we first delivered babies on our own. (Once Chas. Spurgeon's Bible School). 9. The road to QEMH, Nightingale Lane. (Bike provided by SAGU, Waxahachia, TX.)

1. Renamed the "Ghanakust" in 1957 to honor Ghana's independence. 2. Rev. and Mrs. H. Garlock and Akonsi, first Christian, who asked for nurses for Saboba. 3. First "Cracker-box" clilnic (Ruby's version) brought from Accra and set up by McNutts. 4. 1949: First nurse's home. 5. New clinic started. 6. Ozella, Ruby, and Gylima, Akonsi's son and clinic aide. 7. Ann, Becky, and Rev. Garlock— dedication of new clinic. 8. Dewey, Naomi and Stevie Hale and clinic #9 as it was when Helen and I arrived.

CHAPTER TWO

Bekpakpam (Konkombas) of Betchabob (Saboba)

SABOBA MARKET, LIKE A sleeping giant, sprang alive every six days. It was almost two city blocks from our house. As it started to awaken in the morning, we heard a subtle buzz in the distance. The volume gradually increased to a roar by closing time in the afternoon. One lorry, coming from Yendi, nearly always brought our mail. Another came north from Demon through Kokonzoli and still another came south from Chereponi. Only in the driest months, like February, could a truck cross the Oti River from French country on the east; there was no bridge. People who waded the Oti River often encountered crocodiles. We sewed them up and gave them a tetanus shot. It was a mile walk to Saboba Market from the river. Besides local products, one might find some hardware, cloth, sugar, and salt. Homemade soap was often available, but no vitamins. Sometimes they brought oranges, but seldom any other fruit. By mid afternoon, the noise became a roar from last minute bargaining so they need not take their wares home again. Also, they had shared enough of the local pito to be friendly, loud, testy, or combative. Pedestrian and bicycle trails to their villages and homes

43

passed on every side of our house. An afternoon nap on market day was next to impossible. Conflicts often continued from the market to our house and faded away past the clinic. We were always relieved when it did not develop into hand-to-hand combat until well past the clinic.

Dewey, Naomi, and Stevie Hale ate 1955 New Year's dinner with us. It gave us an opportunity to discuss progress and items to introduce to the local council. First, an earthen dam near Saboba would collect water for the people. We would not be forced to haul water a mile or two from the Oti River for building projects, introducing new food crops, or baptizing new converts. Second, a separate maternity building for the clinic. In three rooms, we stored medications and supplies, sterilized equipment, and treated about one hundred outpatients per day. That included pneumonia, tropical ulcers, snakebites, lacerations, leprosy, child welfare clinics, and delivery of the newborn. If you knew anything about Public Health, you had to ignore it. It was better than what Ruby and Ozella started with. Third, a new church building was needed as we expected growth and the mud one was deteriorating. Snakes were honeycombing it and they were becoming dangerous.

That evening we answered letters until midnight. Tuesday would be market day and our letters must be ready to send to Yendi. We were still whittling away by pen and typewriter at the pile of unanswered letters. For form letters, we used carbon paper; we had no duplicator. After a general clinic that week, we decided to go to Yendi to collect our Christmas packages. It was a pleasant surprise when CC took us safely forty miles to Yendi and back. The local Yendi pastor had collected our package slips thinking he could get them to us a faster way than the next market lorry. My diary reads, "The pastor had gone to his farm where no vehicle could go, so we returned to Saboba without packages." On Saboba Market day, the slips arrived in Dewey's locked box. We planned to take the slips to Yendi the next day to collect our packages. We treated seventy outpatients at general clinic. Woe! We met trouble. When we got ready to go, CC had a flat tire. We put on the spare and then tried to patch the damaged tube, but it tore. The nearest tube was one hundred miles in Tamale. By the time we got to Yendi, it was late and the post office was closed. We drove straight through to Tamale even with no spare tire; we had no choice. We bought two inner tubes, one for our spare tire and an extra. We opened a clinic account at the Bank of British West Africa in our names, the final step to being in charge. We were comfortable doing transactions in pounds, shillings, and pence from our stay in England. Every day was Tamale Market and they had hardware, food staples, and fruit. We bought bananas, avocados, paw-paws, and mangos. One lesson required for new missionaries was *how to eat a mango:* "It is best eaten when mushy-ripe while standing over the sink so the juice drips off your elbows!" Helen was learning to enjoy paw-paws too; we thought they took the place of the cantaloupes we missed. That evening we drove eleven miles to the Bible School in Kumbungu to visit the Thomas family.

We left Tamale early on January 8, got our parcels from the post office in Yendi by noon, and reached Saboba in daylight. We now had our Christmas packages in the same town with us, but could not open them! It was Saturday; we must teach faithfulness by example. We washed off the heavy layer of red clay and ate. By then it was time to teach the Sunday school lesson to several young men through an interpreter. They would use the lesson in classes Sunday morning. On evenings, they would give the same lesson at the market, the police station, or some chief's compound in a village within walking distance. If we were not busy at the clinic, we took them in our vehicle to the outlying villages.

Late that evening we opened our Christmas parcels. What fun! Mrs. Vanzant and the ladies in Portales sent a notions doll of useful kitchen articles. We took it apart as we needed the items; it lasted for weeks. Mom Kopp and Mary, Helen's sister, sent personal clothing for both of us. From the time I left America, I could gratefully name the church or individual responsible for each item of clothing on my body from the skin out! There were shoes and hose from Carlsbad, Riverside. We put the nylon hose in a jar with a tight lid and stored them in a kerosene refrigerator to wear home over two years later. Film for my camera, from Dad and Mom, went into the fridge as well; the heat would damage it. Nuts and Mexican food came from Albuquerque.

With all the Mexican goodies from the packages, we took the opportunity to teach Biyimba how to make enchiladas. We wrote it up for his card file; he learned to read that way. A butcher killed a cow for almost every Saboba Market day. We usually bought meat for one dollar and cut it for steaks or stew, or Biyimba ground it for hamburgers, tacos, or enchiladas. Every Monday was washday. The wash water was heated on the wood stove. To utilize the heat, Biyimba put on a pot of pinto beans to boil and a pan of cornbread to bake in the oven. Dinner would be cooked by the time we finished washing on the gasoline machine. Cloth dried quickly and the sun could rot or fade it; we brought it in immediately.

After a week of heavy clinics, we were looking forward to a Saturday of rest. Not a chance! The Hales asked us to do them a favor, as they wanted to fly away again. They had been tied down with the Saboba Maternity Clinic for so long; now they were free. They flew to French Dahomey to check on the Greenaway child. They had been gradually increasing their trips by Jeep to surrounding Konkomba villages and telling the chiefs, "If you will build a runway for the plane, we will come to your area for clinic about once a month." They were also looking for responsible persons in each village to start leper treatment. That Saturday, the Hales asked us to drive their Jeep sixteen miles to Yankazia. It was loaded with lumber to build a small one-room clinic. Pastor Salah went with us. Our car could not have gone where we went that day. The first fourteen miles reminded me of the two-rut, New Mexico farm roads in the 1930s. High centers and washed out gullies slowed us almost to a stop at times. The last two miles was a path. Which tire we put in the path depended on where the scrub trees were. The Jeep had no doors; the tall grass lashed our faces and arms. Dogs and goats could be in the tall grass. We crossed a bridge made of crooked logs, tree branches, and dirt thrown over that. The lumber shifted and we rearranged our load. Teacher Samson Mankrom was in Yankazia when we arrived because it was Saturday. He taught in the Saboba Primary School, the only school in the Konkomba tribe, and served as pastor at Yankazia. He commuted thirty-two miles round-trip on school days. In previous years, U Na (Chief) Febor Jayom had helped Samson go to teacher's training in Yendi and now he was back to help the chief and his people. While in school in Yendi, Samson met the George Anderson family, who presented Christ at Yankazia and the chief accepted the message. Worship services took place in the chief's front room until he and the Yankazia Christians built a mud church. The Hales would build the clinic across the road from that church. The people were clearing a runway for Dewey's plane. This was our first time to meet the Yankazia Chief, a *truly great man*! Teacher Samson led in some inspirational singing; he wrote songs! Pastor Salah interpreted for the worship service as both Helen and I greeted the chief and his people. We were so amazed by the blessed fellowship. We had brought medication and treated the sick people who were waiting. Pastor Salah needed to get ready for Sunday services in Saboba, so we reluctantly left. In Saboba, we washed the red mud off our bodies, ate, and taught the young men waiting on our palaver porch so they could teach the next day. Every day was super-busy.

A daily routine was necessary for both house and clinic. We started by alternating responsibility weekly. One was in charge at the clinic every other week. That was not mutually exclusive. We worked together when necessary, but the one in charge at the particular time made final decisions. Each morning after breakfast, we called the workers of house and clinic to one end of our huge veranda, our *palaver porch.* The workers' families were welcome. We built benches from shipping crates around our beds and the Frank Powers shipping crates around cases of food. We read God's Word and the Daily Light devotional book in English. The English was interpreted into Gylima's version of Lekpakpaln, not yet put into writing. The Konkombas understood him; that was good enough. We prayed in English. They prayed in Lekpakpaln, Dagbani, or Kusal. Every day they called the names of every missionary who had lived in Saboba. At last, we all prayed the Lord's Prayer, not yet that polished, in Lekpakpaln:

"Tite Uwumbor u bi paacham na, binib n san saayimbil; Saanaan n dan. Bi li ngani saageehn dulnyaa wee ni, ki baah ngani pu paacham na. Tiin timi din aawiin aajikaar. Cha timmi aatunwambir pinn timi, ke ti mu aah di cha pinn bin koo timi aataani ni na. Taa cha ti kan ntong. Nyan timi titunwambir ni. Si le yeh nnaan ni mpoan ni mpakm n-yoonn mu kaa kpa ndoon na." (Matiu 6:10-13; The New Testament, Likpakpaln; International Bible Society-*1984*)

After morning prayers, the nurse in charge and the clinic workers went to the clinic. Jobs for the one in charge at the house were: 1) Decide a menu for the day and get three cans out of the locked storeroom: meat, vegetables, and fruit. At first, we helped Biyimba cook. Later we discussed it with him and he did it. 2) Cut the meat into serving sizes on market day. 3) Bake bread until Biyimba could learn. 4) Direct or do house cleaning, laundry, filling of kerosene lights, and fridge. 5) Prepare for extra jobs like teaching in the local Bible School, sewing student shirts, or studying language lesson. 6) Write or type letters. 7) Visit the market for whatever may be useful. 8) Bargain for headloads of wood brought into our yard. 9) Have a market lorry to come and collect the empty fifty-five gallon drums for diesel, gasoline, and kerosene to be brought back full on the next market day. When all this was done and if clinic attendance was heavy, the one at the house went to help at the clinic, so the people would not have to wait past 1 P.M. The next week we reversed responsibilities; however, we alternated delivery of babies or night emergencies even if we were in charge at the house. It took a rested person to treat so many people sensibly in so short a time.

The clinic schedule had to be something we could live with. Mondays, Wednesdays and Fridays were for the general outpatient clinics, usually around one hundred people. We received about fifty dollars per month for operation of the clinic. This was for salaries, medications, and maintenance. The sick people waited on a cement slab leftover from what Ruby and Ozella called the *cracker-box clinic*, but there was no roof over their heads. We used a picture roll and presented a short message with the opportunity for them to accept Christ. Someone responded almost every day. We gave everyone a small chip of wood. That was their ticket to receive treatment; we seldom charged for treatment. If they had no chip of wood when they came through for treatment, we knew they had come late. Unless it was an emergency, they waited until those with a chip were treated. Gylima called the people in, one at a time, for the nurse to see. I wrote home and asked my dad for his mother's school bell; she used it in Kansas and New Mexico. This would speed treatment if he did not call each patient. There were babies with diarrhea, malnutrition, yaws, pneumonia, or measles. Gylima gave vitamins *to all*, while he was interpreting for the nurse. In the afternoons, Gylima and Bileti made paper cups from pages of American magazines and pre-packed child and adult doses of Chloroquin and aspirin for malaria, sulfa tablets for lepers, and vitamins for all. That speeded up all clinics. The people were advised to bring their own bottle in case they needed liquid medication for diarrhea. We gave penicillin injections for pneumonia, breast abscesses, yaws, and infected ulcers. After a time, we began charging them a bit for injections because the people discovered the fast-acting wonder drugs; we could not totally finance the demand. Our helpers washed and boiled the needles and glass syringes and we reused them. Families with an extremely ill member were allowed to stay in one of the four round huts behind the clinic. The local council and chiefs, using local labor, built those. *Extremely ill* meant those with pneumonia, snakebite, meningitis, or tetanus. Newborn tetanus was probably from being born at home on pounded cow manure floors. Adult tetanus was usually from the bite of a crocodile.

Language lessons gradually speeded up clinic work; using an interpreter consumed time. One question we learned quickly was, "E kpa E po waa?" which meant, "Do you have pain in your abdomen?" So many had stomach pain and diarrhea from malaria. We often heard seven languages in one day; that took time. Other than English and occasional French from across the Oti River, there was the local Lekpakpaln, Dagbani (trade language), Twi (policemen), Tchakosi (akin to Twi), and Hausa. Gylima could hear Hausa well enough to communicate with Fulani herders or Youraba traders from Nigeria. The Tchakosis were from the village of Cheraponi and surrounding area about forty miles north of Saboba. Some came to the mission clinic rather than going a bit farther to the Yendi hospital where medication cost more. Sometimes, over fifty percent of those present had tropical ulcers from lack of vitamins, clean water, and soap. There were very few salaried persons in Saboba, so the cash flow to purchase vitamins and soap at the market was almost nil; mostly wares were traded. The people having tropical ulcers, usually on the feet and legs, sat in a row around the high clinic veranda. We hired and trained Bileti, a deacon in the church, to clean the sores with diluted Detol (phenol base) and medicate them with sulfa powder. If infection was clearing up, granulated sugar helped change the acid-base balance and start the healing by granulation. Finally, he dressed it with the clean, white bandages made from torn sheets, rolled, and shipped to us from women in churches in the United States. Bileti sent any newcomers for the nurse to evaluate. If we thought it was yaws or otherwise infected, we injected them with penicillin. One injection would usually be enough to cure yaws. It was caused by a spirochete like syphilis, but not sexually transmitted. It resembled impetigo and was contracted in a similar way from the soil.

Tuesdays were reserved for treatment of about one hundred lepers. Bileti dressed their ulcers on Tuesday. They were not isolated; we delivered their babies. Leprous children went to the local school. One clinic helper's wife and the wife of the Hales' cook were both under treatment. There was a leper camp forty miles from Saboba, but entrance was voluntary. Just before we took over clinic operation, the Gold Coast Government became involved in a research program to test a potential cure for leprosy, using Avlosulfon. We cooperated with that program. Those in the program started on a low dosage of the sulfa. The dosage was gradually increased to a very high amount and maintained for a very long time. The test developed into a proven cure. The government supplied us with just the number of pills for those diagnosed for the research project in Saboba area. Pastor Selah went on his bicycle to villages nearest to Saboba. The Hales flew to the villages in the outlying areas. In this way, over one thousand Konkomba lepers were treated per week.

Thursdays were for expectant mothers. It was called *pregnant women's day*. First, we gave a lecture on pre-natal health care, delivery, post-partum, childcare, or general hygiene. One lecture was about a precipitous delivery at home, where some floors were made of pounded cow manure, or on the road to the clinic. We told them, *"Do not cut the cord!* If the baby is born, but the placenta has not come, lay the baby on the mother's abdomen and carry the two to the clinic. If the placenta has come, allow the mother to walk as she can. Put baby and placenta in the same cloth or calabash (huge gourd) and bring them to the clinic for the cord to be cut." Too many were getting tetanus! They knew how to make an ambulance from a long tree limb, fence post, or pole. They tie each end of a cloth the person was lying on to each end of the pole to form a hammock. They place the ends of the poll on the shoulders of two men. I have seen them carry big fish that way.

For the second time, the week of January 17, Gylima was left alone at the clinic to give emergency treatment only. Bileti could certainly wrap ulcers. Being new missionaries, we were required to attend Northern Territories District Council in Bawku, two hundred fifty miles north, where Franklin and Aneice McCorkle had taken us in early December to meet the Stroud family. Our helper, Biyimba, went with us. We would meet more missionaries, African pastors, and laypeople, and learn a lot. While we were loading CC to leave for Bawku, two people came to the clinic for help. A man had massive burns from a petrol explosion and a woman was still hemorrhaging from childbirth. By the time we treated those and left Saboba, I was not sure whether I was ill or tired. We wore wet medical masks to filter out the dust so we could breathe. Our heads were wrapped to keep out some of the boiling red dust. Missionary vehicles had no air conditioning. The rationale seemed to be that with no air conditioning in our houses the heat would be more traumatic once we exited our vehicle. By the time we arrived in Bawku, I knew I was ill. At the Bawku Hospital, they put a drop of my blood under the microscope and showed me that it was almost solid malaria parasites. With treatment, I was able to attend parts of the conference. I was assigned to the auditing committee, partly because they heard I had worked in a bank. The evening services were for worship. On the final evening, the Tili Naba walked regally down to the altar in his flowing chief's robes. *Some of his wives followed.* He was responding to the call for people to be filled with the Holy Spirit. He lifted his hands to God, and within a short time, I heard him speak in a heavenly language. I was told that what I heard was not Kusal and the joy he expressed made me think he got what he came for. I wept with joy that God so loved the whole world. At the same time, this was upsetting my theology. *What was God thinking* to baptize a man in the Holy Spirit when he had more than one wife? Oh, well, now the chief would know to send them all away except the first one. Not quite! I was told later that he said he could not send wives with their children back to their unbelieving fathers; they would lose their faith in Christ. I was also told that when young men were called to preach, some fathers refused to make bridal arrangements for their pastor-sons, or the sons did not want it done that way. The Tili Naba (Chief), who kept his children in church and did not sell or trade daughters at birth, agreed for them to marry pastors not provided for otherwise. God works in mysterious ways.

As we passed through Tamale on our way back to Saboba, we did some fast shopping and the McCorkles gave us a kitten. We picked up our mail in Yendi. What a surprise greeted us in Saboba! We had another addition to the family, a black and white pup. A note attached read, "We found this plane going north, so have sent one of our pups to you. His name is Buttons. Signed, Elvis Davis and family." A five-hundred-mile plane ride made him a celebrity; our workers found it hilarious! A row of brown spots straight down his back looked as if his pants had been pulled on and buttoned, thus his name. To match Buttons, we called the cat Bows. In the following months, Buttons chewed on our shoes, dug up anything growing, and made us laugh when we might have cried. He slept outside on the porch. Bows slept on a little rug on the floor in our bedroom.

Biyimba helped us unload and said, "Uwumbor tiin timi kitaa," which means *God give us tomorrow,* or loosely, *good night,* and he went to his house. Helen and I washed the sweat mixed with red dust from our bodies, and were about to dive under our security nets when hands clapped. A voice called, "Madam, a woman wants to born." It was a difficult delivery, but we were back in bed by midnight. Helen became ill with malaria by morning and fainted every time she stood up. By that time, we knew more about treating malaria, and we knew Dewey's plane was only a mile away. No wonder we were told that in Africa there were only two speeds: *dead slow and stop*. If people went faster, they got malaria!

On February 9, when Helen was still ill, we delivered a baby for an interesting woman named Ngmakambi. Her husband came with her to clinic and was so attentive. They had children, including Joseph, a local teacher who respected her immensely. Ngmakambi carried her pregnancies in a hernia protruding through the abdominal muscles. Because of this, the second stage of labor was long. Gylima and I had to be her abdominal muscles to push the baby out of her. Both mother and baby got along fine. We named the baby girl Betty; I believe her family called her Bechati. We talked to Dr. Ashworth about a hernia repair for the woman. He said repair might be too traumatic; she had lived with it for years. While Helen was still recuperating and writing letters, she wrote to my parents, "Charlese forgets and calls our dog Skeeter (the name of the family dog in the United States) instead of Buttons. Next time I go west, I'll feel right at home burning holes in my tummy with all that hot stuff. Charlese cooked a grand Mexican dinner for Dr. Ashworth and me on Friday. We drank a lot of water." The dinner was mostly from tins and other food items from America. Pinto beans came from Redfearns, red chili from Powers, green chili, relish, and tortillas from my family and the Belen Church. Olives and pickles were from Tamale. Onions were local. Sopapillas were from Albuquerque WMs. Desert was strawberries and cake from the Lynches in California. Whipped evaporated milk topped the cake. All three of us enjoyed British tea. Our table was polished, six-foot long, two-inch thick, seamless mahogany from the Ashanti forest. All furniture had to be built with solid mahogany, or ants would eat it!

By the time Helen and I got to Africa, Everett L. Phillips was Secretary for Africa at Mission Headquarters in Missouri, in the United States; H.B. Garlock had retired. Both men and their families were special. Everett Phillips wrote that the New Mexico youth department had thirteen hundred dollars for my car, but lacked an additional fifteen hundred dollars. He was going to ask the National Speed the Light Department to write Rev. Holdridge in New Mexico about the urgent need. Then he added, "Inasmuch as I drove a Standard Vanguard for about six months some years ago, I can well understand the problems involved in keeping it in running order. I found it was always wise to have my camp cot and mosquito net with me, for I have had to sleep in some of the most unlikely places when the Standard left me stranded."

We understood this! From then on, we called Casper's Cousin, "The Stranded." I could not imagine the British making a car at all in 1951, since they were being bombed off the face of the earth about that time. Food was still rationed and buildings in heaps of rubble when we were there. Amazing people! I felt sure New Mexicans were doing their best to get a vehicle to us. I wrote, jokingly, to my friend Mae Cohea in Phoenix, "If you know any rich millionaires, tell them we are forty miles from the post office, gasoline, kerosene, and hospital to refer emergencies in Yendi, and one hundred miles from basic groceries in Tamale." Even as I wrote, I had to stop and have the stranded pushed; the battery was dead. They pushed me all over a prairie, while Helen was at the clinic delivering a baby for Piger and Njonabi; they named her Dorcas. It was February 17. The father, Njonabi, was the man that cut our wood, carried our water, kept our yard clean enough to see snakes, and helped care for The Stranded. At the moment, he was putting up a garden fence made of zontamats. After my car started, I hauled water in a trailerload of metal barrels for clinic, garden, laundry, and house. This time of year the well would be almost empty, so men were digging out shale to make it deeper.

Someone dashed us a pullet for delivering a baby. I went hunting the chicken to cook it for lunch. I found her sitting on five eggs she had laid in Bekoon's kitchen, but we had not been told. Bekoon was the wife of the Hales' yardman, Kodjo. They and their daughter Dessie, who was named for Nurse Ozella Dessie Read-Hager, were still living in our helpers' quarters. The Hales had not yet built quarters. Bekoon had told us that her babies were born feet first and were taken out in parts except for Dessie. Ruby and Ozella had taken Bekoon to Yendi Hospital for a surgical delivery of Dessie. She was pregnant again and we knew her delivery date was near. We talked with Dr. Ashworth and Bekoon was scheduled for a cesarean section at Yendi Hospital. After the surgery, she returned to Saboba with a hefty boy named Uwumborbe, *God lives*. Kojo was older, but worked like a young man to feed his young family; he was one proud father! Our hen's eggs hatched. As soon as she lost her last chick to hawks, we *finished her chop palaver*; U kpo (she died). I had written home to my seven-year-old nephew, Jimmy, "We have seven animals, plus various kinds of lizards, rats, snakes, and bats. We have Buttons the dog, Bows the cat, and one hen with four chicks. Buttons and Bows romp and chew on each other. Bows cannot catch these foot-long, redheaded lizards in our yard. He looks but cannot reach the geckos that climb our walls with suctioned feet, click to one another across a room, and compete with bats for mosquitoes."

The Saboba house was nothing like most of the other houses where we visited in the Gold Coast. It was built of rock and put together with mud. The mud part was plastered over with cement, leaving parts of the rock exposed. It looked like a strong rock house, but it needed constant repair and shoring up. At that moment, the house, kitchen, garage, and African helpers' house needed a lot of repair but we only received thirteen dollars a month for station maintenance. The pitched roof over the main three rooms, bath, and storeroom had been covered with corrugated aluminum by the mission just days before we got there. Braided grass on top of metal sheets kept the house cooler. A veranda hang-over, six to eight feet wide, circled the whole house and had nothing but straw over it. It was a cool place to meet our visitors, pray with our workers, teach classes, and have language lessons. Inside, huge arched doorways between rooms, with no way to close them, allowed the air to circulate. Windows had only screen wire over them and fixed wooden louvers in fans we could close only if the house was to be empty for a long period of time or if we saw a fierce storm coming. The wooden exit doors were only locked at night or when the house was empty. In the daytime, we latched the screen doors and napped peacefully. One hot day Njonabi washed our car. Buttons curled up on the damp earth in front of a rear wheel. I started the engine and rolled the wheel of the car over his shoulders. Buttons was yelping and we were crying as the Africans came running. We took turns giving him aspirin for pain all night. It helped, but we could tell when it wore off! We were leaving the next day to go to the Field Fellowship Conference in Accra, about five hundred miles away. Conventions were held in the dry season, as roads were better to travel. We dwellers in the North wanted even a short reprieve from the heat of the dry season. Early on Saturday morning, February 27, we left and took Buttons with us. Ten miles passed Yendi, The Stranded lost a fan belt. We got a ride back to a horticultural station near Yendi. A government man had the exact make of car as ours, but a newer model. He drove us to our car and put his spare belt on our vehicle. We were off again and returned a new belt to him days later. We left Buttons in Tamale with the Cathers. They were Baptist missionaries, so would not attend the convention.

We parked the stranded in Tamale and rode to Accra with

the McCorkles. We met new missionaries, Jim and Delta Kessler and their two daughters, Vangie and Annette. They would live in Accra as the Elvis Davis family had gone to America. At the conference, Helen and I gave our first Saboba Clinic report. Helen was good with records; she reported on numbers treated. We had treated over one thousand people in January. In February, that number had jumped to fourteen hundred. I presented the financial report; we received fifty dollars per month for operation of the clinic. It paid the salaries of the clinic workers and bought medications. We made this a quick trip. The McCorkles decided to stay at the coast for a vacation, so we rode back to Tamale with another family. We picked up Buttons from the Cathers and took him to a government veterinarian at Pong Tamale, sixty miles north of Tamale. He said, "Buttons has no broken bones, but nerve damage. Since Buttons is young, he may walk again." We took him home with us. By March 9, we were back in Saboba and working on our house.

It was time for Dr. Ashworth to check on our clinic. He examined unusual cases we saved for him. He checked our records to see if we were following the laws under which we practiced. For example, we had injection licenses to give penicillin for yaws only. The Ministry of Health was attempting to eradicate yaws. Dr. Ashworth sometimes found we had given injections to babies with pneumonia, mothers with breast abscess, or men with infected gunshot wounds. He would advise us of our infraction. On this visit we had a young mother, named Utchaa, from the village of Nalongni, and her new baby, Rosa, for him to see. Rosa weighed three pounds and three ounces at birth, but cried vigorously and seemed fine. Dr. Ashworth examined her and declared her fit. She lost down to two pounds and twelve ounces before she started gaining and was beautiful in time for our first baby show. One day Helen was busy with general clinic when an Educational Officer brought his wife to the clinic in labor. Helen sent for me to come. The man's wife was sixteen

years old and this was their first baby. I watched her all that
day. We were not unduly concerned about her slow progress; her vital signs seemed normal. The next day, Thursday,
we still observed the young woman while we had a teaching
class for thirty women and checked their progress of pregnancy in prenatal clinic.

While we were busy at the clinic for those two days, there
were about twenty young men tearing off the old grass roof
from our house to put on a new one. It had to be done before
the rainy season. Saboba's Chief Quadin, from the village
of Kpatakpaab, brought men to help and was there to see
the job well done. Grass came two ways and we had to buy
a lot of each, *zontamats and bundles.* Zontamats were put on
top of the aluminum sheets for insulation. They were tied
to a network of boards nailed on top of the aluminum roofing. The beautiful amber bundles of new grass were four
to five feet tall. Men on the ground handed the bundle of
grass ten feet up to men on the roof. Those men unrolling
the bundles on top of the zontamats with the cut edges near
the eaves. They circled the house this way, over and over.
Each layer around the house overlapped the previous layer.
This method took them slowly to the top of the house, where
the grass met from both sides. They pressed it down and
braided it together the length of the house. They secured the
whole roof with chicken wire. That process took a lot of grass
and wire, but there is nothing more beautiful than a newly
thatched roof! DDT was sprayed into every crack in the mud
walls. Along with many bugs, a centipede came wobbling
across the veranda, too numb to run. We put kerosene into
an open sewer to kill future mosquitoes that would give us
malaria. Inside our house, there were still bats and mosquitoes flying while geckos and lizards crawled on walls and
rafters.

Gylima and Helen stayed at the clinic with the woman
in labor. By midnight, Helen reported no progress in labor.
The young woman was stable, so Helen decided to get the

education officer to take his wife forty miles to Yendi Hospital. Helen went with them in case she delivered on the way. I went to bed so I could treat people at the general clinic next morning. Helen returned just before sunup. The young girl delivered in Yendi. Here we learned that the best form of induction of labor was a trip over the unpaved roads to Yendi!

Next morning, I went to the clinic, where sixty-eight people were waiting for treatment. I treated the last patient about noon. Helen had awakened and helped Biyimba cook the noon meal and we ate. We both went to our beds for an afternoon rest. In the daytime, we did not always tuck our nets under the mattress; they were thrown up over the canopy frame. I was nailed a couple of times by a mosquito in broad daylight and noticed the thermometer inside our bedroom said over one hundred degrees, so I got up and wrote letters.

Revamping of the bungalow was a task squeezed in between scheduled clinic hours, church work, sewing, letter writing, language lessons, delivery of babies, and emergencies at all hours of the day and night. On a Friday night, we were planning a long night of sleep when a messenger came from the local pastor. A guinea worm was coming out of his leg and it was too painful for him to walk to the clinic. We drove over a mile to the Hales' house in Toma and planned to leave our car there and walk on to Nalongni where Pastor Salah was lodging; a car could not go there. We found Naomi was frantically worried about Dewey. He had gone to Tamale in their Jeep and he was four hours overdue. We were worried *about Naomi*! She had traumatic epilepsy from head injuries suffered in a car wreck in the United States. Their first son was killed in that accident; Stevie was born later. Naomi's seizures had been increasing so we did not dare leave her alone. While we were there, Dewey rode up on a bicycle. An overload on the Jeep had resulted in two flats when he had only one spare. I wondered why he had not made this trip to Tamale in his plane. Dewey prepared a spare and I drove him about five miles to his Jeep. Naomi had calmed down, but Helen stayed with her. In the meantime, Gylima and Bilete, our clinic workers, walked on to Pastor Salah's house in Nalongni to give him pain medicine to last until he got to the clinic on Monday. Dewey and I returned with the Jeep. Helen and I went home to sleep!

Someone brought the pastor to clinic on a bicycle on Monday. We learned how to treat those who suffer with guinea worms. When you can actually grasp the end of the worm and secure it around a matchstick or tongue blade, you then plaster the whole thing down onto that part of the patient's body. As it gradually comes out you take up the slack. It will eventually end, sometimes after three feet. It may take days to do this and it is very painful. If you disturb them too early, they will go back in and come out another place. We learned that *prevention was best*. One health lesson we taught in the waiting area before treatment was about guinea worms. The eggs collect in stagnant water, usually in the dry season when water is scarce. Drinking water should be boiled. This would kill most germs or eggs and prevent illness. If there is no wood to boil water, then drinking water must be strained through a cloth. A cloth will remove the eggs of guinea worms. Shake the cloth vigorously and hang it in the hot sun to dry and the eggs will be killed by the sun before you need it again. If you do not strain your water, you swallow the eggs; they hatch inside you and come out through the skin. Sometimes when we told the people such things, they thought *our heads were spoiled*. We all learned together.

Early one Saturday morning, a man came to our door doubled over with pain. The regular greetings took place. "A do naa? A te puah? A na puah? A chal puah? A bim puah?" That means roughly, "How was your sleep? Are your father, mother, husband, and children well?" To all we answered, "Naa." That indicates that all is fine. They did not leave out husband or children and we did not explain because that would take time. Some people left those words in to tease us; others left them in as if we had husband or children in America. After all greetings were done properly, the doubled up man said he had pain. We were preparing to take the sick man to Yendi Hospital when a woman appeared. We went through the polite greetings again, chal, bim and all. Then she showed us a very sick child. We took them both to Yendi. The child was treated in Yendi and sent back to Saboba with us. The man was admitted to hospital.

About midweek, we went rabbit hunting to relax. We thought that would help us sleep well. We checked on the Hales and all was well. Back home, we stopped at our helpers' quarter to give them our kill of two rabbits. Someone said, "Madam, a woman wants to born." We admitted Ntubi, from the village of Wudiik, to the clinic and labor was progressing. We heard another voice outside the clinic, "Madam, a woman wants to born." Helen admitted Lasong from Tilengbeni to a mat on the floor; we only had one table and no beds. Both women slowed to an almost dead stop in second stage. As labor increased, it was as if it tore the placenta loose and I delivered Ntubi just past midnight; the placenta came *with the baby*. The cord was eight inches long, not the normal eighteen. As soon as the baby's air passages were cleared and the mother's profuse bleeding was stopped, both were stable but tired. We were definitely experiencing that consultation bit! Helen couldn't actually help me, as she was having a problem down on the floor. The head of wee Boba had appeared with the cord tightly around the neck, *twice*. Helen held the head up so I could cut a loop of cord without cross contamination. The baby came four minutes after the one on the table, but was cyanotic, ashen gray, and limp. Helen suctioned the mouth and nose and the baby soon breathed normally and seemed fine. This reminded me of my state board question in the United Kingdom, "How would you know when a black person was cyanotic?" We were constantly learning *and praying*!

There would be thirty to forty pregnant women at prenatal clinic in just a few hours, so we hurried to bed at 2 A.M. on Thursday morning. In less than an hour, Dewey Hale came and called us. His wife had suffered four seizures within the past hour. We went immediately and stayed with Naomi, giving her sedatives until time for maternity clinic. We ate a quick breakfast and evaluated thirty pregnant women. We weighed each, took blood pressure, confirmed due dates, and gave them vitamins, iron, and folic acid. Sometimes the mothers gave the pills to her children. They said it made their children healthy. Actually, we discovered they were saying their newborn babies were getting larger at time of delivery! Some sold the vitamins for food. They laughed with us when we told them we knew what they were doing and why. We had the women swallow some right at the clinic. It gave us teaching material. We explained that complications such as stillborn, abnormal, or small babies, and bleeding would be less if they would take the pills themselves. Complications we first encountered included five or more pregnancies with no living child, profuse bleeding, small or limp babies, or gas gangrene of the uterus upon arrival. A very common problem was perineal edema and exhaustion of the mother from pushing too early before deciding to come to the clinic. A cystocele or rectocele could delay delivery. Tetanus in newborn from a precipitous delivery on the road to the clinic, or at home on a cow manure floor decreased after classes on those subjects. More and more women were coming to the clinic for prenatal checkups and delivery. The women finally admitted that the more they came for prenatal care the less they bled at delivery and the healthier the baby. We were able to detect potential problems, prepare the mother, and make tentative plans. Up to that date, not one mother or newborn delivered at the clinic had died; we were proud. We delivered healthy twins on Sunday, April 3, and so missed church.

On the last Sunday in March, Rev. Addai, a capable man from southern Gold Coast, had started a revival at the local Assembly. It seemed to be the first time an evangelist came from outside the tribe as speaker. Dewey killed two antelope to feed people during the revival and Easter efforts. He gave us a hindquarter and we shared with our workers. We went with a group on bicycles to villages surrounding Saboba to invite people to attend meetings. Rev. Addai spoke at scheduled clinics before treatment started. He asked if they understood about the sacrifice God made of his Son Jesus Christ. People in the capitol city had known for many years. Only one hand was raised. The native evangelist could hardly believe this to be possible in his own country and exclaimed how much work there was to be done. Evangelistic efforts could not conflict with farm work; the people must eat. That is why the meeting was held in March, usually the hottest month. The heat was also new to Rev. Addai. He said that he could write a book about that week!

The first rains might come in April or May, so the humidity was getting high. We were changing clothing, skin out, two and three times a day. Finally, we had services out under the sky because the local church was so packed and we had seen snakes inside the church at almost every service. Even the snakes were hot and coming out for air. One Sunday morning, the people met a *cow*, dead from snakebite, inside the church. A person might be next. It was definitely time for a new church building. Field Superintendent Franklin McCorkle and his family came for a groundbreaking ceremony for Toma Church. As the ground was broken, the shovel was passed around for all of us to break a bit of the ground. When it got to Helen, the handle of the shovel broke instead; she always made us laugh. The new church would be made of cement walls, floors, and benches, with a corrugated tin roof. It would last in the harsh rains and dry seasons. A parsonage for Pastor Sela and Sunday school rooms would be adobe brick. The locals would furnish the labor. While at Saboba, our transportation problems impressed Franklin McCorkle anew. As field chairman, he wrote to Rev. Everett Phillips in Missouri, "The ladies should receive twenty-five dollars a month, retroactive, for travel for the old Vanguard. Please do all you can to get their new car to them. Charlese is a good driver and knows a lot about car up-keep and repair, or they could never keep this old car going."

By mid-April, it had rained twice, just enough to make the humidity wretched when the temperature reached one hundred degrees or more. As I wrote letters, I put a piece of cloth under my hand to keep the sweat from dripping onto the paper. Storms with wind and dust were getting worse. It blew the grass roofs off the huts behind the clinic. Chief Quadin of Kpatapaab got local men to put the roofs back on. We started cleaning inside the clinic, a repeat of cleaning our residence. We learned that cleaning and maintenance in the tropics must be constant and aggressive. It was a fight with insects building, varmint droppings, and the elements. During this re-roofing and cleaning, we delivered a first baby for a very young girl. Helen named him Rossi after her brother Ross. Women in the American churches were asking what they could do to help. We wrote that we needed baby shirts and blankets, as we gave one of each to every baby born at the clinic. We had just come through the harmattan months, December through March. The temperature of those days and nights were *such a contrast* that pneumonia was a problem. The rainy season posed a similar problem for the babies, April through October. From then on, women's groups and our families sent new and used baby shirts and blankets.

The Belen Bulletin, sent by my parents, was arriving in Saboba regularly, but with month-old news. One announced that my brother, Royce, was home for good from Korea and the Navy. In late April, two very interesting letters arrived. The one from Mrs. Earl Vanzant, State WMC President said, "I have mailed three hundred dollars for the refrigerator and stove fund. The ladies of New Mexico churches are collecting picture rolls and literature for your area. A barrel of bandages is being shipped to you with the freight of Smith and Wichman. Our son and his wife, Clinton and Fretta, are in a revival meeting in Belen. Larry and Homer, our two youngest, got their Salk vaccine for polio at school today." She always added items of interest about her children. Helen had met Homer and Larry as we itinerated. The other letter reported on results of the 1955 District Council in New Mexico. Several new officials were elected: Raymond Hudson as District Superintendent, Earl Vanzant as Assistant Superintendent, Lawrence Green as Secretary-Treasurer, Melvin Sasse as State DCAP (Youth Director), Clinton Vanzant as Vice-DCAP, and Mrs. Earl Vanzant went back in as Women's Director. It seems that Rev. Earl Vanzant, in a youth service on the first night of the Council, had expressed his concern about a car for us. Rev. Glenn Anderson, State Youth Director, allowed him time to receive an offering. The fifteen hundred dollars needed for the vehicle in Saboba was raised! The money was to be paid in cash or within thirty days. That represented sacrificial giving in many cases. Only God, Helen, and I will ever know what that news meant to the work in Saboba and the Konkombas.

"M kpa mpopiin saakpen, Uwumbor u ye maangmangmardaan na pu la." - - "bu pu? Uwumbor u kpa mpoon na tun litukpaan ki tii mi. Waayimbil ye chain la." (Luke 1:47, 49)

1-3. 1954 West African Conference and Dedication of Central Assembly in Kumasi. Burdette Wiles (and Dorris), Missionaries. 4. The Stranded and me. 5. Akonsi, 1st Christian and son, Gylima and me. 6. Typical Konkomba man. 7-8. Our home and fence— Gylima and Bileti. 9. Dr. Frank Ashworth—Yendi. 10. Judy Stroud, Tartain at baby show. 11. Market lorry. 12. In our squaw dresses from Silver City. (Belen, NM has new pastor.)

1. Gylima, clinic orderly, with man and homegrown and spun cotton thread in tunic. 2. Clinic waiting room for teaching. 3-4-5. Forms of ambulances: cow, piggy-back, hammock. 6. True case of yaws. 7. About yaws. 8. Maternity clinic official opening. 9&11. Helen with Zachaeus and me with the "littlest Konkomba." 10. Precious little lady carried her pregnancies in a hernia. 12. Gylema, Bakanti, Yanye, Piger, Yaro, Mary and Obi (God lives).

CHAPTER THREE

At Home in Saboba, 1955

ON EASTER SUNDAY, APRIL 10, the mud church was crowded with one hundred forty-two people. Pastor Salah was enthusiastic to put into effect what he had learned in his Bible School years. With help from local schoolteachers, the Hales, and us, he implemented the first organized Sunday school in Saboba. It was launched on Easter Sunday. Helen was asked to teach the ladies' class with Gylima as interpreter. I was asked to teach the class of twenty-six schoolchildren, ages eight through twelve, with a local schoolteacher, Nakoja, as interpreter. Our interpreters or Pastor Salah could teach when we were detained at the clinic. Some classes were held under a tree. We gave them pictures cut from Christmas cards that portrayed the true meaning of Christmas. They were enthusiastic and called it *magbong* (my book or paper). For most, it was their first. What a challenge! Here were the future pastors, teachers, nurses, and midwives! What I, as a newcomer, did not know was that perhaps the only girls in the class who were free to go to school were Gylima's girls, Yanyi, Piger, and Yaro. Mary and Obi were not yet school age. Fathers who were newer Christians had probably pledged their girls at birth. They may need to fight for their freedom to go to school or to marry whom they choose. On Easter afternoon, we drove the Jeep to Yankazia again. From there we walked over a mile to Nnabuni, where even the Jeep could not go, to see twenty people baptized in water. Many people from Yankazia *footed it* with us; others rode bicycles. U Na Febor Jayom rode along on his bicycle. The people at that small village had made a runway, so the Hale family flew in. Dewey Hale, Pastor Salah, and Teacher Samson did the baptizing. No candidate had on clothing that showed above the waist-deep murky water and nine were women; my theology underwent evaluation again. It was a blessed service. At completion, fifteen others requested teaching necessary for later baptism. Opportunities were snowballing!

The following Thursday, we went to Tamale to shop for groceries and take Buttons for a check-up with the Scottish veterinarian. Rain had produced grass and animals were eating. We saw three antelopes, four monkeys, and two bush turkeys; I shot a hawk. People needed meat. We took our dog Buttons forty miles on north to Pong Tamale. The vet was vaccinating cattle. He was not obliged to do surgery on little animals; he was doing us a favor. He kept Buttons in his hospital to remove the infected front leg. We stopped to visit Baba (Elder) Tiga, the local pastor. This Mosi-man from Upper Volta had pastored in the Gold Coast for many years, like a missionary. Pastor Allason, from Nakpanduri, was visiting Baba Tiga and rode to Tamale with us; he needed to see a doctor. A rear tire blew almost immediately. I was still stressed about Buttons when I jacked the car up before loosening the lug nuts. Pastor Allason tried to help, but his nose started bleeding and we stopped to pray for him. A lorry driver stopped to help us. He said, "Madam, let the car down small-small and then loosen the lugs." In Tamale, we took the pastor to the hospital. We were forced to buy a spare tire for twenty dollars; that really hurt our budget. Rev. Phillips did make the twenty-five dollars a month for car maintenance retroactive to when we got The Stranded;

that helped! I hinted in my next letters to the United States for a pump and light we could plug into the car's cigarette lighter. We got exhausted pumping up tires in the sapping heat. As usual, at Tamale market we bought oranges, onions, bananas, avocados, and knobby tomatoes, things we could not find in Saboba. We bought kerosene for seventy-five cents per gallon; it cost much more in Saboba.

Franklin McCorkle, the Field Chairman, said the term for missionaries to Africa might be raised to *four years*. We asked about our time in England; he said it did not count. With a three-year term, we would be home for Christmas 1957. Even that seemed a *furrr-piece* away! As we got involved in Saboba, time did not seem important. The next day the vet phoned us from Pong Tamale. A phone! We had almost forgotten it existed. The vet said he had taken the leg off and Buttons was still asleep. He would send the dog to Yendi; we were to meet a market lorry on a certain date. We went to Saboba without our Buttons. That is my first recollection of hearing the Africans said, "Madam, don't let your heart *fell* down." Our cat, Bows, got so lonesome without Buttons that he sat in a window and howled like a weird bird. This added to my stress. One evening, I was trying to write letters. I thought some milk might help the cat, so I got some from the fridge. My dress hung on the screen door, the flashlight went out, I stepped on the cat, and spilled the milk. Biyimba said, "I know what is humbugging your cat, Madam." "What?" we asked. "He wants a wife!" Biyimba said and quickly added that there was a wife available in his village. We gave our blessings! Bows, protesting with all his claw-power, was put into a huge calabash with air holes and taken to his wife. We cried again and vowed, "Next time, we will get two."

The six-month rainy season had started. We planted tomatoes, lettuce, and radishes *again*. I was anxious to see if the seed stored in my drums over a year would germinate. Njonabi, our yardman, told us they would die. They died the *second time*! We planted tomato seeds in a tub, so plants were ready to put out when Njonabi recommended it. Some weeks later, we set out thirty-eight tomato plants and planted lettuce, carrots, radishes, peppers, beets, turnips, and cantaloupes.

One day at leper clinic, the attendance was one hundred twenty-three, which is greater than most general clinics. We only had to give them a specific number of sulfa tablets, dress sores, and treat emergencies. Both the local and area leper clinics were growing. One woman, who had a leper spot on her back the shape of the map of Africa, said she *wished she could die*. We started observing depression among lepers. It seemed to be mostly in those taking antihistamines when they were sensitive to the sulfas. It made some sleepy in the daytime, a new feeling they did not like. We explained this in teaching classes before treatment. Soon *they didn't want to die*! They even started joking among themselves about *long naps*. Pastor Salah rode his bicycle to villages ten to twenty miles around to give sulfa tablets as designated by the government program. He passed on teaching such as *long naps* where needed. He presented the Word of God to them about the sacrifice of Christ, God's Son. Some of those people came to church on Sundays, increasing the need for outstations or a bigger church in Saboba.

The next day, Dr. Ashworth came for a routine visit. We had asked several patients to return that day so the doctor could see them. He told some of them to go to Yendi, where he had x-rays and a laboratory for diagnosing. The extent of our surgery was to strap or suture wounds, lance boils, cut off extra fingers, or pull teeth *if* they were loose enough. The doctor stayed for lunch. I played Billy Graham's crusade music on Jimmy's wind-up phonograph. Dr. Ashworth was not too impressed and said he preferred classical music with expression. Next, I played Red Harper's *Old Time Religion* and *Hallelujah, We Shall Rise*. That was more expressive, but definitely *not* what the doctor ordered, so we all had a laugh. The quality of the machine also left somewhat to be desired, but we were fortunate to have it.

Suddenly, Everett Phillips wrote from the Missions Department that our new vehicle from New Mexico might come in about three months. Great! The Stranded had decided to blow smoke into our faces from under the dashboard when we turned on the lights, so we were using it only in the daytime. In a night emergency, we drove with a flashlight held out the window. In the meantime, we had more visitors. Bronnie, Annabel, Judy, and John Stroud came from Bawku. They left nine-year-old Judy to stay with us for a while. How neat it was for the parents to share their children with us *African aunties*. They were brave to leave Judy when our car was giving us trouble. Still, they knew that Dewey's plane was not far away. Judy did not get homesick. We helped her get rid of some boils. One day we saw her reading a medical book. When we asked what she was learning, she said, "I'm reading about puberty." At her age, I could not read and had never heard that word! She was still with us on Saturday, April 23, when we went to pick up our dog, Buttons, but *we met his absence*. Four days later, we went again. A man said they had put him on a Saboba Market lorry. We rushed back to Saboba but could not find Buttons at Saboba Market. Then we were called to the Saboba Police Station, where they had a little yapping black, white, and brown female dachshund. It was *not* Buttons! An attached letter read, "Dear Madams: I regret to inform you that your Buttons died in surgical shock. I am sending you a daughter of my own dog. She is a dachshund, eight weeks old. I do hope it will help you forget your other one. Take her to Yendi for shots in another four weeks. Yours Sincerely, Dr. Campbell." I was not prepared for this! If I could not have Buttons, I wanted none; I could not even look at her. Helen said she was beautiful and promised to feed her and keep her out of my sight. The agreement was quickly forgotten, as our hearts were won. We named her Tartan because of the Scottish doctor and because she had three colors in her coat.

This wee, short-legged lassie was a novelty in Saboba, but I *never forgot* Buttons! We soon found that our dog, Tartan, had a problem. She roamed and carried many things onto our porch. She went to the police station living quarters, two blocks away, and brought a policeman's stick and shoes. They knew where to come looking for them. We never knew when she did these things.

Right after we got Tartan, we had a baby show at the clinic. We gave away seventeen prizes of pretty items of clothing that people had sent for babies. Prizes went to the prettiest and healthiest by age categories. We went through the age groups and picked the individuals. When we asked for their birth certificates, my second delivery in Africa, Edna, got the prize for prettiest baby in the six-month-old group. We gave her a little white dress. Irene, delivered by Helen and named for her mother, got the prize in a younger category. We declared there was *no bias*! We planned a demonstration of how to boil an egg, mash it, and feed it to their babies. We told them to test the egg in water. If it floated and stood on end, it was rotten. We tested the egg; it sank to the bottom of the pan on its side. We boiled it and cracked it; it was *rotten*. We said, "When it looks like this, don't feed it to your baby." When people *dashed* us eggs as a thank you, we had Biyimba test them by putting them in a deep pan of water. If they floated, we called them Chinese eggs, or "chicken-too-young." Biyimba could have those that floated if he wanted them. After what happened at the clinic that day, we decided to do some serious research on African eggs before we gave them away! We tied a ribbon around Tartan's neck and Judy put her on her back in a cloth like the African mothers were carrying their babies. She carried her all during the baby show; Tartan loved it and the women laughed. While Judy was with us, Titchau from the village of Kisabuini delivered at the clinic. We asked her if she would like to name her baby after Judy and she did. When Bronnie and Annabelle came to get Judy, they brought oranges, avocados, and fresh eggs, things we could not get locally. They were with us for my birthday party on May 3. The three Hales came with a piece of African cloth from Stevie. A card read, "Happy Birthday, Auntie Charlese." He was almost eighteen months old, cute, and precious. Helen had baked a cake, made ice cream, and gave me a blouse. Afterwards, the Strouds left with Judy, what a *vacancy*!

A week after my birthday, Helen and I got a letter from Dave and Claudia Wakefield. They and their four children lived in French Togo in the foothills of the Bassari Mountain. We could see the top of the Bassari Mountain from Saboba. The letter instructed us to walk about two miles to the Oti River on a certain day. They would drive to the river on their side. We knew there was no bridge; we expected to see a canoe for crossing. The rains had not been heavy enough to flood the river yet, so some Africans helped us splash across. We had given tetanus injections to Africans who had been attacked by crocodiles doing this very thing. It was much cooler at their house in French Togo than in Saboba on the British Togo side. They had sixty outstation churches and a technical school. Ruth, their eldest child, joined the other three children with enthusiasm to tell us what part they contributed to area projects. The whole trip was a nice change, but we waded back across the Oti Saturday evening. Our Sunday school helpers came and we studied the lesson together so they could more easily interpret for us Sunday morning. Some could not read. In the night, Ngmanyindo came from Nalongni to *born* her first baby. The baby's head was in a posterior position, so she had difficult labor. Helen and I were consulting and praying all night. Because of this, the interpreters taught the Sunday school lesson we had studied together on Saturday; that's what it was all about. The little mother in trouble delivered; we were glad we came back from Bassari.

On Friday, May 13, we went to Yendi to pick up packages for the first time since my birthday. Six were for Helen;

thirteen were for me from all over New Mexico. More than half were bandages for the clinic and we even got excited about that; we were almost desperate for them. My Mother Spencer's school bell came from Belen! I almost cried. Next morning at prayer with all our workers, Gylima, the clinic helper, said he was going to shine that bell and keep it locked up for protection. Then he got serious and asked, "Madam, isn't this sin palaver God's palaver?" I asked, "What are you talking about, Gylima?" He replied, "Well, isn't God the one who threw the devil down to earth?" Then he laughed his great, thunderous laugh, and I knew he needed no specific answer. Many people came to the palaver porch just to visit or join us in prayer. One day, two teenagers came. They said they were Tako and Kayil, brothers. I asked them if they had, *"Same father, same mother?"* One answered, "Same father; same mother." Then I asked, "How can that be? One is so tall, the other shorter. You are so different." One replied, "That's *just the way our mother born us.*" When I asked a question and they didn't know the answer, I asked, "Why don't you know?" One replied, "Madam, my father never taught me that." They expected to learn everything they knew from their parents. A world of respect! I wondered what years of public school would do to that custom; even the primary school had not been there long.

Just one week later, we left the clinic with Gylima again on Friday, May 20 and took the three-day trek to and from Tamale for food. We bought bacon and potatoes in tin cans. We did not yet know much about the local white yams, as the people were keeping them stored to feed their own families until the new crops produced. They stored very few items because of the heat. Sometimes by the time the rains came, they had eaten what they stored and new crops had not yet produced. They called it the *hunger season*. Unlike us, they did not have a vehicle and seventy-nine dollars a month to run to Tamale to buy food for their families. I was feeling guilt-ridden, but we could not farm. One evening in

Tamale, Aneice McCorkle was extremely upset and we discovered it was because her husband and daughter, Franklin and Amonna Sue, were out after dark hunting frogs to feed their pet crocodile. Franklin, or *Elder McCorkle* as nurses Ruby and Ozella called him, told us how to tell the number of years a person had been in Africa. The first year you are in Africa and a fly falls into your glass of drinking water at a meal, you ask for a new glass of water. The second year you take a spoon and dip the fly out. The third year you grab that fly, squeeze him, and say, "Spit that out!" The fourth year you just say, "Protein is protein." Franklin read this and accused me of adding the fourth year!

We hurriedly returned to Saboba on Sunday to be there for clinic on Monday. Helen and Gylima treated the people. She was taking the clinic more than her share again, while I was improving our living conditions. Every pair of hands we could persuade was whitewashing parts of the outside of our bungalow with an alkali, a whitewash. It looked nice, protected the mud parts from rain, discouraged varmints, but used a lot of water and emptied our well. I hauled water for the house, clinic, and garden. After the house was whitewashed, we painted a black twelve-inch border around the bottom of the house. The coal tar, thinned with kerosene and creosote, was a sealer, so water running off the roof would not erode the mud walls around the bottom and allow the house to cave in. The border also discouraged varmints like ants, centipedes, rats, and snakes. One day the yardman came running, "Madam, I hear the rain crying, utaal cho (rain is coming)!" That thunder was music to my ears. The rains came, the water level in our well slowly rose, and our garden produced.

We tried to have a language lesson each afternoon, but it was difficult to concentrate because of the heat and we were mentally tired. A windstorm usually hit each afternoon if the rainy season was trying to *start or finish*. We closed doors and windows, which made it dark inside, so we lit a storm lantern to write letters or study language. That made it even hotter and we sweat. Women glow; men sweat. We sweat! We had bought mosquito boots at the Tropical House in London to wear during language lessons or writing letters as mosquitoes collected in the shadows, like under tables. The boots were canvas and fitted loosely at the ankles so snakes biting could not reach our skin. They tied at the knee with a drawstring. Letters from Helen's Mom usually ended with, "Sleep under your nets, use your pith helmets, boil your water, and wear your mosquito boots." We did. An example of why to wear boots came in the form of a twelve-year-old boy bitten by a snake on May 26. We had learned several things. *First*, people with a snakebite usually waited too late to come to the clinic, so cutting at the bite site was of no use; it just made another hole from which to bleed. *Second*, we learned that because they came late, injections into the muscle would not work fast enough. If we gave them the anti-venom serum in the muscle as the instructions suggested, it would take several expensive ampoules and be absorbed too slowly to save their life. *Third*, each ampoule may cost up to forty dollars. A minimum of two or more was recommended via the muscle. Before this was absorbed, the snake's venom would have a head start at killing the person. To give two ampoules instantly, without evaluating the need for it, would be more than they or we could afford financially. *Fourth*, we learned to test the blood as soon as they came. We had no laboratory. They may be bleeding from every orifice, scratches, their eyes, and the bite site. We took blood on our finger from any area and rubbed it between our fingers to evaluate the viscosity. If it got sticky and coagulated within five minutes, we waited. We gave them Vitamin K and other vitamins by injection or mouth. We gave them a sedative, but certainly no aspirin. This was to make them lie quietly, so they would lose as little blood as possible. We assumed the loss might become heavier, so they needed to retain all their blood for strength. If in testing, it was like water and did not get sticky, we knew the venom was hard at work; we went straight for the vein! We injected an entire ampoule of the serum directly into the blood, but ever so slowly. It may take thirty minutes. We tested every few minutes and it was amazing how quickly clotting would return. Sometimes, however, they would lie in a pool of blood before we got it reversed. We wrapped the part with pressure bandages. Nothing really helped until the body restored the process of clotting the blood. We have used as many as three ampoules, but few times. We watched closely for any reaction to the serum itself, so we could treat that. We encouraged victims to bring the snake when they came, as we had a book by which we could identify the particular type of snake. The ampoules listed the type of snakebite it was meant to counteract. I stress that this was *our method*. We learned what worked very well and we lost almost no adults. Babies were almost impossible to save. The amount of venom per pound of body weight must be enormous compared to the adult. I shall never forget one father who beat the ground and cried when his one-year-old child died. The child had stuck his finger in a snake hole! They brought the snake; it was a dreaded carpet viper. The snake must have been hungry and saved up a massive dose of poison for his next meal. We could do nothing fast enough to save the toddler. Two times a year the snakebites increased. First, as the rains increased and the water level rose near the surface, the snakes were forced up closer to the ground or out completely. Secondly, in the hottest season, snakes came out to cool off. Dr. Ashworth came the last day of that week. He observed the twelve-year-old snakebite boy and left him in Saboba, saying, "He seems to be recuperating." He said we really should send every snakebite patient to the Yendi Hospital; we knew he was right. However, we found that they would not always go. It was partly the time element; they said they might die before they got there and they would rather die at home because of certain burial customs. Dr. Ashworth was also to inspect Naomi Hale's mobile clinic work on these visits, so she invited all of us to eat turkey dinner at their house that day.

Five young men from the local church wanted to go to Bible school to become pastors. Dewey Hale talked us into taking on more responsibility. We helped them establish a local prep school for those wanting to enter Bible School at Kumbungu, eleven miles north of Tamale. It was the only Mission Bible School available to the young Konkombas. It was taught in Dagbani, the trade language of the North. Most young Konkombas spoke Lekpakpaln only. We planned to teach these young men English in the classes and to put their language into writing, using international phonetics. This would help us learn Lekpakpaln. The young men learned easily; Lekpakpaln was harder for us, but we were learning. The classes were 8:00-11:00 A.M. each weekday. In the meantime, Dewey said he wished the Bible school in Kumbungu were taught in English so other tribes did not have to learn Dagbani or any other tribal language but their own. All government primary schools introduced English early, but taught the first year in the local dialect. At some level, they switched totally to English, as the Gold Coast Government functioned in English. The Bible school at Kumbungu did eventually switch to English, but Dewey Hale had returned to America before it happened.

We were also learning practical lessons, like how to settle palavers. Our yardman beat up his wife right in the house we provided for them. We called them to our porch, where we greeted strangers (visitors), prayed every morning, and settled palavers. This was definitely in the last category. The man said she refused to prepare his chop and give him water. She said she needed a new cloth and he would not buy it. He said he must first feed his family before there was money for cloth. "Oh, Mercy!" I thought, "This is sounding too much like America, fighting over money and clothing." We talked and prayed with the couple. As we got raises in our allowance from America, we gave our helpers raises. We really could not afford a yardman, but how could we use our time to cut wood and carry water when we needed to be treating the sick, delivering babies, learning a language, teaching health, teaching Bible, and going to the villages to speak with the people? Finally, the man looked at me and asked, "Madam, did the moon die today?" I was sure I did not know. Suddenly, I knew; it was the *end of the month, payday*! I paid him his salary. Several months later, I saw the wife at church in a new cloth.

A letter from Rev. Phillips informed us that the 1955 Chevrolet Handyman 210, six-cylinder, heavy-duty springs, heavy-duty shocks, and green tinted windshield *had been ordered!* The cost would be one thousand eight hundred ninety-four dollars straight from Flint, Michigan to the Gold Coast. All we knew about the color was that it would not be black or navy blue. What excitement; we were happy campers!

As June neared and I was thinking, "Happy Birthday, Dad," I received a letter that he and Royce had been in a bad truck accident on the border of Arizona and New Mexico. When I told the Africans at Morning Prayer, they prayed for them as though they knew them personally. It was my week at the house, so I wrote home. Dad and I always hunted rabbits together, so I wrote him, "This is how I use my gun in Africa. Twice this week, Tartan barked unusually loud. I went out to see why and each time she had cornered a cobra." Even as I wrote, Tartan barked loudly again. I discovered the Chief's cows had walked right over my garden zontamat fence, in one side and out the other. I wrote the Chief a note. He sent little cowboys who removed the cows. Preteen boys, if they were not in school, cared for their father's cows. Cows were his "money in the bank." Young cowboys chose a cow from the herd and rode it, so they were truly cowboys! They wore nothing, except perhaps a straw hat they may have woven for themselves from grass. The veteran missionaries declared that Genesis 3:7 says, "And God saw that man was naked, so

God put a hat on his head." After lunch, as tired as we were, we took a very sick baby to Yendi and I mailed what I wrote that day. Mom wrote that Dad and Royce were improving and that Dad had gone to stay with my sister, Mae, in California to recuperate.

A killer of babies was discovered the first week in June. A pregnant woman, who was scheduled to deliver at the clinic, had her baby at home. When she brought the baby to the clinic, we were shocked to discover it had tetanus. She had lost all her babies except the one just older than her newborn, and it had pneumonia. We quickly used this as an example in our teachings. It must have registered, for we delivered eleven babies at the clinic in July. We also noticed that the general clinic attendance was down when the rains came. Men were busy plowing with the short-handled hoe and women planted the seed even if they needed to go to the clinic or bring a child. That *chop palaver* was a priority! Rains were coming, so water was becoming more available and cleaner. They took more baths and we treated for fewer guinea worms. They could eat more of their stored food, as they felt there would soon be more if they planted and rain continued.

By June 17, the rains came in earnest. Our garden was growing. We had planted turnips, carrots, and other vegetables, but learned that the growing season was too short to develop underground tubers. Our house helper, Biyimba, planted pawpaw seeds and a banana plant where the water drained out of our kitchen. When the plants came up, he thinned the bunch to have a male and a female pawpaw tree. There were still no mango trees in Saboba, and they were supposed to grow easily in the North. Saboba was just too dry. The Ashanti forest, where tropical fruit grew in abundance, was about two hundred fifty miles south. We decided to attempt a trip to Tamale once more before the rains made it impossible. The roads were mud with deep ruts from the large market lorries. It was hard to decide whether to straddle the ruts or drive with the wheels in the ruts.

The next time we felt brave enough to go to Yendi for mail and packages, Tartan was old enough to get her rabies shots as advised in the note from the vet, so we took her. The Yendi veterinarian refused to inject her, saying that she was too young. We could hardly wait to open our packages. We even enjoyed the funny papers people used for packing. A pattern evolved, people in Belen gave items to Mom; she packed and mailed them. A gallon of washing machine oil came from the Galloways, enough for our duration in Africa! Sweet-smelling Avon products came from Mrs. Boster in the same package. The light and pump I asked for to plug into the car's cigarette lighter came, but did not fit The Stranded. It might fit the Chevrolet when it came. There was garlic salt, Hershey syrup, and Old El Paso chopped green chili. We looked forward to eating our own peppers soon. The plants were three inches tall. We welcomed the clothing people sent as we changed three or more times a day, partly from sweating, but also bathed and changed each time we came from the clinic. Washing and hanging them to dry in the hot sun shortened their lives.

The first two weeks in July, Helen and I made eleven shirts, using feed sacks from my parent's store. They were for the young men in the local Bible school. For some it was the first shirt, other than a T-shirt, they had owned. For the larger students, we put a yoke and facings of front and collar out of a matching solid color. That way we could get one shirt out of one sack. As I was sewing, Helen made buttonholes and sewed on buttons. The shirts were nice and they were proud. One day while we were yet sewing shirts, an African came and told us Tartan was sick and shaking. We knew she was off her food and had mange. She went places that we never knew about. She could have contracted any disease. We stopped our sewing and went to see about her. She was foaming at the mouth; the African said she had rabies. We took her out behind the garage. Helen held her collar and I shot her in the head. We nearly fainted. We left our sewing for later and went to bed. That evening, I wrote letters. In one, because I was so angry, I said to my Aunt Leonora in Phoenix, "Africa is not fit for a dog." Later she replied, "What about people; are they less delicate?" I wrote in reply, "Yes, animals live or die, mostly because of humans. They can't convince a vet of their age for rabies shots, boil and filter their water, wear mosquito boots, or wash their hands after fellowship. They can't wear a pith helmet or sleep under a net so flies can't lay eggs under their skin and hatch worms. They can't wash their grass with potassium permanganate, as we do our uncooked veggies and fruit, to prevent hepatitis and other illnesses. They will not sit on the porch and watch as their friends romp in cow manure-infested dirt; they join their friends and then come to love us. God says we are to care for the animals. Genesis 1: 26. So much for my sermon." My Aunt Leonora mentioned several times in letters that she would like to come to Africa near to my furlough and travel home with me. She reported on her children. My cousin Lester was in law school, Robert was at UCLA and had an MG and Cathy had gotten married.

Ann Symonds and Becky Davison, the British nurse-midwives, came to visit us in July. After the heartbreak of Tartan, it helped to have company. We had corresponded with A and B, as we called them, while we were in England and they were in the Gold Coast. Now, Ann and Becky had just returned from furlough in England and would be with us until July 22. Then they would go to Nakpanduri Clinic, where they had been stationed most of their years in the Gold Coast. Dorothy and Vivan Smith, whom we visited at Nakpanduri six months ago, would move to Walewale to operate a midwifery clinic. Addie and Polly, the area missionaries for Walewale, would return from America in August. That would make six single ladies in the North. For the moment, we were four women at Saboba for two weeks! On a Tuesday while Helen, A and B, and Gylima had leper clinic, Biyimba and I washed clothes. While the wash water heated on the wood stove, I had fun bartering with Mananyi, a teenage girl, for more wood. The rains made it harder for the women and young girls to find wood to sell. We were forced to pay more per headload than in the dry season. We bargained for each headload although we knew about what we could pay. We got to know them that way. Njonabi, the yardman, called to me, "Madam, I find, I find, I no see the cong-cong for water." The five-gallon can he carried water in was lost. I said, "Hunt it; I did not eat it." He thought it was hilarious that I might eat a cong-cong. We both laughed and went off to find the tin can. A storm hit; lightening was fierce! We killed the gasoline washer engine, as we were on an open porch. Our days often went differently from scheduled. Naomi Hale had invited the four of us to dinner; Ann Symonds' birthday was near. It was also the second anniversary of Helen's and my waving good-bye to the Statue of Liberty. We provided cake and ice cream for the grand party. Little Stevie and Mama Sarah always made our visits with the Hales delightful. The road was like a river as we drove home. A very sick man awaited us at the clinic. We treated him and then went to finish the wash and hang it out to dry.

Biyimba was learning to cook, but as we taught him, it still consumed time. We bought a three-burner butane stove with money from women in the New Mexico District. It took time to request the money, buy the stove, get it hauled this far into the bush, and set it up for use. We kept the wood stove to boil the drinking water, heat the wash water, and boil the beans on washday. On July 25 (my mom's birthday), Ann and Becky left Saboba. They promptly were stuck in the mud and Dewey went with his Jeep to get them on their way to Tamale. We planned to drive that same road in less than a month. Since we had no phone, we waited for a letter to see if they got to their clinic station safely. Communication methods made the clinics at Saboba and Nakpanduri extremely isolated. When A and B did write, they said they had bought a huge set of dishes for Helen and me from the Thomas family who were leaving to America on furlough. The dishes were a thank-you for our hospitality.

The Konkomba family homes nearest to our house were about a block away in several directions. The Saboba Market area, Gylima's house, some Moslem families, a few Fulani, Hausa, and other Nigerian traders were southwest. The police station and all roads out of Saboba were northwest. Kpata-paab, Chief Quadin's village, was northeast. If you walked a path from his village to the police station, you would pass between our house and the clinic. The path was nearer to the clinic. Probably the nearest occupied mud huts with grass roofs was Yando's compound southeast of our house. Just at the edge of our yard was Yando's fetish tree. He had worn a path crossing the open field to that tree, where he made sacrifices of chickens and animals. When we first got to Saboba, I made the mistake of nailing a target to that tree for practice. A young man came to tell me it was Yando's fetish tree and that I must not shoot it. I had seen someone making sacrifices under the tree now and then. One morning we were awakened by the repeated blasts of the handmade muzzle-loader guns. We had been told at the clinic, as we repaired hands with fingers blown off by those guns, that they were used to let everyone know an important person had died and to frighten away evil spirits. We knew instantly that Yando, the head fetish man, had died. In the distance came shrill cries, drums, and blasts from other villages in reply. Helen and I had been to visit Yando. When we heard he was ill, we went again. We asked him if he had heard that God had sacrificed Jesus, His own Son. He said, "People have told me about that." We told him a little more and he agreed for us to pray with him. Our interpreter prayed with him; the rest we left to God. On the morning of the guns, they hoisted white, blue, and yellow flags over their huts and an effigy of a man in the native attire. A white helmet was put atop the tallest hut. They brought a flag and put it under his tree near our house. This was not altogether a sad time for the people. They killed and ate chickens, sheep, and cows with plenty of grain and yams. They drank pito, the local brew. Hundreds of people danced nonstop to loud drums night and day. His wealth would be at their disposal for a few days as they indulge in the funeral customs. I was called several times that week to shoot snakes in our yard. Either the dancers were running snakes out of the bushes into our yard, or the snakes thought there was an earthquake and were coming up from fear. We got little rest, day or night, for that week. Through the years, the tree died and the path from it to Yando's house dimmed.

The day we planned to go shopping in Tamale, the local talk was that ten big market lorries were stuck seven miles west at the Yombateau River Bridge. That indicated we might not be shopping in Tamale for at least another month. We had post office slips for packages from Las Cruces, Clovis, Belen, and Raton. They would wait in Yendi, as we must personally sign for them for security reasons. Even if our vehicle could get through the mud and over the bridge, too many stranded trucks blocked our way. Lorries would be stuck there until the rains slackened. The garden that had died at least three times because of no rain was now under water. It had produced two ears of corn, a handful of cherry tomatoes, radishes, a few dwarf turnips, and a cantaloupe that was solid larvae inside. A fly had stung it. Only the peppers were doing well. In the dry season everything got brittle and cracked, while wood curled and warped. Now we were learning about the rainy season; shoes and books got moldy while wood swelled. Drawers and doors would not shut, or could not be opened. We learned that the dry heat cracked the negatives to our pictures. In the rainy season, they got moldy. We started keeping the unexposed film in the refrigerator and mailing the negatives to America. The ivory crocodile and Gold Coast icon, bought at a Kumasi carving shop during the convention in December, were finally mailed to Dad and Mom. The ebony bookends went to my sister and her husband for birthdays and Christmas.

On August 14, we had a very ill lady to transport to Yendi. Lorries stranded at the Yombateau River Bridge had been removed. The bridge had been under water for days and the side rails were broken and gone. We drove across sixteen-inch planks for each wheel. At another place, we waited while the road crew repaired the approach to a bridge with tree limbs, rocks, and dirt. Even then, the bottom of the car touched rocks and logs as we rolled slowly over them. It was Sunday, so we could not get movies at the post office showing my new niece, Roxanne, and nephew, David. Since we got that far we decided to try going on to Tamale; it was time for our typhoid boosters. Between Yendi and Tamale, we saw our first gorilla in the wild. He walked across the road ahead of us, reached up, and held onto a tree limb as he watched us pass. He seemed as tall as a man; it was awesome.

The McCorkles had a movie projector in Tamale. We were all disappointed that there were no movies. We had to say, as the Africans did, "That will be next time." At the evening meal, four-year-old Amonna Sue was so sleepy that her mother and I were feeding her until I told her the freckles on my arm were caused by not eating my peas. She awoke, grabbed the spoon, and shoveled them in. Franklin and Aneice told us Pauline Smith and Adeline Wichman had recently arrived from furlough in America. We decided to go sixty miles north to Walewale on a roughly paved road and meet them for the first time. Amonna Sue was allowed to go along. She sat between Helen and me on a stack of books. She read from the Bible about *Jesus fishing with Moses* and other stories. Then she said, "Auntie, when I get to America and the teacher wants to show me how to read, I will tell her thank you, but I already know." In Walewale, Amonna Sue was happy to be with her four African aunties and Nimbu. He was a young African helper who had only been in Tamale with the McCorkles while A and P, as we sometimes called them, were on furlough. During the noon meal, Polly and Addie told us that three metal drums for Saboba Clinic had arrived with their freight. The barrels contained bandages, baby shirts, and blankets from New Mexico women's groups. Edith Whipple, National Women's Director at headquarters, had found money for the freight! After a first meeting with Polly and Addie, we safely returned Amonna Sue to her parents in Tamale, shopped a whole day, and then went home to Saboba. As we passed through Yendi, we got the packages containing the movies. "Patience, little donkey," my cousin Kathy Wister always said. It would still be a matter of weeks before we could return to Tamale and view those movies.

Back in Saboba, about sundown on Wednesday, we unloaded our car. There was a month's supply of groceries with a basket of fruit and the seventy-two-piece set of dishes from Ann and Becky. We bought some items from the Thomas and McCorkle families who were leaving on furlough within the next few months. There was a pressure cooker, chair, mop, broom, shovel, rake, and three trees, which were three feet tall. There were three, fifty-yard rolls of chicken wire and a coil of barbed wire for the fence we had pooled our birthday money to buy. With all this plus three people and their suitcases, the vehicle was so heavily loaded that it felt like we were driving with the brakes on, but we did not get stuck. We were so tired and it was getting dark so we took time to light the kerosene fridge. With considerable frustration, we discovered a *whole case* of matches bought in the United States would not begin to light. The case read, "Guaranteed to light in damp weather." We saved them for the dry season and found others. The Servell fridge had an open flame under it to heat the gas that cooled it. The fire was dangerous, as it would sometimes flare up if the wick were not kept strictly trimmed; houses had burned because of kerosene fridges. We always killed the fire and serviced ours before we left on a trip so it would be ready to light when we returned so tired from travel. After that, we found time to open some packages and saved others to open the next day.

Early next morning, we were back in our routine. I taught the local Bible school students. Helen took the maternity clinic on August 17. Clinic numbers were increasing in every category. We had delivered twenty babies in the previous two months. One mother reported that she had lost all six of her babies at birth. We gave injections of penicillin to women with this type of history in case it was a result of syphilis. The husband had to be willing to pay for himself and all his other wives, about twenty-five cents each, before we would inject the pregnant woman. This lady was given penicillin. In due time, she delivered a healthy baby and happily gave God credit. That afternoon, Helen and I picked oodles of tomatoes, radishes, and leaf lettuce from our garden and took some to the Hales in Toma, as Naomi had delivered three babies for us while we were in Tamale. We stopped to inspect the big new Toma church being built. It was going up slowly but surely. In the evening, we put away enough dishes to serve a convention. We later left them in Saboba and many nurses used them.

When a fierce rainstorm hit next morning, we were made aware of how necessary the fence around our house was and that we had made our journey to and from Tamale just in time; we were *marooned again*. Goats, sheep, cows, and fowl had discovered our veranda to escape the heat or rains. Who could blame them? My head was not far from a window where heavy breathing, sneezing, mooing, or cackling critters often rudely awakened me. Their hot breath actually blew into my face through the screen wire. On a trip to the bush with three helpers, we cut, trimmed, and hauled eighty fence posts. Every post was crooked as a dog's hind leg, as the trees were not very tall. We painted them with coal tar laced with DDT, kerosene and selignum (creosote). Njonabi dug holes for posts and the one hundred sixty yards of chicken wire we brought from Tamale was nailed to eighty posts topped with barbed wire. I made two gates from Frank Powers shipping crates; every board was spliced. We had cuts, blisters, bruises on hands and painful backs for days. Our birthday fence was complete! However, another problem developed. The animals moved their sleeping quarters to the clinic porches. I sent word for the chief to send someone each morning to sweep away the night's residue and then we scrubbed it with Detol (Lysol) water.

1-3. Trek to the Oti River for a hippo-burger. 4. Cholada, Tege, Biy-imba (the cook), Torba (the yardman), and Nina. 5. Pastor Salah (lower right) and church elders with me. 6. Rev. Brown and family at Yendi. 7. Sad news from Phoenix, via Aunt Leonora. (Re: Mother of Mae Livengood-Cohea.) 8. Vangie, Annette, and Benny Kessler.

1. Techimentia Clinic. 2. Midwife and clinic dresser. 3. Techimentia Assemblies of God Church. 4-7. Clinic opening and dedication. Missionary Burdette and Doris Wiles. 8. House the locals were building for American nurses or midwives. 9-10. Biyimba (Amos), Helen and I went to dedication. 12. The Konkomba girls' sewing class (11. just a bit of humor.)

Chapter Four

From Vanguard to Chevrolet, 1956

D URING A SHORT LETUP in late August rains, Missionary Dave Wakefield came from Bassari. He got stuck in the Oti River, trekked past our house, and continued on to the Hales' house. We did not see him. The Hales were not at home, but Dave borrowed their Jeep to get his car out of the river. We first knew all this was happening when he brought the Jeep to us and asked us to return it. Daylight was almost gone and he was exhausted. When I heard Dewey's plane come in, I drove the Jeep to their house through almost impassable mud and water. They had dropped down in Yendi and collected our mail along with theirs. We had letters and package slips. Floyd Thomas arrived with them to see what was going on in Saboba. He said his family would be in Albuquerque, New Mexico in about a month to visit his wife's brother, Everett Smith. It had not been three years since we saw the Thomas family in London, so they must have taken early furlough for reasons unknown to us. Naomi Hale drove me to the clinic in their Jeep.

The next day, Dr. Ashworth made his way through the mud for an official visit to Saboba Clinic. The good news for the doctor was that the tropical ulcer count had lowered from one hundred to seventy per day. This was due to penicillin, vitamins, Bileti's surgical dressings, and an increase in rainwater for bathing. The doctor reminded us again of our injection license for *yaws only*. We had saved one case for consultation. A young girl had brought her baby to us asking how to end its life; it had severe cerebral palsy. We told her only God should give or take life, but our hearts were broken for the little mother. She said no man would marry her with this kind of child. She allowed us to pray with her, although she did not attend the local church. The doctor said nothing could be done for the child. Some days later, the little mother came back to the clinic alone. She had taken the child to a local medicine man; he had done as she asked. In the 2000s, there are medical men in America who might have obliged her.

Our support checks for September 1955 were burned in a plane crash in the Canary Islands. We received loan checks from the General Council to operate the clinic and eat until ours could be replaced. The report of the crash waved in and out from Liberia on our wireless; people had died. Two weeks into September, we were forced to transport a very sick woman to Yendi hospital. As usual, we took our package slips to the post office. We took three helpers with us, as the possibility of being stuck was real. Gylima, *the PhD*, said, "Madam, this is *faith in action*; we *believe* we will get stuck!" At times, we could not see the ruts under the water and we hit high center. Our helpers bounced us out. The deep water sometimes touched the fan and we stopped to let the engine dry. They walked along through the water to show me where the edge of the road was or put rocks and boards in a puddle so we could cross. We bent a tie rod and came home with a crooked wheel to add to previous problems of a bad battery, loosened exhaust pipe, one bumper hanging on, and the other one bent, letters missing off the license plate, a broken door handle, and lights that worked part-time. The contents of the packages lifted our hearts. A bag of rice my Mamaw Layman contributed had broken inside one box. When we opened it, the rice scattered on the floor. We swept it up, washed it, cooked, and ate it. In the same broken parcel was a cake mix. For a visit by Dr. Ashworth, Biyimba prepared to bake the cake. After removing the plastic bag containing the mix, there was some content left inside the cake mix box. He brought it, asking if he should add it to what was in the plastic bag. We *assumed* the plastic bag had broken, and said, "Yes, add it to the cake before cooking." The cake was beautiful, but one taste told us we had made a wrong decision. The extra content had been *talcum powder* from another container!

As the rains decreased, we went to Tamale and saw movies of David, my nephew, on his first birthday. In the movies, big Dave was beaming on Davey exactly as he had on Jim when I visited them in Norfolk. There were also movies of my dainty niece, Roxanne, born just as we left England. Helen wrote a poem:

> *To see you in the movies was really quite a treat.*
> *Honestly, I couldn't leave my seat!*
> *So I begged and begged the movie man*
> *those movies to repeat.*
> *I saw two darling bonny babes having, oh, such fun.*
> *With Grandma, and Grandpa too, ever on the run.*
> *I saw Royce with a pretty maid, but alas, the movie ended!*
> *We're sending that roll back at once,*
> *With hopes that can be mended.*
> *The parents new, a good job do; of that, we have no doubt.*
> *We only fear those lively babes will surely wear them out.*
> *Please keep the movies rolling, across the deep blue sea.*
> *You'll never know how much they mean*
> *to Charlese and to me.*
>
> —Lovingly, Helen.

What a wonderful way to celebrate our *first-year anniversary* in Africa. We mailed the movies back to the United

States; they had been in the tropics long enough. Another reason to celebrate, our Chevrolet was aboard the *S.S. Taurus* on its way from New York! The year without a dependable vehicle had been tough. We had not been inside Dewey's airplane since the day we arrived in Saboba. In order to get to our station, my co-worker had twice broken a promise made to her mother not to fly. In both cases, we had no choice. When we needed to send a patient to the hospital, we sent them to Dewey for a plane ride or to a market lorry driver. We left them to bargain for the fare. Then we borrowed the Standard Vanguard for six cents per mile. The American men who loaned it to us admitted they would dread the job of keeping it road-worthy! Thus began my positive reputation about car-care. The youth in our American churches provide all kinds of vehicles, duplicators, and communication equipment like loud speakers. The program was growing by leaps and bounds. How fortunate we were, compared to earlier missionaries who did not have this kind of support. By having to wait, we learned how important Speed-the-Light was.

Our garden flourished with the heavy rains. The green chili peppers were eight inches long. We found someone in Tamale to take a bag of peppers five hundred miles to people in Accra who were from Texas and loved peppers the way we did. We attached this few lines of a quasi-limerick to the bag:

The content of this plastic bag are fine if you can take it.
But we must warn you, they are HOT, so eat them bit-by-bit.
In Mexico, we like 'em hot; we hear you like 'em too.
Hey, *Pennsylvania's* ketchin' on and eatin' not a few!
C & H.

Back in Saboba, anticipation of the arrival of the Chevrolet made the month drag! We were both running a low-grade fever every afternoon. The Paludrin tablet, taken with breakfast, probably suppressed our having a full-blown case of malaria, but wasn't stopping the fever. We started planning the five hundred-mile trip to get our car at Takoradi Harbor. Gylima and Bileti would be left at the clinic again to help in emergencies and to dress ulcers. We decided to give them two weeks off to work on their farms before we left. They had taken no time off since we arrived a year ago. We felt it would also help our language skills to be without our good interpreters. One day while they were on leave, it was Helen's day to treat sixty-three people inside the clinic. I dressed seventy-seven ulcers for those seated around the edge of the veranda and was sunburned on my back. In the process, a big man with a scowling face went raging down the row of people picking out young boys and beating them with a whip. A woman and man bent over one boy to protect him. All those naked young boys grabbed their straw hats and went flying down the road. The little cowboys had left their herd of cattle unattended and came to the clinic for sores to be dressed. The cows had gotten into that man's field. Later, the cowboys returned as spry as ever, sat down in line and I dressed their tropical ulcers. After the last ulcer, I went to the house to check on the men who were painting our cement floors and wooden louvers in windows and doors. A couple had dashed us a chicken for delivering their baby, so I cooked it for lunch. When I went to the garden for tomatoes, cucumbers, peppers, and runty carrots, I heard voices. Inside, among the vines, were three young cowboys furiously eating the eight-inch chili peppers from tip to stem, seeds and all. They fled before I could dig up enough Lekpakpaln to talk with them! Fresh veggies made our meal delicious. By the time we got back with our new car, the rains would have stopped and all signs of a garden would be gone. We would be back to the vitamin bottle and trips to Tamale market for fruit.

That evening we were practicing our accordion and guitar together when two policemen brought an old man to our veranda. He was splashed in blood. We set up a first aid area on our *palaver porch* and Helen sutured his head. We asked, "Who did this?" A policeman replied, "We did. This is the man who has been poisoning teenage girls because their fathers are not pledging them in marriage to the men he recommends; he tried to run from us." Helen said, "Hand me those forceps, I'll add a stitch for every girl he killed!" We had been helping parents whose daughters he poisoned. We felt helpless, as we were new and did not know their poisons. The police took their prisoner and left. We circled a pile of furniture in the middle of our front room, jumped the wet border of maroon cement paint around the linoleum, and got to our beds. Tomorrow would be pregnant women's day.

Friday of that week was exactly one year since we walked that precarious ramp at the Takoradi Harbor; time had flown. It was time for inventory both at church and at clinic. There were fewer complicated maternity cases because of prenatal care and teaching. There were fewer babies and children dieing from malaria, tetanus, and pneumonia. Baby shirts, blankets, and bandages were arriving regularly. One-third fewer tropical ulcers reflected a decrease in cases of yaws. We had treated around fifteen hundred per month in general clinic. Hopes were high that a cure for leprosy was possible. With our method of treatment, adults seldom died of snakebite. The chances of recovery for children with snakebite had improved, but infants usually succumbed to the venom of the viper. Services were being held in the big new cement church. The walls were not complete, but the roof was anchored to pillars and protected the worshipers from rains. There were constant testimonials in church: "I was sick, I went to the clinic, and heard about the blood sacrifice of God's Son. I want to make Jesus the Lord of my life." Increasingly, people told of healings through prayer. Two young men in our local Bible school had been accepted to the three-year Bible school in Kumbungu. We went to bed feeling elated about what God had let us see in the lives of the people. When hands clapped, we suspected someone was calling us to the clinic. No! Our post had come with a telegram! Our car had arrived in Takoradi harbor, *one year to the day* from our arrival!

Gylima and Bileti, our clinic workers, had returned from leave. We went to Tamale where we had been instructed to abandon The Stranded. Paul and Virginia Weidman and Faith, their teenager daughter, had driven north to Tamale from the port city of Takoradi. Helen and I joined them for the return trip south. I recall very little of that trip because of my extreme anticipation. Since the mission convention in March, Paul Weidman was Secretary-Treasurer of the Mission Committee, replacing Bronnie Stroud, who lived far north at Bawku. Most transactions involving mission money took place at Takoradi harbor when people or their freight arrived or departed. He had been sending our fifty dollars a month for clinic medicines and twelve dollars for station maintenance; we enjoyed the humorous notes and announcements he added. We took possession of our new car at Takoradi harbor on October 21, my sister's birthday. The 1955 station wagon was aquamarine with green tinted windows, *but only had two doors!* How would we get sick people into the back seat? This was to be an ambulance; we had forgotten that item in our order! We stayed that few days in the home of the Weidman family. They seemed to know so much about Africa. We were latecomers, but learning. From Takoradi, we drove to Accra, the capitol, to register the vehicle and update our Gold Coast and International Driver's Licenses. The drive east along the Gulf of Guinea was beautiful, much like the Pacific coast in America. There were leaf cactus plants with apples on them like in New Mexico. We took pictures of a big one and ate a picnic lunch nearby. In Accra, we bought a few things and mailed them home for family and friends at birthdays and Christmas. We wished for our October checks so we could buy food to take back north. The postmaster in Accra kindly tried to intercept them. He found letters from our families, but no checks. They would be waiting for us in Saboba, where we could buy very little food.

The trip north through the jungle was breathtaking as always. We could take our time and see things. Missionaries and Africans alike were impressed with our vehicle. There were waves and cheers of "Akwaaba, Akwaaba." ("Welcome, welcome, Madam.") Along the road children called, "Baturi, baturi, Akwaaba, Akwaaba." ("White person, welcome!") They even called, "Airplane! Airplane!" When we left the Ashanti Forest and crossed the Volta River Ferry at the town of Yeji, the blacktop roads ended and we had to dedicate our new car to God. The dust started boiling in around the doors; we turned red. Still it could have been worse; we *could have had four doors* instead of two! It never let dust in as badly as the Standard Vanguard, but we started plugging up holes that we found. We even wished it did not have a rear tailgate door to fold down. However, that was convenient for loading and unloading. We piled in stalks of bananas; missionaries in the North would be glad to see those. Farther north, we passed laborers making the roads passable after the rains. It was our turn to call to them in Dagbani, *the trade language,* "Na tuma! Na tuma!" ("Thank you for your work.") The Lord knew we meant that from our hearts! Nearer to Saboba, the people lined the roads calling, "Welcome, Madam!" in their language. You could tell they liked the beautiful car. Finally, there it was in Saboba! Biyimba and Njonabi, our house and yard helpers always came to welcome us home and help us unload. Njonabi's wife, Piger, even came to help sometimes. Biyimba was yet unmarried. Gylima, his wife, Bakanti, and their girls had built a house between our house and the market to be nearer the clinic. They had previously lived in Nalongni with his father, Akonsi. If Gylima saw the lights of our vehicle, or someone told him we had come, he came to help unload and report on the *clinic palavers*. That day, Helen stepped out of our car and instantly screamed; she almost stepped on a snake. It was halfway down a hole before I shot it. Biyimba and Njonabi pulled the snake out and *finished his chop palaver*. We counted seven new holes. The snakes must have felt safe with no noise above them, so they come out to have a ball while we were gone. It took time in Africa to realize we must scream but not run, for if we got our eyes off the snake we never found it again. Biyimba and Njonabi filled all the holes and pounded them closed.

We had a lot of post, including a few parcels. I learned that my Dora friends, Lola (Bates) and Doyle Wilson and daughter, Sharon, had moved to California. My brother, Royce, moved their furniture. My Phoenix friend, Mae (Livengood) Cohea sent a family picture so I could see Bill, her husband, and their children Billy and Burla; Tim was not yet born. A letter came from N.D. Davidson and family in Oregon. They were my pastors in Phoenix when I left to attend SBI in Texas. He said they knew the Kesslers who were in Accra from the Oregon District.

Our garden was completely dead. This was where we came in a year ago. We would not see a cloud for almost six months. We dreaded the heat, but were not on a back screened-in porch, with both sleeping on a three-quarter bed. We now had good transportation. We could thank God, officials at the mission headquarters, and officials in our districts (states), our families, friends, and laymen on both sides of the Atlantic Ocean. Biyimba, at ten years of age, started washing dishes for Ozella and Ruby after they *brought him back from the dead*. We thought he saved our lives daily! He desperately wanted to learn to cook and by the beginning of this second year, he had his cardex of menus and recipes, could read them, and make them. U pung umung, paa! (He really tried himself!) He wanted to marry, but the girls were promised when they were born. His mother, Gaemba, was a widow. She refused to marry again so had no money to buy brides for her sons; she said God would provide. She had at least four other sons whom I knew well. *Bileti* was surgical dresser at the clinic. One of Gaemba's sons, *Jagir*, was a leper. We named one of his sons Zachaeus, as he was so tiny when he was born. Jagir was a deacon in the Saboba-Toma Church and had a beautiful family. *Makuba* led the cow that brought Biyimba to the clinic when his life was saved; he was attending our local Bible school and planned to go to Northern Ghana Bible Institute at Kumbungu soon. *Torba*, Gaemba's youngest, was yet at home. *Long time customs* in the tribes were that when the girls were infants they were pledged to men who paid for them with hours of labor or animals for years until they were of age to marry. When a girl had her first baby, those who bargained for her would know she was old enough to get married and they may come to take her along with her first baby. A village chief and his elders may have bargained for her. When she was taken she might become wife number two, wife number three, four, or more to a man in that group. They might even agree for her to go to a younger man who needed a first wife at the time. The girl of age may not agree to go to the man chosen for her. Before independence day, the British government officials had a method to free her, but the elders sometimes kept the girls unaware of this method. She was kept fearful, as she was told of killings in freedom attempts. To be free, she must be aware of this method and be willing to fight for her freedom. A girl in Saboba must travel forty miles to Yendi. There in front of the District Offices the girl must hold to a flagpole. When the British District Commissioner appeared, she told him her story. Investigations were held; compromises were made, and sometimes people were killed in the process. If the young girl won her freedom, the young man who got the girl must *watch his chop palaver* for a long time. Poison food or an arrow may be used even years in the future. Vendettas were neither forgiven, nor forgotten quickly, *if ever*. We sewed up people who erred years ago!

November became very busy with clinics daily, among deliveries and emergencies like pneumonia or snakebite. The Hales flew to Liberia for Thanksgiving on November 15 for a whole month. Mama Sara was not returning with them; Stevie was older. We had a going away party for Mama Sara. This kind of social event was new to them. We had Teacher Nakoja to interpret; he knew what a *social* was. He kept telling them they must sip their punch *small-small* as they talked with friends. Usually, they washed their mouth out with the last mouthful of drinking water and spat it away. That was good, as eggs from guinea worms and other varmints settle to the bottom. Biyimba told them how our water was strained through a cloth, boiled, and then dripped through a chalk candle filter before being cooled in the fridge, something yet impossible for villagers. They were still hesitant and laughed nervously as they drank their punch *to the last drop*. While the Hales were gone, we continued to make time to work on the growing cement church. The cement foundation and floor were there. The roof was built atop cement and rock pillars a number of feet apart. It got the people out of extremely hot or rainy weather. Not all cement walls were complete between floor, roof, and pillars. Helen helped the WMs ladies to plaster and paint walls after the men poured the cement and it set.

We planned a time to get our mail from Yendi, until the Hales returned mid-December. Once when we went, we met a new British District Commissioner, Reginald Wallace. His wife, Barbara, a retired doctor, was on crutches. Their young daughter, Elizabeth, would soon return to England for school. Phyllis, another British lady, seemed to be a companion to the disabled wife. A celebration was planned in Yendi to welcome those new arrivals. Helen and I were invited and we went. Early in the day, we set up camp in the empty Yendi mission bungalow. That included sweeping up hundreds of bats, dead and alive, and throwing them outside.

We put mosquito nets over two beds and dressed for the big welcome. The Gold Coast Police Band provided the music. The new government agent invited Dr. Ashworth and us to dinner at his home after the activities. That was partly for the new agent to become aware of expatriates in his area. After the beautiful, posh affair, we crawled into our *canopied beds* and slept like royalty in spite of the remaining bats that slammed into the nets. The next morning, we collected early Christmas packages from the post office and returned to Saboba. What a change from last year when the box, with no key available, was locked in our storeroom for the Christmas duration. One package contained a Presto Cooker from First Assembly in Albuquerque. My sister, Mae, sent personalized tea napkins. She tagged some articles with the names of my nephews Jimmy and Davie.

Dr. Ashworth said the Minister of Health from Accra and the Regional Medical Officer from Tamale would pay a visit to Saboba Clinic with him in December. We heard the Governor, Sir Charles Arden-Clarke, might be with them. We were not concerned, our African helpers knew their jobs better than a year ago; we certainly knew ours better, too. Between the usual clinic demands, we cleaned the clinic thoroughly. The visit went well. Then, well into December, our school-age children's Sunday school class started practicing Christmas songs in English. Konkombas, like teacher Samson Mankrom, were good songwriters in their language. We included songs they wrote about Jesus. Gylima helped us write the Christmas story in Lekpakpaln, including Joseph, Mary, the baby Jesus, wise men, angels, and shepherds.

When Dewey and Naomi flew back from Liberia, two Canadian ladies came with them. On our visit to the Cheraponi Chief's compound, the two Canadians went with us. The rains were over, so the roads were dry but full of holes, and bridges were damaged or gone. We went around one bridge and passed through the dry arroyo (creek) bed. We stopped the car at the bottom and took pictures. The next arroyo was not so deep but its walls were too steep to drive into safely. We took a shovel, cutlass, some boards, and my gun for meat on most journeys. We decided to repair the bridge with boards, stones, tree limbs, and sod. As we drove across, it fell in behind us. If we returned that way, we would need to build the bridge again, but in the dark. At Cheraponi, we formally greeted the Tchakosi Chief, routine in any village. We asked permission to hold the meeting and he agreed. He said he knew Dewey Hale was flying in his plane to Nasoni and Tamboun, two nearby Konkomba villages, to give the people medicine, leper treatment, and teachings about God. The mass of children had feathers, beads, or both around their wrist, neck, hips or ankle. At the side of the house stood an earthen pot upside down with feathers and other remains of blood sacrifices. This compelled us to tell them about the sacrifice of God's Son, and that another blood sacrifice was no longer necessary. They said, "We can see the chicken blood; we cannot see the blood of this Jesus on a cross." Our message required *faith*, a concept not easily explained. They say, "He de, like He no de." ("He's there, like He's not there." Or, "We do not know where He is.") However, six strong-looking men came forward for prayer to accept Christ as their Sacrifice. We had no church there and it was *forty miles from Saboba*. I felt overwhelmed by challenge, but full of joy. As this was happening, the Chief removed his ornate hat and put it on the head of his three-year-old son, who was clinging to his leg. The small boy had on a white, flowing robe similar to his father's. What a picture! We called him the *little chief*. Because of the damaged bridge, we chose to return to Saboba through Wapuli, a trek ten miles longer. Helen and I had been discussing how much we wanted a turkey for a Christmas dinner. As we rode along, suddenly I thought I saw a turkey squatting in the brush by the side of the road. I applied the brakes and Gylima ran back with a flashlight. He returned with a *domestic turkey*. He said it might have fallen off a lorry going to French Togo, as there were no villages nearby. In Saboba we put the turkey in a metal drum covered by screen wire for air; it fussed all night. Next morning we tipped the drum to remove the turkey and there was a snake curled on the ground under the drum. The poor turkey had felt it moving. We staked the turkey out until we felt it would not run away.

On Wednesday evening before Christmas, we had the party for our employees, their wives, children, and the local pastor. We had candy and popcorn for the children. They probably would have *preferred* eight-inch chili peppers! So would I, but the garden was gone. The wrapped gifts were mostly clothing. We had laid aside the choice items from packages. We added a comb, pencil, or other small item. Our workers were *special*. We had not been to Tamale since we brought our Chevrolet to Saboba with four new tubeless tires on the ground and two spares. We were a bit surprised that we could have a Christmas dinner for ten people, five American and five British, having not been to a store for two months. Dr. Frank Ashworth, Government Agent Reginald Wallace, his wife Barbara, their ten-year-old Elizabeth, and Phyllis had come from Yendi. The five from Saboba were Dewey, Naomi, little Stevie, Helen and me. Dr. Ashworth carved the perfectly browned turkey. We served dressing, sweet potatoes, carrots and peas, cranberry sauce, and pickles. A chocolate cake with Merry Christmas emblazoned on it and a mince pie were dessert. All were from tin cans or cardboard boxes except the hot rolls and the turkey! After the meal, small wrapped gifts were exchanged. We had decorated a dry, leafless tree with ornaments from my sister's early Christmas box. In December, the trees were dry because of the arid heat and not because of a cold winter. Elizabeth Wallace and Stevie Hale, for whom we did most of the tree bit, thoroughly enjoyed the day. Opening of the gifts could best be described as *hilarious!* For example, the doctor had teased me a lot about my Mexican food, so we gave him a cup of uncooked pinto beans, stationery, and a can of mixed nuts. He said he was going to take the beans home to England and show his dear mother how he had suffered. He gave us a box of chocolates, a set of bubble bath and soap. In one week, Africans *and baturi* enjoyed blessings from our families and churches in America and England. Dr. Ashworth was due for leave soon. He said, "Government reports say it has been proven that if employees stay in the tropics over two years, money is lost as work output is cut in half." He was not certain he would return.

Christmas was on Sunday that year. The people rejoiced at their first Christmas in their new, unfinished building. My Sunday school class presented the Christmas skit they had practiced for a month. It had the live baby Jesus. The school-age boys sang Silent Night. What a change from Christmas a year ago! We knew more about the people, *felt at home*, but were tired. After the planned pageant, most all the church went caroling to chiefs' compounds, police station, and the market. With the help of Gylima and Bileti, we had kept the full weekly clinic schedule during all the activities. In spite of our having had a nagging fever, we delivered twelve babies in December (one stillborn breech, possibly from syphilis) and made us new dresses for the upcoming council in Tamale.

Even with a new vehicle, journeys were dusty, over washboard roads, and tiresome, especially at night. One must be alert when driving; animals, bicycles, and people darted here and there, and small square rocks could rip a tire. It still took one day to go to Tamale, one day to shop and one day to return to Saboba. On January 2, we went to Tamale for our second Northern Territory's District Council. It had been in Bawku the previous year. We bravely passed the Yendi Post Office with package slips in hand, because we did not want to haul the contents to a convention. In Tamale, we deposited our three monthly support checks in the bank. We had agreed the previous year to pool our birthday money and put in a fence; this year we decided to put ceilings in our house. We went shopping for lumber and nails. At the open market, we saw so much food *outside of tin cans* that it was shocking. We were so tired from clinic and Christmas that it was even hard to attend the convention. There were twenty-two missionaries present. We met Harold—he preferred to be called Hal-and Naomi Lehmann and their teenager, Gretchen, for the first time. The three had just returned from furlough in the States. Their one son, David, was married and did not come with them. As we visited, I discovered they pastored in Oakland when I lived with my parents in San Francisco during World War II. One day in a service, I heard someone ask Gretchen why she was crying. She said, "The smells! I did not realize how much I missed the smells of Africa." I thought, "That is both touching and amazing; will I ever feel that way?" The Thomas family had gone to the United States; the Lehmanns were camping in the new bungalow at Kumbungu to teach at NGBS along with the Andersons until Homer and Thelma Goodwin returned.

Parts of Tamale were strange to us yet. To find places for so many to sleep at the conference, we were placed in the middle of the village. Even today, I do not know where that mud house was. A small, high window, with a wooden fan to close when it rained or blew dust was open to all the world, for mosquitoes, odors, the beat of drums, and (please) a small breeze. Suddenly there were hands clapping. I sat upright in bed. A male voice said, "Ago-o, we need a mid-wife." It was Hal Lehmann. We were not sure whether it was worse for one to go alone or stay where we were alone. I was chosen to go; Helen decided to stay alone. On the way, Hal explained, "A pastor's wife is about to deliver their firstborn. She is near term and so small that the husband felt he could not come to District Council and leave her at home in Bunk-purugu where they pastor. That town is thirty miles from Ann and Becky, British midwives at Nakpanduri, but they have not yet arrived at District Council." I was wishing I knew a bit more about her medically, but I followed this sage missionary and his torchlight through a maze of back alleys formed by mud houses. Finally, we came to where Pastor Dokurugu and his family lived in the Chogou Parsonage. In the *stranger's room*, just one of the round mud huts, lay a tiny, new Susanna squirming on the floor. That made two of us who had arrived into this *strange new world*. Karen, the new mother, was fine. The young Mamprusi pastor, E.J. Namyela, was a new father. There were several African women in the room. I cut the cord and tended to the mother; one of the women bathed the new baby. Helen and I were so tired from house repairs and clinic operation that I hardly remember what transpired at that council.

After hearing our cat and dog fiasco, the McCorkles gave us two kittens, not yet weaned. We had no idea when we'd come again so we took them. On the way home, they got hungry. We stopped to pour some milk; they could not lap. We stopped at the Yendi Post Office to get our belated Christmas packages. By the time we got to Saboba, the kittens were weak and staggering. We fed them from the tip of a plastic spoon. This continued for weeks, but they never woke us at night. As they got older, they stood on three feet and held onto the spoon with the fourth. Konkie, the female, weaned herself, but not Damba! He would have forever used that plastic spoon if we had obliged. We named the cats after the Konkomba and Dagomba tribes.

The packages picked up in Yendi were full of things we forgot existed. An album for Roxanne's pictures came from my brother and his wife. Shoes came from Dobyns' church in Albuquerque. Red and blue materials with rickrack and thread for fiesta dresses, probably purchased at Pennington's Store, came from the Silver City Church. We made the dresses immediately and wore them every Monday when Biyimba cooked beans and cornbread on washday.

Recently, some juju man made fetishes against Makamabi, a Christian woman. He cut a piece from her best garment in her room as she slept, mixed it with blood and feathers and plastered it up above her door. Some said her husband paid the fetish priest to do that. She took it down and burned it. Then she came to church, told the story, and declared that God could protect her. After a few weeks her husband, Nabiche, came to church and accepted the blood of Christ as his Sacrifice. He brought his fetishes and we watched them burn outside the church. It had not ended there. Their teenage daughter, Mananyi, loved to barter with us over prices of headloads of wood. After attending Sunday school one morning, she went into a coma. We treated her for cerebral malaria and took her to Yendi Hospital, but she died. We brought her body back to Saboba as we had promised the family. The parents had a Christian funeral for her. Some of their older children and people in the village did not agree to this and the parents were forced to sleep at the police station for protection. Their younger daughter, Nabibiche, continued to barter with us to buy their wood.

Construction at the clinic and our house was buzzing. The local council had agreed to build a new maternity building. Then, to protect the people from wind, rain, and sun while waiting for any clinic, they put three walls around the cement slab left from what Ruby called their *cracker-box clinic*. They built a continuous bench inside, against the three walls, and put on a corrugated tin roof. At our house, carpenters were putting in the ceilings. It made an attic for critters to stay in, but kept them away from us. The new ceilings could not be attached to the delicate mud walls, so carpenters made it into a hanging ceiling using upright two-by-fours, of various lengths, attached to rafters above. We wondered if it would be too heavy and collapse the old mud house. Bats flew against our mosquito nets only occasionally now. Lizards quit falling on top of the nets and dropping stones or their own droppings onto our nets or into our coffee cup at breakfast. Even geckos could not walk upside down on the ceiling, but they still walked the walls and clicked to each other. The snakes still lived in the grass roof, but we saw them only above the verandas where there was neither aluminum nor ceilings. Occasionally, I shot at snakes in the grass roof. When anything fell on my head from the grass roof, I froze until it hit the floor and I could turn to see what it was. Our ceiling project ended, but building at the clinic continued.

Just before Dr. Ashworth went to England, we invited him, the Hales and two European United Nations Plebiscite Observers to a farewell Mexican dinner; we wore our fiesta dresses. As usual, the doctor reminded us that our injection license was only for the purpose of eradicating yaws. The next day, in spite of our hesitation because he was our Medical Director, we mailed a cartoon cut from a Saturday Evening Post to the doctor. In it, a patient was on a grass mat, and a medicine man was complaining, "Oh, these wonder drugs, they've got my patients immune to bat's eyes and lizard dust!" We signed it, "Yaws truly, the Saboba nurses." The doctor went on leave without responding.

Water was getting difficult to obtain and the hippos were challenging the local women for the scant water left in the Oti River. The police had gotten permission to kill any hippo that threatened the safety of the women. One day, Teacher Nakoja, a visiting British man and his wife, and Helen and I trekked to the Oti River bank on bicycles. We saw huge hippo tracks and finally found where the police were butchering two. They gave everyone some of the meat. We ground ours and made hippo burgers.

On February 28, after treating one hundred eight lepers, we planned to go for a village visit. Biyimba was going with us so he prepared our lunch earlier than usual. Then we heard those familiar words, "Madam, a woman wants to born." Our first observation was that she had one *big palaver*. She was already saying to Gylima in Lekpakpaln, "My eyes are turning, my eyes are turning." Americans might say, "The house is going around." Neither is true. To decrease the vertigo we let her inhale a bit of ammonium carbonate (smelling salts) and lowered her head. Believe me, we did some *consulting and praying*. We thought this might be our first mother to die on our delivery table. She was bleeding profusely and continued to bleed until the baby and placenta came at the same time one hour later. We had no blood, but we gave her what fluids we had to increase volume. She survived, but the baby did not. That was the first of three babies we lost in one week, all for different reasons. It was too late to go for the planned village visit, so to relax we played music. I enjoyed strumming chords on Helen's guitar to accompany our singing. Helen played classical guitar and was learning to play my accordion even better than I did. She heard the song, *I'll Meet You in the Morning*, at my Grandmother Spencer's funeral and wanted it, so we wrote home for the music; it eventually came.

It was leap year, February 29, 1956 and Helen and I were stuck in the bush treating seventy general outpatients. In the waiting shed mothers sat with thin cotton cloths around themselves and naked babies in their laps. Some babies obviously had pneumonia. The harmattan had made the early mornings cool. We passed out baby shirts to cover the babies' chests. The next day was Thursday. After maternity clinic, we finally went to the village for the outstation visit. We asked permission of the headman to tell them about another sacrifice. We had brought pictures from used Christmas cards and told them the story of the coming of Jesus to be that Sacrifice. When we gave a card to the Chief, he sent for some eggs to pay for it. He had pieces of the Moslem Koran sewn into leather amulets attached to his cap. We explained that our cards were free and had no power. When we gave cards to the children, they fought among themselves. The group pushed against us so hard that we had to get into the safety of our vehicle. We said, "Next time we come, we will bring more if you promise to sit down quietly so everyone can get one." There was a next time and they got their cards. Dated literature was printed in later years at an Assemblies of God

Press in Accra, but none was more colorful or told the story better than some of those old Christmas cards did.

The first week in March, we went to the Yendi Post Office for packages. In one, there was an excellent pair of pliers from Dad. We had written him that I did a lot of repair work on the car, washing machine, and other items. Helen teased me about being so thrilled over a pair of pliers. Part of the thrill was that Dad had sent something important to him. He trained me as a mechanic's helper by sometimes *conking* me on the head with pliers and Mom trained me as a carpenter's helper when she dressed up old houses. Helen declared that she was more thrilled over the *chili peppers* and pinto beans. She had come a long way from the Jalapeno pepper she thought was a pickle in New Mexico! We delivered three babies in March before we left Saboba to attend the required annual mission conference at the beautiful oceanside, tropical port city of Takoradi. We had been there six months ago to receive our new vehicle. Biyimba went with us as far as Tamale and joined another vehicle taking the African helpers to Takoradi so they could visit while traveling. Biyimba was in demand because of his *Edna Spencer light bread* and his New Mexico *enchilada casserole*. The cooks in Takoradi needed help in catering and enjoyed working with peers.

The McCorkles rode from Tamale to Takoradi with us as they had sold their car and were flying to America on furlough after the conference. They suggested we take a detour by way of Bole National Game Reserve. Helen and I had been too busy to enjoy the many wonders of the Gold Coast. I was driving our new vehicle. Franklin sat in the front passenger's seat making a list of all the animals we saw. Aneice, Helen, and Amonna Sue were in the back seat. In a low gear, the Chevrolet moved slowly up an embankment and out of a sandy arroyo bed into grass that was taller than our vehicle. The road turned sharply and there, in our path, stood a water buffalo with a horn span as wide as our car. We bumped eyeballs with him! His eyes flashed with terror!

From the back seat Helen called, "Franklin, write down the date, time and what we are seeing so when someone finds us dead they will know what happened." After a long moment, the huge animal took a graceful leap and disappeared into the tall grass, but not before I got a rather poor picture. Speculation was that many more were around him in the grass, but we did not wait to find out! Aneice had packed her usual good lunch so we had an Ashanti Forest picnic, including the ants and gnats!

In Takoradi, we stayed in the Weidman home again, and slept downstairs in the same room and beds as we did our first night in Africa. The rhythm of the waves lashing the shore relaxed us and we slept. The conference included the usual reports from Bible Schools, printing press, and clinics. In 1955, the Saboba Clinic had four thousand new cases and thirteen thousand return visits. This represented six thousand visits for general outpatient treatment, four thousand visits for surgical dressing of tropical ulcers, five thousand leper visits, over one thousand maternity visits and sixty-six deliveries. The financial report was the same as last year; we *still got fifty dollars per month*. Missionaries, including Helen and me, had a few dollars transferred from our personal account into the clinic fund monthly in America; that made up the fifty dollars. Helen and I ended our report with one suggestion, "Because we sometimes feel so alone in the clinic work, we suggest a Clinic Committee be established. All new nurses need support and to know objectives and decisions are within mission goals and Gold Coast laws." A letter was read from Ruby Johnson. She planned to come at the end of our term. Wow! A replacement! However, she needed a co-worker. One new family had arrived from America in time for this conference. They were Dale and Betty Brown and their *five children* from Oklahoma City. The previous year, when the conference was in Accra, the Kesslers, Helen, and I were so new that we were not allowed to vote. The Browns were in that position this time. We tried to make this a relaxing time and planned to stay a week after the conference. We went shopping for items we never saw at Saboba. We went to the harbor, as the *M.V. Nigerstroom* had docked. It arrived every three months from Holland. Biyimba, Helen, and I went aboard. This was Biyimba's first time to see the ocean and a ship of that size. His reactions were our enjoyment, probably a reversal of when we first got to his hometown of Saboba! The stewards who had been on board with us a year and a half ago served us tea in the lounge. They took us on a tour of the cabins and we showed Biyimba the one we had occupied. We went to the helm and the captain showed us some new radar equipment. He told us the ship would be newly christened the Ghanakoost when the Gold Coast received independence and became Ghana within a year. We watched them unload a car using a crane.

After the conference, the Weidmans took the McCorkles to Accra to board a plane to the United States. Helen and I were allowed to stay in their house for those few days and Biyimba lodged with the helpers. Helen and I were writing letters to mail at the coast when Biyimba called, "The phone, Madam. Someone wants to talk with you." What, a phone call for us? We re-discovered the phone each time we came out of Saboba. Burdette and Doris Wiles were calling from the harbor. They had arrived from America with their seventeen--year-old son, Dick, and their ten-year-old daughter, Cheryl. They would be stationed in Kumasi in the Ashanti Forest. Biyimba and other helpers joined us as we went to help the Wiles get their equipment, car, and baggage through customs. This was not their first term; Burdette knew the process. We just provided an extra vehicle and helpers. In fact, Burdette Wiles had just been voted in as field chairman *in absentia* since Franklin McCorkle, the outgoing chairman, was going to America on furlough. On the way back to the bungalow, a brake line ruptured on my Chevrolet. We got it repaired, but I felt sad that my car wasn't new any more! The Weidmans returned that day.

We hurried back north. The Lehmanns were moving into the Tamale mission house that the McCorkles vacated; someone must oversee the printing press. We got to Saboba two days before Easter Sunday. As you topped a small hill just before reaching Saboba, you dropped right off that hill onto a plateau. It contained Toma straight ahead, Nalongni where Akonsi lived a bit off the road to the right, and other villages. The tallest building you saw a mile ahead was the Toma church under construction. We first reached Maja's house on the right and Chief Oden's compound on the left. The next on the left, directly across from the Toma church, was where Deacon Beso and wife, Victoria Bilijo, lived with their extended family. They were the *backbone of the Church*. Akonsi, the first Konkomba Christian, was Beso's uncle but acted as a foster father and raised him. A mile or two beyond the church, in a loop of the Oti River, was the end of the road; no bridge crossed the river. Inside that loop could be called the village of Saboba. It contained our mission house and clinic, the police station, and Saboba Market. Chief Quadin's village of Kpatapaab, Yando's village, the Moslem Village of Zongo, and the market were between the mission complex and the river. That plateau, one huge community of villages, could be referred to as the *Saboba Area*. When the people were expecting someone, they watched that hill for a vehicle to appear; all inhabitants knew you had arrived! It still took about fifteen minutes to reach our house. That gave our helpers time to get ready to unload our car and be there to say, "Welcome Madam, we have a snakebite."

The first day of April was Easter. While it was still dark, the people gathered at the church and we all walked up the road to the top of that observation hill beyond the Toma church. The people said this was their first introduction to a sunrise service. They sang with all their hearts; the family harmony was perfect. Pastor Salah read the first Easter story as the sun came peeping into the day. We walked back to the church, taught our Sunday school classes, and Pastor Salah led a blessed worship service. Margurite Shirer was in Saboba on a nostalgic visit. She and her husband had brought Ruby and Ozella into Saboba for their very first day. After the Easter morning service, Mrs. Shirer, Pastor Salah, Helen, and I went to the village of Cheraponi to read the Easter story to the Tchakosi Chief and his people; he remembered Mrs. Shirer. She presented the Easter story partly in Dagbani, the trade language many understood. The Africans do not call it preaching, they say, "Give the Word" or, "Pass the Word." Several people chose to follow Christ that day.

Back in Saboba, we tried to write letters as Billy Graham waved in and out, on shortwave from Liberia. It rained and we were forced to close the shutters. We lit kerosene lamps, but they kept blowing out as wind blew right through shutters. The evening service at the Toma church was sparsely attended because of the storm. Since we were terribly tired, we went to bed early and it was good we did. A rash of emergencies filled our days and nights for the first part of April. A schoolteacher was badly burned with gasoline. We treated a small girl and a thirty-year-old man for snakebite. The girl recovered gradually. In spite of using the antivenom serum, the man lost so much blood that his *eyes were turning*. We treated him for two days and prayed a lot. Finally, we found him sitting up as he said, "I am well; God lives." I delivered a premature, breech baby; it died. Helen delivered a mother who was a severe leper and that baby died. Both babies weighed less than three pounds. The mothers were both from Kpatapaab, the Saboba Chief's village. The third one within a week was from Sambol and a repeat of the low birth-weight, but he was alive. Helen wrote a poem about him:

> *In Memory of the Tiniest Konkomba*
> *A wee, tiny baby came to our house one day,*
> *Weighed a pound and a half, 'twas all.*
> *The thing that he wanted and wailed for quite loudly,*

Was a wee bit of milk, 'twas all.
In blankets we lost him; a tiny Tim was he,
Only twelve inches long, 'twas all.
Such wee, wee hands and feet; so perfect, yet so small.
He flung them high in glee, 'twas all.
The tiny shirts we made him revealed our love, not skill.
Worn with a wee diaper, 'twas all.
Just two days and two nights and then he went away.
Stayed such a short, short time, 'twas all.

HRK

Dedicated to Charlese who did her best to make our little guest's stay permanent. Date: April 1956. Helen Ruth Kopp.

Two serious palavers surfaced while we were at the coast and involved us one way or another. A Christian man told us, "A man is trying to buy a lock of hair from either of you nurses so he can make a juju out of it." When the Christian would not do it for one pound, almost three dollars, the offer was raised to two pounds. The Christian still refused and came to tell us. I said, "Helen, if a lock of our hair was worth over five dollars, how much are our livers worth?" We were grateful for the police about a block away. The second situation was that a man had just gotten out of prison and returned to Saboba. He was saying that a local young man who once worked for us had married his promised wife while he was in prison. This latter problem surfaced strongly on Friday morning, April 13, at the clinic. I had been tending a delivery since three in the morning; there was little progress. It was near general clinic time and Helen was busy teaching in the waiting room. Gylima and a man were having a verbal battle. It was not good for this to happen at our clinic, so I physically pushed Gylima inside the clinic and shut the door. The other man left, but was soon back with a knife and called Gylima to come out and fight. Gylima wanted to go; this was demeaning to a man. I ordered him to stay inside the clinic. I told the man with the knife to meet me at the police station about two blocks away. I got in my car and left. As I was talking to the police, the man arrived. The police reached for the man's knife. The man jerked the knife away and cut the policeman's hand. I went back to the clinic. That night, we were in bed and almost asleep when we heard a loud commotion. We knew that if Gylima met that man with the knife anywhere, someone might be killed. When the noise seemed to come between our house and the clinic, we threw on our clothes, got my gun, and went to our car without turning on our flashlights-never mind the snake! We drove to the Hales' house and learned that same man had threatened Dewey with a knife while we were at the coast. Dewey got his revolver and we stayed alert for the night. We heard noises but no one came to the house. The next morning, we went home. On the way, we stopped at the police station, and asked, "Is the man in jail?" The policeman said, "No, he is still walking." At the clinic, people told us the man had stolen a bicycle and left town. The following night, it rained hard so we felt fairly safe. We were able to relay that story to the British Government Agent from Yendi within a few days when he brought his wife and her companion nurse to visit us. The two ladies were going on leave to England soon. They agreed to be judges at our second annual baby show scheduled that day; he went to transact business.

CHAPTER FIVE

UN Plebiscite in British Togo: Techimantia Clinic

AFTER THE BABY SHOW and when the Government Official returned from his official duties, the group returned to our house to eat lunch. Biyimba baked a cake and we decorated it, "Bon Voyage, Barbara and Phyllis." Family members of government officials did not stay in the tropics even as long as the officials themselves. Money was a factor in mission policies, resulting in longer terms.

The clinic work was becoming so demanding that we could hardly help Biyimba at all with house cleaning, laundry, cooking, and boiling drinking water. It was too much for one person; he actually got sick. While he was off, we hired his younger brother to help with the housework. Torba hated it. Njonabi wanted to farm, so he quit the yard work. Torba took the outside job. It included cutting wood and carrying water. To him, that was also women's work, but better than inside work. Then we hired a very young fellow named Cholada to help with dishwashing, house cleaning, and laundry. Any new person required a lot of teaching time, something we did not have with clinics, language study, and Biyimba ill. It took time for a new person to learn why Biyimba was so strict about boiling and filtering our drinking water. He knew that if we got sick there would be no medical help for his people. One day a fierce storm struck when Cholada was washing dishes. He disappeared while the dishes were still in the pan and a storm lantern lit. We looked for him. Workers found him two miles away at his mother's house! Rain, lightening, and thunder on a tin roof terrified him! He returned the next day, smiling.

By the end of April, we needed a change and my birthday was near. We drove one hundred miles, by way of what we lightly called the *Gushiago moto-way*, to visit with Ann and Becky at Nakpanduri. Animals sleeping on roads were a problem. The difference between goats and sheep was that a goat's tail stood up and the sheep's tail hung down. In addition, goats run from a lorry while sheep slept quietly and let a lorry run over them. The lorry drivers explain it, "The goat runs from a lorry, because he did not pay his fare; the sheep paid his fare, so he is not afraid and does not run; the dog runs barking after the lorry because you forgot to give him his change from paying his fare. The cows or oxen will stand and dare you because they know that if you hit them you will need to sell your lorry to pay their owner." What a surprise met me in Nakpanduri! Polly, Addie, and Mrs. Shirer had arrived from Walewale for my birthday. That evening all seven of us went for a village service. The Bimobas were most amused; they had never seen seven white women in one place in their life! Helen and I went home Saturday morning. In the afternoon, we had a girls' sewing class, taught the Sunday school workers, and ate supper with the Hales. Dale and Betty Brown and their five children had come from Yendi; it was another birthday party. The Browns had settled into Yendi mission house since the convention in Takoradi. They had owned a construction business in Oklahoma before selling it to finance their Africa plans. Dale agreed to look at our stovepipe, which was leaking smoke and water into our kitchen. He drove to our house, where he drew a picture of how the problem could be corrected. It had been a long day; we fell into bed. By morning, we had each delivered a baby! On May 3, my actual birthday, Helen said, "Charlese, get in the car, Biyimba and I are taking you to a drive-in for your birthday." I got in. She drove a few miles up the Cheraponi road. She parked the Chevrolet and they set up a birthday meal on the tailgate. They had baked a cake!

In May 1956, talk among Africans and expatriates, was mainly about an upcoming United Nations Plebiscite. Expatriates were not allowed to voice political opinions. Across the Oti River, east, was French Togo. We lived in British Togo, a part of the Gold Coast since World War I. The Gold Coast was to receive its independence from Britain within months. The United Nations was asking little British Togo to vote on May 9 whether to join French Togo or be a part of the new Ghana when Gold Coast independence happened. The voting area was a narrow strip the full length of the east side of the Gold Coast. That included the Nakpanduri, Saboba, and Yendi. United Nations observers had been in Saboba for months. The day before the voting was my day to treat lepers. Helen was at the maternity clinic with a difficult case; it was Ngmayun of Toma. Suddenly, Dave Wakefield appeared at the clinic from French Togo. He had come for Dewey to fly him to Tamale to shop, before the rains made it impossible. Dave had parked his car on the French side of the Oti, waded the river, and walked to Hales' residence where he *met their absence*. We did not know they had flown to the coast. Dave might have asked us to take him to Tamale to shop, but a runner from the Chief's compound appeared demanding to know about the stranger from French Togo. Perhaps he had come to influence the voting. In fact, Dave had heard of a plebiscite, but did not know the date. He got himself back across the Oti River *at once*! While we were still treating patients, we noticed there was a second vehicle in Saboba, and it was not market day. We were told the driver had been dispatched to *deal with Dewey Hale*. Someone had reported that he had definite opinions about the voting. It apparently never occurred to Dewey that someone might think we shared his opinion. The car left. About the time we were treating the last leper, another car came straight to the clinic. Saboba traffic was getting heavy! It was Dale Brown from Yendi. He had a telegram from mission officials; he was to remove us from Saboba immediately. They had learned that Dewey and Naomi Hale were in Accra. That would leave us in Saboba during the voting the very next day. We treated all people present at the clinic, but the round huts behind the clinic were full of very sick people. Three babies had pneumonia. In one hut, the baby boy born breech the night before weighed less than three pounds. We were supporting the mother while observing the small infant. Her baby was the *100th delivery* since our arrival! The mother was from Kpatapaab, Chief Quadin's village right behind the clinic. We told Gylima how to care for them while we were in Tamale and we went to the house to eat and pack. Gylima was with Ngmayun and would call us if her difficult labor changed. We had no way of knowing how long we would be gone. Suddenly a fierce storm hit; it blew right through our wood shutters. Our floor was swimming in water. Roofs were blown off the round houses behind the clinic. Dale Brown realized we could not leave quickly and said, "Look, I have Betty and five children in Yendi, which is also in the plebiscite area; come when you can." He left; we understood! While Helen stayed with Ngmayun, Gylima and I went to Chief Quadin's village, and asked him to provide a house for the sick people now in the huts with no roofs. He agreed to do so. The mother of the three-pound baby was from his village anyway. Gylima knew what to do from there. We stayed with Ngmayun until she finally delivered at 9:30 P.M.; she would be fine. We left before we knew whether the newborn would live or die; he was not good. We killed the fire under the fridge, locked our house, and assigned Biyimba as watchman. He always had a key;

missionaries might come by to sleep. We could not take an African with us on this journey; they had to vote the next day. Our return depended on the outcome of the voting. It was midnight when Helen and I left. The natives were restless; light from campfires showed people dancing. We never stopped once in the forty miles to Yendi, where we spent the night at Dale and Betty Brown's house. Next morning, we drove sixty miles on to Tamale. It was out of the voting area and we needed to shop anyway. We bought wire to go around our garden as the winds blew the zontamat fence down onto the garden. I mailed two tiny Bolgatanga baskets to Niece Roxanne and Nephew Davy and a wee elephant for Nephew Jim for birthdays. We stayed in Tamale until after the result of the voting was known. The majority of voters chose to remain a part of the Gold Coast. French Togo, east of the Oti, would remain unchanged. The results decreased the danger and we returned to Saboba. We learned that Ngmayun's new baby had died. Little Paul, from Kpatapaab, had lost half a pound since birth, but was healthy. We put him on a supplemental formula and he started gaining. One afternoon we put up our garden fence, so we were ready for the rains to come. Then, to prepare our walls inside our house for paint, we filled cracks as Helen sang, "Back in the plaster again!" Several Sunday school boys came to help us. We paid them a bit and gave them a sack of Christmas candy. In our one bedroom, we painted my two walls pastel green and her two pink. To decorate the windows, I sewed valances from material received in packages. It had fruit and flowers on it and the words, "Home Sweet Home."

For weeks before the voting, we did not go into the villages for outstation visits. The second night back we went to Sobiba, about four miles from Saboba. The headman said, "Our whole village will repent and be Christians." We explained that every person must choose for himself. Six men, their wives, and children accepted Christ as their blood Sacrifice. When Dewey and Naomi returned, we talked with them. They had received threatening letters saying they had told the people how to vote; the Hales denied it. Before Dr. Ashworth left to England on leave, he instructed Helen and me how to treat Naomi Hale's convulsions in a crisis. The Hales said he had also given them a letter saying they should return to America within the next three months as Naomi's seizures were becoming more severe and frequent.

One Saturday night, after teaching the Sunday school lesson in preparation for Sunday, we sat on our palaver porch and just listened and rested. Children were singing and playing childhood games, the frogs were croaking, bats were screeching, crickets were chirping, cattle were lowing, and drums were beating near and far. It had been a year since the big funeral behind our house; they were having a memorial for Yando. Those drums were a bit too near and loud. The next morning, we went to the Toma church for Sunday school and worship. Sunday evening we rode our bikes and many walked past the Toma church to the village of Nalongni, where Akonsi, the first Konkomba Christian lived. There was only a path. We had the evening church service at his house, as he was old and could no longer join his wife, Mayen, and an auntie, Majin, who still walked to church.

The Ziemann family went on furlough from Kumasi. Burdette, Doris, Dick, and Cheryl Wiles, who arrived during the recent conference, assumed the mission work in Kumasi and all Ashanti Forest area. A letter from Chairman Burdette asked us to leave the Saboba Clinic with Gylima for a short time and help open a new clinic in the Ashanti Forest area. We were nurses and trained in job excellence. Each time we left Saboba clinic without a midwife, our conscience smarted, and so did the Hales. We instructed Gylima on what he could legally do at the clinic. The Hales were not far away, but they had outstation clinics to fly to at the same time. We killed the fridge, locked up our house, and told the yardman to watch. Biyimba went with us; he had neither wife nor children yet. On June 7, we headed south to Kumasi. From there, we were to go seventy miles into the Ashanti Forest to Techimantia. There in the Brong-Ahafo Region, we were to open a general and maternity clinic. Naomi Lehmann packed us a lunch when we stopped in Tamale. At the edge of the Volta River, the three of us were eating lunch inside our vehicle. A tropical rain had delayed the ferry crossings. A man in a small French car came around the trucks, down the hill, and parked crossway in front of us. This placed him to be first on the ferry. He walked past us without making eye contact and walked up a steep hill where huge trucks were lined up. The driver of the first truck got out and railed at the ferry operators for delaying him. Suddenly, in our rear view mirror, I saw a big truck coming down that hill. No driver was inside! There was no time or place for us to move. My emergency brake was set and the gear in low; I pressed on the foot brake. When it hit, our sandwiches flew through the air and our vehicle lurched forward and hit the little French car broadside. The impact tipped it up just enough for the two tires on the far side to dig into the earth. It stopped all three vehicles from going into the Volta River. The driver of the truck ran to the bush and was not found. The owner of the little French car came down the hill and *was very friendly*. He said, "Looks like you have enough trouble; I will take care of damages to my own car."

We drove on and off the ferry with no problem. The front and rear body was damaged. The rest of the road through the Ashanti Forest was roughly paved and we slowly drove to Kumasi. Down one steep hill, a lorry had gone off the edge. We stopped; the people had gone. The front of the lorry was looking straight up at us with the name, *WHO KNOWS THE END.* The next morning, the battery in our vehicle was dead and would not take a charge. We could not prove it was damaged in the accident; we bought a new one. Kumasi was a good place to get the body repaired at UTC Swiss Motors, but we were without transportation again.

Burdette Wiles drove us to Techimantia. I had to shut my
eyes as we met logging trucks zooming around curves on the
narrow, unpaved, rain-slick, clay roads. Some logs were several feet in diameter so the truck could haul only one. Vegetation reclaimed the roads in spite of many workers who
hacked away with cutlasses to keep it cut back. Tiny orchids
and huge poinsettias could be plucked from the car window. Techimantia was in the tall mahogany trees. As we got
near the town, the children lined the road calling, "Akwaba,
Akwaba, welcome!" Finally, on foot, we were led through a
cocoa plantation to greet the Chief. I broke out in hives all
over, even in my hair. It was the first time I had reacted to
chocolate since I was a teenager. Since that day, I have been
allergic to chocolate again. The Chief appointed someone to
give us a tour of the village. We first saw the clinic. It was
new and yet unfinished. As we walked through the village,
we passed an Assemblies of God Church. We waded a small
creek and went up a hill. They had cut down some tall trees
to make a clearing and were building a neat bungalow for
nurses. They hoped we would stay. Since that house was not
yet completed, they took us back to the other end of town to
where we would sleep in a tiny, one-room house near the new
clinic. It had high openings for windows, but neither screens
nor panes, just solid wooden fans to shut out rain. It was too
hot to shut them. Only our mosquito nets were between the
jungle and us. The people also found a place for Biyimba to
sleep. During the first night, we heard shrill screams in the
night that sounded like a woman. The next day we asked
about it and someone explained, "It is a little tree bear that
cries to frighten away predators so it can come down to eat
in the night." I agreed; it would frighten anything. The next
morning, we were awakened by a group of people chanting and dancing as they came toward our house. They made
a frightful, banging noise. We discovered some men were
rolling a metal barrel to our house. Women were swaying
gracefully with containers on their heads and chanting as

they came. A man announced, "Chief says we are to place this drum at your house and the women are to keep it filled with water for you." We were not the only ones frightened by unfamiliar things. The local people said they had heard about the fierce Konkombas of the north. They were leery of our helper, Biyimba. On our first Sunday at their church, he won their hearts with his miraculous story of healing from yaws! When we got our repaired car, we made trips to the police station nearest the accident site. We wanted the driver or owner to pay for the repairs. The police court ordered him to pay eighty-five dollars, but we never got a shilling. Speed-the-Light paid for the repairs with money from New Mexico.

The Local Council would hire a midwife and a nurse practitioner, and pay for certain items for the new clinic. We ordered medications and equipment for sterilizing linen and supplies. We made pillows and stuffed them with kapok. We made pillowcases. We bought beds for the wards and ordered local tailors to make mattresses. We drew pictures of a delivery table for a local carpenter to build, along with some small tables and chairs, which he knew how to make. We had been in the Ashanti Forest about a month; we needed to return to Saboba. We would return to open the clinic when the medicines and equipment arrived and the furniture was made. We had good memories of Techimantia.

It was an emotional experience, but a closure, to cross the Volta River again where our car had been hit. As we went through villages to Tamale and on to Yendi, we were as a *horse headed for water*. We collected our packages and letters at the Yendi Post Office. Helen read our letters aloud as I drove to Saboba. One letter reported that Helen's Patomic District was going to finance a fence around the clinic to keep the animals from sleeping on the verandas every night. I learned that my youngest brother, Royce Ray, had married while we were working in Techimantia. They sent pictures. That meant I had missed the weddings of my only sister and both my brothers. A letter from my oldest brother, Calvin Lee, said, "Our daughter, Roxanne, was recently dedicated by Rev. and Mrs. O.W. Keys. They were teachers at SAGC, in Texas, but now pastors in Belen, New Mexico." Calvin said he and his family planned to meet my ship in New York in 1957. That would be about a year yet. We felt a combination of elation and sadness, so we got the songbook from the glove compartment and sang our way to Saboba. The building of the Saboba maternity clinic was progressing. Gylima had delivered babies of mothers who chose to come to the clinic and kept up with regular clinic schedules. Our garden had okra, green beans, Swiss chard, chili, radishes, and tiny cucumbers ready to eat. We could only grow vegetables three months of the year, so they were delicious and precious. The packages we collected contained both edible and inedible items. We were so delighted with a paper towel rack from Ma Toothman and women in Mountainair that we installed it at once! We felt it dressed up our kitchen.

The Wakefields from French Togo wrote that Ruthie, their ten-year-old daughter, would come for a two-day visit. Then the Browns from Yendi let their two oldest daughters Rhonda and Lisa, nine and seven years, come and stay a few days. We played jacks, pick-up sticks, and Scrabble, and enjoyed being kids again. Biyimba cooked palm nut stew for the visitors and they loved it. The American visitors joined with a group of young African girls who came each week for sewing and first aid classes. They memorized verses from the Bible in Lekpakpaln while throwing a beanbag from one to the other. The one receiving the beanbag must quote a verse in her language. The young American girls also got to help when three schoolboys, Bimunjir, Tige, and Nakiwu, came to help make songbooks for twelve English-speaking students. They backed the books with colored construction paper. Besides the English songs, the school-age boys were learning the names of the books of the Bible, the Beatitudes, the Ten Commandments, the Twenty-third Psalm, and the fifty-third chapter of Isaiah. At stages in their learning, the students presented a program before the local church congregation to show what they had learned. We were busy teaching adults, too. Since the men expected their wives to have something to take to market to sell, we were trying to give them an alternative to brewing and selling pito, the local alcohol. We taught the women to make light bread and doughnuts, and introduced them to new domestic garden greens for their stew.

A year ago, the rains had marooned us by mid-August. In 1956, it had rained only three times. Our well was dry and the new yardman, Torba, was forced to carry water from a dirty source. We were pleased, however, that sparse rains allowed us to put one hundred fifty posts in the ground at the clinic. We stretched chicken wire around the bottom and two rows of barbed wire at the top. We planted twelve fruit trees, some inside the clinic fence, and some at our house. Our hands were raw and blistered. At last, it rained on the afternoon of August 14. We caught four barrels of water from guttering on the kitchen. That morning, while Helen treated over one hundred lepers, Biyimba and I did the washing, baked a cake, and cooked a Mexican dinner for nine. The Browns from Yendi had come to get their daughters and brought our mail. One letter informed us that the next Northern Territories District Council *was to be in Saboba* in January 1957. What a shock! The Hales, Helen, and I would feed and sleep some thirty missionaries for almost a week. We started making out menus with Biyimba and writing home for items we could not buy in Africa. It would be the dry season, so there would be no garden. About the same number of northern pastors would be present. The Africans would lodge them and the local Konkomba women would cook for them.

We had a run of *difficult and unusual* clinic cases. 1) A young girl in her late teens came after being in labor at home for days. Her whole abdomen was full of gas gangrene. We took her to Yendi immediately, but it was too late. We tried to use such situations to stress the need of prenatal care and coming to the clinic in early labor. 2) A small boy of about nine years fell on his father's cutlass, piercing his abdomen and liver. When we saw him, Gylima said, "Madam, if not one thing it's another." I was amazed and asked, "Gylima, where did you hear those words?" He said, "Oh, Madam, you say that all the time." Dr. A.K. Korsah, son of the Gold Coast Attorney General, was in Yendi Hospital since Dr. F. Ashworth went on leave. Dr. Korsah *just happened* to be at Saboba Clinic to check our records when the child arrived. We said, "God really loved that small boy to *have a doctor waiting*." Parts of the boy's intestines were hanging outside his abdomen; Dr. Korsah did surgery instantly. Dewey Hale flew the boy to Yendi Hospital, where he recovered completely. 3) At a Wednesday general clinic, a juju man came for help. He said, "I mix medicine for women who are unable to have children. If she gets pregnant, she pays about six pounds." That was about twelve dollars! He said, "After I mix the medicine, I take it to a Moslem priest who writes on paper, 'This woman shall conceive.' We wash the writing off with water into my medicine mix. The woman sips that for thirty days. I will bring some of my medicine if you will wash some Jesus writings into it." Ah, this was getting too *ecumenical* for me! I asked, "What did you come to clinic for today?" He said, "Constipation." I asked, "You have no medicine for that?" He said, "No, only for women." Wow, *specializing!* 4) The family of a woman who had a history of postpartum psychosis brought a newborn to us to keep for a while. They said the mother did not know she had the new baby, but continued to breastfeed her older child. The other women in her village were afraid of the newborn because of his mother's illness and would not wet-nurse him. We named him Joshua. He weighed six pounds, less than when he was born a month prior in Yendi Hospital. His eyes were sunken and he seldom opened them. His skin color was gray and he was so dehydrated. After a few days, he was fun to have around, but washing bottles and diapers was an added chore. Cholada complained bitterly; washing diapers was 'women's work.' 5) While night deliveries and hundreds in outpatient clinics continued, one of the local schoolteachers went into a coma from typhoid fever; Dewey flew him to Yendi. Then Dewey Hale became ill with typhoid fever. We took one of our two cans of fruit and some Jell-O to Naomi for him. We took Naomi and Stevie to Yendi for typhoid immunizations. It was time for our typhoid boosters. I got mine first and we went back for Helen's five days later. We could not afford to feel ill at the same time; too many people were depending on us. The schoolteacher died in Yendi Hospital, so public health officials came to Saboba to search for the source of the typhoid. 5) We got so busy that Helen got infection in the site of a mosquito bite; her leg swelled huge. We quelled the infection, but the area broke down into a tropical ulcer. We took pictures of the missionary making use of the rolled sheet bandages, thus becoming part of those grateful for the work of American Women's Ministries. Partly because of Gylima at the clinic and Helen at the house, our days were usually filled with laughter. They were both genuinely humorous. The Africans called Helen the *funny one*, and me the *quiet one* or Madam Fixit. If they reported a broken item, my reply was, "Well, let's fix it."

One evening we relaxed on our veranda with Baby Joshua nearby. We listened to tapes sent from Helen's family for her birthday. Each family member greeted her; I had met most of them. Biyimba and I had baked Helen a chocolate cake and we were eating it. We started hearing voices. They got louder and people with storm lanterns soon covered the pasture near us. We were concerned and asked Biyimba about it. He said, "Someone called that a thief-man had stolen something." As in all thefts, people within hearing distance joined the hunt. By the time we went to bed, I had broken out in hives from head to toe from the chocolate. I had forgotten to take an antihistamine *before* I ate the chocolate.

That night Helen and I both dreamed about our families; we seldom dreamed. For my birthday, we had visited Ann and Becky at the Nakpanduri clinic. So near Helen's, we decided to visit Polly and Addie in Walewale. We left our little Joshua with Bakanti, Gylima's wife, who had several girls but no boys. We stopped in Tamale to view the movies Lois and Cecil had sent from California of their beautiful Ladean; two sons followed her. We encountered two broken bridges and feared we might not get back to Saboba, but we did.

During September we delivered seven babies, and little Joshua's mother came to get him. She just appeared and said, "I know you have my baby, and thank you very much. I am now ready to take him." We prepared a bottle of milk, but she put him to her breast and off they went. We were sad, but saw him later at the clinic baby show. Workers were still building on the maternity clinic; we were still working on the new church. Everything took so much time. We were still having the local language and Bible classes for the non-English-speaking teenagers desiring to go to school at NGBI. We were still having sewing classes with the teenage girls, but their hand-sewn feed-sack dresses were becoming too small before completion. One day Biyimba said his *heart fell down* and I asked, "Why?" He showed me his apron, which had holes where it rubbed on the cement kitchen sink. He had to interpret for me anyway, so I gave him some cloth and he sewed right along with the girls to make an apron for himself. The girls colored Sunday school papers for fun time; Biyimba joined in that, too. It seemed surprising that I could say to teenage Biyimba, "Go cook a chicken in the Presto Cooker." That was no problem to him, but he had never held a crayon in his hand. On one market day, the teenage girls popped corn and sold it at the market to pay for one more cement bench being built inside the new church. We wanted more benches in time for the District Council the following January; many people were coming. A mighty electric rainstorm hit and broke up the market. Our corn poppers fled for home, calling, "Madam, that will be next time," or "Uwumbor tiin timi kitaa," meaning, "Bye-bye," or literally, "God give us tomorrow." Again, the rain literally came in one side of our house and out on the opposite side. We watched lightening roll across our front room in a ball of fire. Afterwards, we mopped up water with throw rugs.

Suddenly, we were called back to Techimantia. As usual, we cooperated; it was all God's work. Burdette Wiles said the mission and chiefs were about ready to dedicate the new clinic. Things in Saboba were such that we wished we did not have to leave. We were about to move into the new maternity building. We were talking about building a second bedroom at our house, or a *stranger's room* as we referred to it. Konkie was about to have kittens. Our tomatoes were just getting ripe enough to eat. Our part of church-related activities would go undone. *No wreck this trek!* After driving ten thousand miles in exactly one year, we had not needed our two spare tires. In Kumasi, we had them and two other new tires mounted on the Chevrolet. We kept one of the slick tires for a spare. We had gotten so much done with the new car and with lowered stress, but we never forgot the "Stranded" Vanguard; it was better than nothing! As we drove from Kumasi to Techimantia, we were again overwhelmed with the beauty of the jungle. Trees were at least twice as tall as any pine tree in my memory. The underbrush was a solid network with the gorgeous hanging flowers. At our cozy little one-room-near-the-clinic, we again used one fruit crate for a table and two more to sit on. We had two cooking pans, two dishes, and one dishpan. In one pan, we made tomato soup; in the other, we boiled water for tea. In one dish, we mixed fruit salad and scooped half into the other dish so both could eat. We washed dishes, clothing, and took a bath using the one dishpan. People did not need to bring water; it ran off the roof, flooded the metal barrel, and produced healthy mosquitoes. We were showered with oranges, bananas, and a few coconuts. We drank orange juice for breakfast, ate fruit

salad for desserts, and snacked on oranges. That was a welcome change from the North, where we paid dearly for fruit.
Previous experience had taught me well; I avoided cocoa
plantations. Multiple insects tormented us as we worked
at the clinic, even with screens on doors and windows. The
Avon insect repellent from Mrs. Boster in Belen saved our
lives. In the late afternoons, we got on our army cots under
our mosquito nets and wrote letters. At nights, both torchlight and kerosene lamp attracted gnats. They came through
the nets *to be friendly;* we turned off our torchlights and went
to sleep early, as we were tired. We learned that the local
Christians gathered at the little church every evening for
town-wide devotions before going to bed. The pastor had
a circuit of ten churches so he could not always be there.
One evening a woman came forward to repent. They prayed
with her and then each one had a part in admonishing her,
"You will forsake your fetish ways. You will burn your jujus.
You will accept God's Son as your Sacrifice and not go to
the medicine men to make other sacrifices. You will come to
church regularly. You will not chew cola nuts or drink the
local pito." Biyimba seemed interested; perhaps he would
introduce that practice up north.

Before the clinic dedication date was set, we were
required to go back north for a four-day Minister's Institute
at Kumbungu. Helen and I stayed with Homer and Thelma
Goodwins and their two children, Nova and John, in the
new bungalow. They had arrived to teach at Northern Gold
Coast Bible Institute. Their two older children, Sydney and
Betty, were attending Southwestern Bible College in Texas.
(I met Homer in New Mexico in 1940 when he was itinerating. I visited their family in West Texas as I was itinerating
in 1953 and they greeted me in Dagbani.) NGBI was taught
in Dagbani, the language of the Dagomba in Yendi, Tamale
and Kumbungu and the trade language of the Northern
Region. As Helen and I were eating a meal with the Goodwins, Thelma said to Homer, "Doesn't Charlese remind you

of Meta Wederbrook in the church at Hereford, Texas where we pastored? She does her hands the same way when she talks." Homer observed me for a bit and said, "Yes, she does!" I told them I did not know anyone by that name and none of my extended family was Assembly of God members as far as I knew. The subject was dropped. Wheeler, Eileen, Paul, and Alice Anderson had vacated the old bungalow to go on furlough to the United States. The Lehmanns still commuted the eleven miles from Tamale to help with the NGBI teaching load, but it just changed the house where the Lehmanns would camp while they helped in Kumbungu.

After the seminar, we drove north to Saboba to get our mail and check on the clinic. Helen got three more boils on that leg; some became tropical ulcers the size of a quarter. The doctor put her to bed for a few days. We were spreading our strength thin, but there was no let up. One morning Helen awoke very ill with a high fever and hard pains all over her body. It was dengue fever (break-bone fever), a *gift* from gnats and mosquitoes in our wee house in the jungle. It hit me while I was delivering a baby at the clinic; I fainted. Gylima finished the delivery. For hours, I heard lovely organ music; I was hallucinating. The textbook says one never dies from dengue, but from *complications* associated with it. The Africans say, "You never die from dengue fever, you just *feel like you will*." I said, "You just *wish you could*." At the clinic, we often asked the people where they hurt. They would say, "All my body, Madam, all my body." With dengue fever, we learned what they meant! Hal Lehmann came from Tamale to inform us that the District Commissioner had set the date for the dedication of the Techimantia clinic on November 5. He found us both very ill. He knelt by each of our mosquito-netted beds and prayed a fervent prayer that was ever so welcome and encouraging. We had also been informed of the date for the dedication of the new Saboba Maternity Clinic, also on November 5! We were to be in full uniform for both. This was an utter impossibility; the two clinics were over four hundred miles apart. Techimantia Officials moved their date to November 14. That gave us nine days between the two, until the Yendi District Officials, thinking they were obliging, moved their dedication up to November 10. Three days between was better than none; we just kept quiet!

In Saboba, on November 10, a grand dedication and ribbon cutting ceremony by local, district, and regional government officials took place at the new maternity unit. The sugary speeches about their hard-working nurses embarrassed us, but the anticipation of a maternity unit in Saboba almost brought tears of joy to our eyes. Everyone was taking pictures. Afterwards, we served tea at our house to eighteen dignitaries and missionaries. Many of them bragged that our bungalow was painted and dressed up beautifully. At that moment we almost forgot the hard work of two years it had entailed. In the evening when all had gone, we packed our suitcases and camping items for Techimantia. Our cat, Konkie, forced us to stop packing to admire the three babies she produced. We named one Midnight, as he was coal black. One we called Beastie as he was white but had a black mark in his forehead. The third one we called Carco, a carbon copy of her mother. Konkie got one baby at a time from the box in the storeroom, took it to our front room, and let it nurse. She returned it and got another; three at once just overwhelmed her.

The next morning we left; Techimantia was a nine-hour drive. Burdette Wiles had hired an African midwife and surgical dresser. We made the beds, put up curtains, sterilized equipment, organized record keeping, and *officially* put them to work. The government doctor found time to visit, inspect the facilities, and observe the clinic in operation. On the big day, November 14, Rev. Wiles prayed the opening prayer and gave a welcome address. There were chiefs present in their colorful attire, umbrellas, medallions, and crowns. Photographers from the press snapped cameras and interviewed. For two hours, there were speeches by chiefs, government officials, and doctors. Between speeches, a band of horns and drums played music, the Methodist girls' choir and other groups marched and sang. A Catholic priest came from Sunyani, forty miles away, where Helen and I had previously visited their clinic. Finally, Burdette Wiles directed the actual dedication and finalized it with prayer. We stayed another five days. The African midwife and dresser were capable professionals, so we left. Burdette would pay the salaries and manage the money provided by the local council. He would actively recruit American midwives. Until he found them, we would supervise the operation from Saboba by an occasional visit. As we packed our car to leave, the Chief of Techimantia dashed us a turkey and about two dozen eggs. We took the turkey to Kumasi where Doris Wiles and her cook added the trimmings to celebrate Thanksgiving. We went to town for our very last shopping before the convention in Saboba in January 1957. On the day before Thanksgiving, we ate a huge turkey dinner with the Wiles family. Dick, their son, was leaving for school in America. Doris was tutoring their daughter, Cheryl.

On Thanksgiving Day, we drove four hundred miles to Yendi. The Dale Brown family had the table set for a big turkey dinner and said, "We were just hoping you'd get here in time." They had gotten our mail and the postman had even let them get our packages, as they knew we would come late. We drove on to Saboba that night, where Gylima and Bileti were very glad to see us. They had held regular clinics and even delivered babies when women chose to go to the clinic. We were left with about a month to prepare for Christmas and the Northern Territories District Council. We sent out a form letter, "Dear Fellow Missionaries: The five missionaries at Saboba are eagerly looking forward to having you as their guests January 4 through 9. To make your visit as comfortable as possible, bring linens, washbasin, bucket, cot, and mosquito net. Fill your thermos jug with ice cubes and bring a lantern for your room. There will be ample space for all. If you sing or play a musical instrument, bring that talent along. Pass word to your African pastors that sleeping quarters and food will be provided, but they should bring a sleeping mat, mosquito net, and personal eating utensils if desired. Expect a refreshing as we pray and plan for the future. Signed: The Saboba-ites."

We dug out our two Christmas records for the wind-up for the *fourth year*. Our Christmas packages came from America as usual. A tiny, six-ounce sack of pinto beans came. We put it in the front room as a conversation piece. People continued to tease us about our love for Mexican food, including pinto beans. We had a Christmas party for our house and clinic helpers. Pastor Salah and the Hales were always included. Then we were invited to a Christmas party in Yendi, mostly for children of expatriates. The British District Commissioner and his wife sponsored it. Their ten-year-old daughter, Elizabeth, would fly from England again.

For the Toma Church Christmas program, one of the schoolboys read the Christmas story from the book of Luke; another schoolboy interpreted into Lekpakpaln. They sang Christmas carols and their songs about Jesus. Gifts were presented for regular attendance and for memorizing parts of the Bible. They preferred clothing as rewards rather than toys or candy. I have seen a child walk the dusty path to church with a pair of boxer shorts folded on his head and a little pair of thongs on top to secure them. At the door of the church, he put on both and entered. After church, the process was reversed; clothing was prized! On Christmas evening, Christians went caroling to the compounds of Akonsi in Nalongni, Chief Oden in Toma, Chief Quadin in Kpatapaab, the police station, and the Saboba Market area. Someone carried a storm lantern on his head to lead the way and watch for snakes. They beat drums, rang bells, and sang their Christian songs and Christmas carols. For that Christmas, Helen gave me my favorite book of Africa photographs; it is called *Navrongo*. She made a card with a blazing sun and wrote, "I'm dreaming of a hot, parched Christmas, just like the ones I never knew (before 1954). Where the treetops wither, and children run thither, happily around our house. I'm not dreaming; 'tis the harmattan, with every Christmas card I write. May your days be blazingly hot, and your eyes with the dust blood shot. May the tropical sun, like Bethlehem's star, ever shed its rays upon your path." Realistic! Water, please!

As scheduled, January 4-9, the convention lasted five days. The clinic schedule proceeded as usual. We prepared three meals a day for fourteen people and ourselves; the Hales fed the same number. Food like pancake mix, cake mix, and cooked cereal from Christmas boxes helped considerably. We prepared afternoon tea with snacks at our house for all thirty-one missionaries, so all could have time to visit those who ate regular meals at the other house. We had not shopped since November in Kumasi. The packages from America made it unnecessary and we could not have found the items in African stores anyway. We worked with Biyimba so that he knew the menu for every meal, every day. He knew the recipe for every dish. We wrote it all down; he was learning to read. In our storeroom, we lined up the cans and items by day. Helpers for Biyimba came with the visiting missionaries. Some would help Biyimba cook and boil drinking water; others would wash dishes. They slept in our helpers' quarters. They cooked and ate their food together, went to the services, and seemed to enjoy the whole thing as we did. Dr. Ashworth had come back from England and made a visit to the clinic during the convention. All missionaries knew him, but it was especially nice for Ann and Becky, the British midwives.

Sleeping almost thirty extra people posed a challenge. Seven single ladies slept in our house: A and B from Nakpanduri, A and P from Walewale, C and H from Saboba, and teenager Gretchen Lehmann. Helen and I went back to our original screened-in porch to sleep on two cots. Gylima could easily call us there for medical emergencies and deliveries in the night. Two ladies slept in our bedroom and three were on army cots with nets in the front room at first. They soon chose to move to our open palaver porch at the opposite end of our house. They said they felt safe because of our fence and their mosquito nets. The harmattan made the nights so cold that everyone called for blankets before morning. We had not used the new maternity building yet. It had two rooms, the labor room and the larger, four-bed ward. Therefore, it housed two families with their cots and nets. They ate with us. We placed a barrel for water near their veranda. The bath suite they shared was almost exactly like the one in our bungalow. While the Local Council was building the maternity clinic, they built two new rooms onto the local primary school, and a small one-room government rest house; neither had been occupied yet. Families who slept there ate with the Hales. David Wakefield from French Togo was speaker for the District Council. He and his wife, Claudia, slept in the Hales' home and ate with that group.

As expected, there were about thirty-five African pastors present from northern Gold Coast. They slept in local Christian homes. The Council consisted of both business sessions and precious times of worship and dedication. In fact, our new Saboba-Toma Church was dedicated during that convention! Local Chiefs, Quadin and Odin, came. An impressive group of chiefs, including U Na Febor Jayom of Yankazia, hired lorries and came from surrounding villages with their people. A brush arbor, built onto the back of the huge new church, was necessary to accommodate the numbers; progress had been rapid and phenomenal! (I visited that church in 1987; because of the cement and stone pillars, it is still standing in the 2000s.)

After the convention, a letter came from my Aunt Leonora in Phoenix. It contained an item from a local paper dated December 19, 1956. My friend, Mae (Livengood) Cohea had lost her mother, an Assemblies of God minister in the Arizona District, in a car crash in the city limits of Phoenix. It was a shock! A more encouraging note from Hal, Naomi, and Gretchen Lehmann in Tamale read, "Thank you for everything you did to make the District Council in Saboba so pleasant and profitable. The Nakpanduri nurses sat with us and praised your ability to plan and then execute the plan. Gretchen remarked that the meals were super, not the convention type." The credit went to Biyimba for that!

Within the month of January 1957, twelve members of my Sunday school class were leaving to attend boarding middle schools outside the Saboba area. From these would come our future pastors, nurses, midwives, teachers, doctors, and elected civil officials. They would attend classes on "Who We Are and What We Believe." They completed all requirements, were baptized, joined the Church, and we had a fun-filled going-away party for them.

By this date, Raymond H. Hudson was the Superintendent of the New Mexico District Council, Assemblies of God, with headquarters in Albuquerque. In 1942, they were in Bible College when I was in High School at Southwestern Bible Institute (SBI) in Fort Worth, Texas. In 1953, they were pastoring in Hobbs when Helen and I traveled in New Mexico. On January 24, 1957, I wrote a letter to him and his wife, Onie Marie, "Since sending you our Christmas letter in November, we have been more than busy. After dedication of the two clinics, one in the jungle (Ashanti Forest) and one in the grasslands (Saboba), we started planning for the Christmas season and for the Northern Territories District Council to be held here in Saboba. Our almost completed church building was dedicated during that council. Because of the wonderful way the New Mexico people responded, Helen and I were able to operate the clinic, feed our half of the visitors, and enjoy the services. After March 6 there will be no more Gold Coast, it will be the new, *independent nation of Ghana*. It *appears* the change will be calm, but pray toward that end."

We could not possibly know what a drastic change was coming. The very next day on Friday, January 25, we were working at the new church when Dale Brown arrived with a cablegram for Helen from mission headquarters in America. It said her mother was not expected to live and that since her furlough was so near, she had permission to go home. We had been gone from America nearly three-and-one-half years; terms were usually three years. We talked with Dewey Hale about flying us to Accra and he agreed. From Accra, we could telephone Helen's home. *If her mother were still alive,* Helen would fly home. We had flown into Saboba in Dewey's plane; now we would fly out, the only two times we were ever in his plane. We went to our house so Helen could pack. She went into a drum and got new clothing, toothbrush, and other items to pack. It happened so quickly; almost none of her belongings in the house were disturbed. We *figuratively* slit our wrists and mixed our blood to declare that we would return to Africa with no one else. We looked at Addie and Polly, Ann and Becky; they stuck together. We agreed it would be too hard to come with a new co-worker each time. If God so chose, we would stick together like the other single ladies.

CHAPTER SIX

My Heart Fell Down Paaa! Gold Coast to Ghana

O N SATURDAY MORNING, DEWEY flew Helen and me to Accra in his single-engine plane. Right over the dense Ashanti Forest, the motor died. The plane lost altitude and took a couple of dives as Dewey scanned the panel. Then the engine sparked and the plane leveled off. Dewey explained, "We ran out of gasoline sooner than I expected. I had grounded the plane until I had time to overhaul the motor, but I hated to refuse to help you. As soon as I saw the gas gauge pointing to empty, I just switched over to the reserve petrol tank." I had been making a new use of a Tupperware since just after we left the ground; I was so airsick. After the adrenaline rush caused by the danger, the nausea almost left. I was asking questions, while Dewey was showing me as well as telling me how he solved the problem. Helen reached from the back seat, hit me on the shoulder with her fist, and said, "Shut up, Charlese; let him drive this thing!" Flying was a problem for me, but I don't think anyone hated it as much as Helen did. Once again, we had no choice. We landed safely in Accra. While Dewey was refueling the plane, Helen was trying to phone her family in the United States. She could not get through quickly, so she got a tentative plane reservation to America and continued phoning. We could not leave Naomi alone in Saboba overnight. Dewey and I flew back north, not knowing whether Helen would fly to the United States or not. I was quiet and in shock. The return trip was uneventful, except we arrived in Saboba after dark because of the slow engine. The bush runway had no lights. Dewey made one dip down toward the ground and saw the aluminum roof of the airplane hanger; he was crossway with the runway. We went up again; he knew where the runway was. Africans came with storm lanterns to each side of the runway and we landed between them. Naomi was fine. I went home to an empty house, but our helpers came with support.

When I did not receive word whether Helen had flown to America, I assumed she had gone. However, I made a trip to Tamale on Monday and found that the Lehmanns had talked with the Kesslers in Accra by phone. Helen had been successful in contacting her family. Her mother was still alive, so she had taken the flight on Sunday afternoon, January 27, as scheduled. I returned to Saboba where the Konkombas said, "Madam, don't let your heart *fell* down." But it really did. I wrote to friends and family in New Mexico, "Do not send any more packages. If anything, send money I can use while returning to America in the near future." A package came later; it contained a girdle. I had forgotten they existed! It reminded me of the time we were using American magazines to make paper cups to pre-pack clinic medicine. One page showed the lower half of a woman wearing only a girdle. Gylima said, "Madam, I don't think women dress like this in America." I said, "I hope not" and explained. Another time Gylima found a picture of a UFO in a magazine and read about it. He said, "When I was a young boy, something like this landed between here and the river. The lights were so bright they frightened us. It is our custom that when anything frightens our whole village or we do not understand, we run toward it in a group instead of from it. The people lit torches and ran toward it. When we got near it, it went straight up same as it had come down. We were amazed; it never came again." In one package, there were pink and blue booties. Gylima and his wife, Bakanti, had only girls. I told Gylima that if he would hang a pair of the blue booties in his grass roof his wife would produce a male. He roared with laughter! Gylima had worked with Americans so long; he understood our humor.

Helen and I planned to visit a French Togo Game Reserve before we went to America. Since she could not go, the Yendi District Commissioner allowed an employee, Phyllis Jones, to go with me. We went ten miles east from Yendi and crossed the Oti River on a very slow ferry that actually drug on the bottom of the river as it crossed. We were instantly in French Togo. We stayed with missionaries both going to and returning from the reserve. We joined in prayer each morning with them, their children, and workers. Their dedication and projects were impressive: primary schools, technical schools, Bible schools, clinics, agricultural projects, and more. Phyllis spoke French. I spoke almost none but understood a bit more than I spoke; I had taken the subject at SBI in Texas. We stopped to refuel my lorry and I asked an African to fill the tank with *petrol*, the British term for gasoline. Phyllis intervened just in time; in French Togo, the word petrol means *kerosene*. Roads in French Togo were worse than those in the Gold Coast. We crossed bridges where the tires had a plank apiece. We repaired some bridges before crossing. Near the huge animal reserve, we parked our vehicle; the missionary family taxied us. We could be free to list animals we saw. Their car was newer than mine was, yet the doors required bailing wire to hold them shut. Having just driven their roads, I understood. Roads inside the reserve were worse; I was glad my lorry was parked. The animals were beautiful and our list of antelopes, monkeys, and big cats was impressive. The Africans said they had neither giraffes nor zebras.

A visitor may kill one antelope, on the way to or from the reserve, but not inside it. Only an arroyo bed fenced them in. We saw animals right at the arroyo bed, but none on the side where they would be in danger. When we returned to the mission house that evening, the mirror inside my cosmetic case was broken. I had taken it for hand lotion, sunscreen, and lip lubricant; the roads were indeed rough!

Phyllis and I retraced our journey back to the Gold Coast. At the Oti River, they had been forced to stop using the ferry because of the low water. It was after sundown and many men were there working. When the sun goes down in the tropics, it is suddenly dark. The men were filling in the river with dirt to make a crossing, but it was unfinished and soft. They kept saying, "Come, we will get you across." I knew they would even if they had to carry us, but I was terrified as I drove onto the soft dirt made softer by water under it. The station wagon sunk into mud several times, but the Africans spoke true; they got us across. However, in Yendi, the District Commissioner knew about that river situation and was not as kind as the Africans were. He was totally responsible for Phyllis as an employee so he got his prayer words all mixed up as he described his version of our decision to cross in the dark. I drove on to Saboba that night. Next day was a general outpatient clinic.

Being alone, I had clinic *every* day and delivered *every* baby whether night or day. I responded to *every* emergency and there came a deluge of difficult cases. I transported two cases of spinal meningitis to Yendi. One was an adult man, the other a small boy. A walk-in, a woman with no prenatal care, came with a ruptured uterus. When I got to Yendi with this third case, Dr. Ashworth felt it was dangerous for me to be driving as tired as I was. He sent word to his house helper that I was to go to bed in his guesthouse immediately. He sent an ambulance to Saboba to collect all that would agree to come from the round houses behind my clinic. Two babies with pneumonia and sick adults were brought to Yendi in the ambulance. I had no idea how long I slept before I awoke and returned to Saboba, where I hoped to sleep all night. At about midnight, Dewey came for help. Naomi had been convulsing for some time and did not show sign of stopping. We feared this would eventually happen and it waited until I was alone. I went to their house. I prepared a paper and had Dewey sign it that he would take responsibility. Then I gave Naomi an injection of sodium pentothal as previously instructed by Dr. Ashworth. She gradually quieted. The rest of the night I sat by her bed with caffeine sodium benzoate available in case she stopped breathing. Soon after daylight, I went to the clinic. People were waiting.

By February 13, I received letters of concern from New Mexico Churches, my family, and Helen. She had written as soon as she got to America. She seemed still in shock, as I was. She wrote of her concerns about leaving early and my being alone. She said she had heard from my mom and dad. She was busy nursing her mother, who had suffered several physical problems for years and now a stroke. I started packing Helen's belongings to send to her. A letter from Burdette Wiles in Kumasi said the Mission Executive Committee did not want me to be alone for long. What could anyone do? Dewey decided he must get Naomi home *ASAP!* I helped pack their household and personal belongings. Naomi could help very little; one day she told me *she was pregnant.* If I had known that, it would have taken more than a signed paper from Dewey to persuade me to give her the Pentothal. I hauled a load of their belongings to Tamale to be shipped to them later. Naomi was flown to America exactly one month after Helen left. Pan American Airways required a nurse to accompany Naomi; it could have been me. I refused, so a nurse from Liberia went.

Before Independence Day, Ann and Becky came from the Nakpanduri clinic to visit. I was in awe of their gigantic abilities. I asked God to let me learn from them. They could learn languages, as I noticed the British did in London. They said it was good to be away from their clinic at the moment, as Nakpanduri was in British Togo and opinions about independence were hot. They said someone admitted, "Yes, if necessary, I could kill you; you are British." However, they returned to Nakpanduri clinic even before March 7, the date set for celebrations. I was never threatened, as I was an American and had no interest in their politics. On March 6, I drove the one hundred miles to Tamale to witness the lowering of the British flag and the raising of the new Ghana flag. I saw no violence, but it was emotional. The occasion took on the form of a durbar, a formal reception. A circle of covered bleachers was provided for observers. After the flag ceremony, departing British officials circled the edge of the arena and stopped to bid each major chief farewell. In response, the chiefs of any renown and his entourage made the same rounds to greet other chiefs and the departing British officials. As greetings were taking place, members of the various tribes were gathering at designated places on the parade grounds to do their particular tribal dance in costume. Tribes chose their best dancers. Each tribe was known by its respective headdress, noisemaker, and attire. Konkombas appeared with their long-horned headdresses covered with cowries. Some people were in awe and even intimidated. I got impressive photographs. After the celebrations, I went home to Saboba, where I had lived in the same house three years, but in *three countries*. First, Saboba was in *British Togo*. At the plebiscite, it chose to join the *Gold Coast*, which became *Ghana* on March 7, 1957. Hal and Naomi Lehmann allowed their teenage daughter, Gretchen, to return with me to Saboba for a month. Hal warned me nicely, jokingly and sincerely, "Just don't influence her to become a single missionary!" One word described Gretchen; she was delightful! Once after our evening meal we were playing table games and writing letters when Gretchen said, "Auntie, I'm hungry." I said, "Well, there's the fridge." She said, "Auntie, I can't eat the fridge; I want a pickle." I said, "Gretchen, you can't sleep on a pickle." Her reply: "Auntie, I don't want to sleep on it, I want to eat it." We soon crawled under our mosquito nets for the night. Before we went to sleep, I called over to her, "Gretchen, I thought you said you could not sleep on a pickle; look under your pillow." There was the pickle-in a plastic bag. This kind of humor may be labeled childish, corny, or a bad joke by those who are entertained by sordid innuendos on TV. The world could use some childish, innocent jokes! I am bored and not amused by what is labeled comedy; much is an insult to any intelligence. In a society that talks so much about self-esteem, people (including Christians) get their sit-com entertainment from putting someone else down and watching them suffer. A commandment addresses that in Matthew 22:39, "Thou shalt love thy neighbor *as thyself." You (thyself)* do not enjoy being put-down; TV is sick!

While Gretchen was in Saboba, a woman who delivered at the clinic named her newborn girl Gretchen. A very ill woman came to the clinic for treatment; we knew she might die. Within days of treatment and prayer, she got better and went home. The family slashed the bush and made a road into their village so we could visit them. One evening, Pastor Salah, Gretchen, and I drove there. When we got near, the bright lights of the vehicle frightened the children. They fled into the bush, but slowly returned as we were greeting the chief and his elders. When Gretchen spoke to them in Dagboni, the trade language, it delighted them all. I spoke and the pastor interpreted into Lekpakpaln. Several accepted Christ as their Sacrifice and, I believe, that was the beginning of the Church at Gbenja. Eventually, they had their own pastor.

Time went so fast. We were invited to another huge, gala function in Tamale honoring the departing British Governor General, Sir Arden-Clark. After that celebration, Gretchen did not return to Saboba with me. From Tamale, I drove five hundred miles to the annual missions conference in Accra.

Jim and Delta Kesslers lived there with their daughters, Vangie and Annette. In addition, the Kesslers had a new son,
Bennie, whom we were all anxious to meet. Seeing this newborn reminded me again of how much I had missed in the
early lives of my nieces and nephews. My youngest brother
and his wife recently informed me they were about to make
me an auntie again. I would possibly see their first baby
soon.

When I went south, I enjoyed the Ghana newspapers. I
found an article that said their people would now be called
Ghanaians and that the members of Parliament had chosen
English as the official language of Ghana for three reasons:
Their Parliament had long functioned in English; there were
many tribal languages and it would be difficult to choose
one above another; English would make it easier for their
youth to travel the world and compete in sports. After the
conference, on the way back north, I took three days to check
on the clinic at Techimantia. I observed their treatment and
did an inventory of medicines and furniture. I greeted the
chief, his elders, and others in the village. I did not sleep
there; I commuted the one hundred forty miles roundtrip
while lodging in the Kumasi mission guesthouse.

I was alone in Saboba for seven months after Helen left.
Naomi left a month after Helen. I was the nearest medical aid available for some fifty thousand Konkombas; they
expressed gratefulness. The Yendi Hospital was one hundred miles from some of those. I learned, *after the fact,* that a
group of six men traveled from Saboba to Tamale to ask the
Mission Superintendent to allow me to remain until other
nurses were found. When I learned what they had done,
I felt more strongly that I should stay. April 21 was Easter
Sunday. The weather was dreadfully hot and humid, as
the rainy season was threatening. The Easter service at the
church in 1957 was blessed and joyous. It also illustrated the
advancement made in the past year. I *typed* programs! Pastor Salah was Master of Ceremonies. Mr. Gylima Akonsi led

the congregation in *Lik Uwumbor Apibo (Look to the Lamb of God)* in Lekpakpaln. Mr. Nakoja Namuel, a teacher, led the schoolboys singing, *Wonderful, Wonderful Jesus*, in English. I presented the Easter story in English using visual aids. Mr. Sampson N. Mankrom, a teacher, interpreted my presentation into Lekpakpaln. Mr. Isaac Bowa, the District's Member of Parliament, interpreted Dewey Hale's message, "The Power of the Resurrection." One day after Easter, I delivered four babies in twelve hours at the clinic. It would not have been noticed much, had there been two of us. Within that week, Dewey took Pastor Salah and me on a tour of the villages where the Hales had general outpatient clinics, leper treatment clinics, and small churches. I was doing the work of two in Saboba, now I would be responsible for clinics Dewey and Naomi had started. I combined a farewell party with a birthday celebration for Dewey; Biyimba baked him a cake. I invited Dewey, his helpers, my helpers, Pastor Salah, and local teachers. The Africans felt the loss of Helen and now the Hales. We played children's games like Spin the Bottle. In a few Days, Dewey Hale flew to Liberia where he had a sale for his plane and flew on to America. Some time later I heard his wife, Naomi, had given birth to a healthy baby girl. In a way, I felt I had saved both their lives.

Friday, May 3 was general clinic. I treated almost one hundred people in outpatient clinic. The rains had started coming seriously and since it seemed I would not be leaving soon, my yard worker and I were planting tomatoes, peppers, beans, corn, radishes, and okra. In three months I would be eating the produce or gone to America. Suddenly Biyimba, the cook, called that lunch was ready. He had a surprise for me; *he had baked me a birthday cake!* Clinic workers, house workers, their families, and the local pastor were there. They had a party and played Spin the Bottle as they observed at Dewey Hale's birthday. I felt like weeping from emotion! Near that date there was a son born, I believe to the Yankazia Chief. They named him Dewey-Charles. This may have sprung from their sudden loss of Dewey, when I stayed to help even longer. After the excitement, I went to take a nap. I was terribly tired. Some time later, I awoke hearing voices in my front room. I went to investigate and found Hal and Naomi Lehmann waiting for me to awaken. They said, "You are really frightened up here alone; the door was unlocked!" Besides coming for my birthday, the next day would be Saturday and I could go with Hal to villages. He must observe the NGBI students in their Easter break practical work. Hal, Pastor Salah, and I went in an open Jeep. Naomi stayed at my house. Before we left, I said to Naomi, "This will take us all day so I don't know what I will do about a bathroom." Hours later, we greeted the chief at Cheraponi; we visited the students at Nasoni and Tamboun, Cheraponi, and were on our trek back to Saboba. Hal slammed on the brakes and said, "Charlese, I see a Texaco station over here; I'm sure there is a Conoco on your side!" There were no petrol stations in those years; Pastor Salah waited quietly.

One afternoon, two policemen came to my door. They handed me a subpoena to appear in court at Yendi. I was to be a character witness about an African. I was shocked and said I could not do that. They said I would be arrested if I did not go freely. It was to be about the man who came to the clinic with a knife to fight Gylima. He had left Saboba in the night on a stolen bicycle. Since the Saboba Clinic incident, the man had killed somebody. I was to tell what happened at the clinic. The man received a heavy prison sentence. Gylima said, "Never mind Madam, you will be old and in America before he is out of prison." I wailed, "But what if he escapes?"

Because we were so busy at the clinic, sometimes a disaster would happen, like burning up a kettle of boiling needles and priceless glass syringes. Rather than blaming some already overworked soul, someone would call, "One, two, three!" That was to announce a disaster. We all stopped whatever we were doing and said in unison, "It's all your fault!"

This was followed by spontaneous laughter and the incident was never mentioned again. This philosophy helped, especially if we had delivered babies the previous night and slept little. One day after quite a heavy clinic, I ate lunch and went the forty miles to retrieve my mail and to take a sick person to the Yendi hospital. It rained lightly most of the way. On the return trip, I discovered one stream had swollen. As I entered the water, I saw a crocodile. The water became so deep that it hit the fan and killed the engine. I pulled the car a few more feet with the starter so I could raise the hood and let the engine dry. When it started, I drove to a small hill, slanted my car sharply to one side and opened the car doors to let the water run out off the floorboards. I drove on home, looking forward to a good night's sleep under my safe, cozy net, but Gylima was waiting. While I was gone, he had been treating a comatose male infant for possible cerebral malaria. The family of the child attended the church, so we had prayer with them. I offered to transport them back to Yendi hospital and they agreed. Torba, my yardman, and I filled my car with petrol while Biyimba made two sandwiches for us to eat along the way. It was dark when Gylima and I left with the father, mother, and sick baby. I took my gun along since Gylima was a good hunter. We crossed the deep stream of water with no problem; it had waned a bit. About twenty miles from Saboba, between Kokonzoli and Demon, I noticed the gas gauge indicated empty. I did not believe it, as I had held the funnel while Torba filled the tank. Then the motor died. We checked under the bonnet (hood). With a torch (flashlight), we followed the gas line back and inspected the tank. Everything seemed intact, but the gasoline was gone. It had cost over a dollar a gallon. In America, it would have cost less than twenty-five cents. When I checked under the bonnet, I smelled gas around the fuel filter so I took the top off and made sure it was replaced tightly.

The village of Demon was a few miles ahead. Gylima and the child's father could not have persuaded anyone that a white woman was in the bush without gasoline for her car; I was forced to walk. Imagine the fear of the mother and father! They were left alone in the dark and in this strange vehicle. Their child may even die in their arms. Gylima and I literally picked up each foot and put it down as fast as we could. Suddenly, Gylima asked, "Madam, are you afraid?" I answered, "No, are you afraid?" Then I noticed he had my gun, I wailed, "Gylima you have my gun; you are afraid!" We could meet a snake or lion, but we both laughed hilariously, as usual. By midnight, we were telling our sad story to the Demon Chief in a patio surrounded by little grass-topped mud huts. He informed us there was no lorry or petrol in his village. Then we asked him if someone had a bicycle. I was ready to pay someone to take a message to Missionary Dale Brown. The Chief said no young man would go eighteen miles through the bush on a bicycle at night; there were too many lions! Finally, the Chief said the man owning a corn grinder another mile down the road had gone to Yendi that day to get petrol, but no one seemed to know if the man had returned. We walked another mile and found him there. He said he had suffered all day to get the petrol and would sell it to no one! He said he must start his corn grinder before sunup. I told him I would have the gasoline back to him before sunrise. He said, "White man never lies." Reluctantly, he brought out a four-liter tin of petrol. The Africans tell a story about how important it is to tell the truth. It seems a monkey was shipwrecked in the Gulf of Guinea, off the Gold Coast. He caught a ride on the back of a big fish. The fish asked the monkey where he lived. The Monkey said, "The Gold Coast," hoping the fish would rush him to the nearest shore. The fish asked the monkey, "And do you know gari?" "Oh, yes, I know him," the monkey lied. If the monkey had been from the Gold Coast, he would have known that gari is a *food*, not a person. The fish dived and let the monkey drown.

Gylima and I retraced our trek back to my car. He walked

in front with the petrol cong-cong (gasoline can) on his head and the torchlight in his hand to watch for snakes. I walked behind with the gun. When he handed me the gun, he said, "Let me remove the bullet." Then, I really teased him, "Gylima you *were* afraid; you even had my gun loaded!" We laughed again, but I found myself more jumpy on the way back. Gylima said he felt like the prisoner with the warden following behind with a gun. Back at the car, we put some of the petrol in slowly while checking for leaks. We drove to Yendi. The gas gauge indicated we had used very little of the liquid gold. In Yendi, we rushed the baby to Dr. Ashworth. He admitted him to the hospital. Gylima and I woke up the Brown family. I went to bed. Gylima and Dale Brown took the petrol back to the corn grinder before sunrise, in another vehicle. Dale inspected my vehicle. No one ever found where the petrol went! The sick child and his parents returned to Saboba by market lorry. They brought a paper from the hospital. The diagnosis of cerebral malaria was confirmed. The doctor wrote that the treatment Gylima had initiated had saved the baby's life until he could be treated at Yendi hospital. The grateful family dashed me eggs. The live child was pay enough! I tell these stories, partly to show how important Gylima was to his people, the missionaries, and ultimately the church in the area. Many of the people at church would say, "I was sick, went to the clinic, heard the Gospel, believed Jesus Christ to be my Blood Sacrifice and now I am a Christian." Mostly, Gylima had interpreted, or given the Word himself if we were out of town. He and his beautiful wife, Bikanti, and their five daughters: Yanyi, Piger, Yaro, Mary, and Obi, were faithful to attend church as a family. In a language lesson, Gylima sat with me while we put the last song, *When the Roll Is Called Up Yonder (Bi Ya Ti Ye Ti Yimbil Pacham)*, into the Konkomba Language before I left on furlough in 1957. I gave the stack of songs to Hal Lehmann to be printed into a book. It represented the work of every missionary who had lived in Saboba.

Dr. Ashworth came for his final visit before I went to America. A doctor in charge of the leper program also came. On Tuesday January 27, they discharged fourteen lepers as *cured* because of the sulfa drugs we gave them in the field test. Because of my heavy schedule in the Saboba area clinics, it had been three months since I had checked on Techimantia Clinic, so I went the three hundred seventy miles. Biyimba traveled with me. In Kumasi, I telephoned my brother in New Mexico. He, his wife, and little three-year-old Roxanne, whom I had never seen, were planning to meet my ship in New York. We agreed on a date, the first week of October. Missionaries advised me not to fly into busy America, but rather go by ship so I could rest for about two weeks on a boat; they knew I was very tired. The rains in the jungle were heavy. The last seventy miles of the road from Kumasi to Techimantia were slick; wet clay and heavy logging trucks on them were dangerous. After I completed an inspection of the clinic, Biyimba and I visited the people again in the little church at their nightly devotions. Then we visited the local chief and bade him farewell, as I knew I would not come again. By August 4, we were back in Saboba. Along with all the packing, I delivered six babies in August; including a breech for Yimbinya from Toma.

One morning at prayer on the palaver porch, Biyimba said he wanted to talk with me about something. He said, "You know my father died and my mother, Gaemba, never remarried. No one was there to buy me a wife, but I have found the girl I want." I asked, "Is she free to marry and is she a Christian? Does she know when she marries a Christian it is *until death parts you*?" He said, "Oh, yes she knows all that. He brought her to meet me. She was beautiful and her name was Makpa. I asked her all the same questions I had asked Biyimba. To all the questions she answered, "Oh, Biyimba already told me that." That was a happy time. Right when I needed to be packing seriously, Torba, Biyimba's youngest brother, became acutely ill. We took him, unconscious, to Yendi Hospital. Dr. Ashworth officially diagnosed cerebral malaria. It had attacked his kidneys, so he had black water fever. One of these is usually fatal, but *two!* We were in mourning as we packed and made inventory of the house and clinic.

On September 1, I went to Yankazia to greet U Na Febor Jayom and conduct a clinic for the last time. Rains had been heavy and I was not sure we could reach there. Pastor Salah went with me. We drove fourteen miles to Wapuli with no problem, but the last mile to Yankazia was impossible. The vehicle slipped off the road into a flooded, bushy area. Pastor Salah and I tried to get it back onto the road, but failed. The water was moving the vehicle gradually downstream. Pastor Salah ran to Yankazia and I was there alone with the moving car for about forty-five minutes. Then I heard chanting and saw a group of men appear over a hill. They bounced the car along in the water onto ground where I could start the motor and help pull it out. Sadness was overshadowing the village, as the chief's wife had recently been killed. They were building a new church across from the clinic when the rains came heavy and a mud wall fell on her. Still, U Na Febor declared it *wonderful* (full of wonder-amazing!) that we would come this last time to hold a clinic for his people. After clinic, we had a combined farewell and memorial service in the chief's throne room. I hooked the tape recorder to the battery of my car and taped the meeting. U Na Febor Jayom gave a personal testimony of when he accepted Christ. Then he sent a message to the American Christians, "When my people of Yankazia accepted Christ as their Lord and Savior, it was as if a bright light, like the headlight of a lorry, was turned on in our village. The people are happier, healthier, and busy helping each other. Our village has never been the same. Thank you for the clinic, too." This statement caused me to remember Matthew 4:16: ""The people which sat in darkness saw great light; and to them which sat in the region and shadow of death light is sprung up." In Likpakpaln, "Nima aanib bi bi mboumbooun ni na, bi kan nwiihn saakpin. Bin bi mboumbooun ni, ki san nkun ijaawaan na, le nwiihn woln bi pu." Matu 4:16. Teacher Samson Mankrom, his wife, Tani, and his mother, Binimpom, were there. Little David (Mankrom) Nabegmado, almost three years old, was there with Binimpom, his foster mother. She was playing an eighteen-inch-long gourd as a percussion instrument and presented it to me. Another woman gave me a round gourd with a handle; she was using it as a tambourine. I had ordered a white blanket from a man whom I saw weaving one from their locally grown cotton. He had completed it and I paid him. The chief dashed me a live goat. That was the highest honor I had ever been paid. We took it to Saboba in the back of my station wagon. The group of men who had helped us get there followed us along, chanting as they went, and bounced the lorry safely through the wide, shallow river again. (Of those present that day, Teacher Samson had already been to school in the United States before I got to Africa; Little David Nabegmado came to America several times after my retirement; and Samson's third daughter, Sarah, phoned and e-mailed me from New Jersey, United States in 2003!)

On Sunday, the first day of September, the people had a farewell service for me at the Saboba-Toma Church. There were tears of joy and sadness. We remembered the good times, but I was leaving. Late Monday morning Naomi Lehmann arrived from Tamale to help me with the two last days of packing. She had packed for furlough before! *Been there, done that*! I knew I must keep busy; a deadline was set to board the ship! Naomi forced me to stop and eat a bite and drink tea. On Tuesday morning, Chief Oden and a group representing the Toma-Nalongni area and church brought me *a goat*! Some young men killed and dressed my two goats. We put some of it in the kerosene refrigerator. Some we gave to wives of my helpers to cook stew for a farewell banquet on the palaver porch that evening. They cooked rice. The pastor and teachers were there. Their chil-

dren came. Even as we were eating the banquet, Saboba
Chief Quadin came from Kpatapaab with eight of his elders.
They dashed me a goat! It was the third one in less than a week;
I was *overwhelmed*! On Wednesday morning, Christians and
other town people filled the yard by 7 A.M. I knew they had
not eaten. Bachi and Jabob worked as if I were paying them
ten pounds a day. So did Gylima, Biyimba, their wives, and
other women. We were missing Torba, my regular yardman;
he was still in Yendi hospital! I worked only a few minutes, rested, and worked again. Some of the men killed and
dressed the last goat, but there was *no room in the inn (fridge)!*
Also, we wanted to empty the fridge and kill the fire under
it. We lined a garbage can with U.S. newspapers saved from
incoming packages. We put the extra meat inside so Naomi
could take it to Tamale; it would not do to leave gifts behind!
Pastor Salah was planning to go to the coast with me so I
would not travel alone. He went home to pack. I thought
we'd be gone by noon, but even Naomi did not leave until
2 P.M. To close up a station involved more than I thought. I
locked five metal drums to store in Tamale for Helen and me;
either could use the contents upon returning to Ghana. Mr.
Adam, Education Officer from Moslem Zango village near
the market came to help me take down my radio aerial and
sort out dozens of keys; he tagged the keys. Some keys went
to Gylima for the clinic, house keys to Biyimba as the watchman, and the others to Rev. Dale Brown in Yendi. He would
have to work his area, the Konkomba areas north and south
of Yendi, and the Cheraponi area; missionaries were getting
scarce! Gylima would continue to treat general patients at
the clinic but not deliver babies inside the clinic, only if they
called him to their home. He could take supplies from the
clinic in a bag for home deliveries. He would continue to
work in cooperation with the Leper Control Agent.

At 6:30 P.M., I was ready to leave Saboba. Makuba, Biyimba's younger brother, prayed in English and Lekpakpaln; he
was on leave from NGBI. He had led the cow on which Biy-

imba rode for treatment years ago when Ruby and Ozella saved his life. Finally, Pastor Salah and I were on our way and waved to them. Bakanti, Gylima's wife, was crying; so was I. I made a last round to Kpatapaab to greet Chief Quadin and his people, to Moslem Zango and the market area, to the police station and teachers' quarters. At the school, Teacher Samson Mankrom could hardly look at me. In the Toma area, we paused at the church and greeted the people in Beso's house and in Chief Odin's compound. People waved from the roadside even west of Maja's house and up to the hill where we went out of sight. We went forty miles to Yendi, where Pastor Salah and I visited Torba at the Yendi Hospital and prayed with him. Dr. Ashworth said that he was better and it was a miracle. I took Pastor Salah to the local pastor's home. Betty and Dale Brown had saved supper for me. I gave them the mission books and keys. Teacher Nakoja was in Yendi and came to tell me good-bye. He paid me one pound and four shillings, the balance owed on Yanyi's wedding dress. I had ordered it for them from Mrs. Mutrage, a seamstress in Tamale. Yanyi was Gylima's oldest daughter. Eventually they married in Yendi and Nakoja sent me pictures. He wrote, "I hope you agree that our wedding was beautiful!" The Newell family from England had replaced The Wallace family as Yendi District Commissioners. They checked on Torba at the Yendi Hospital and the wedding for Teacher Nakoja and Yanyi. They promised to keep me informed. After I ate and said farewells to the Brown family, the pastor and I drove another sixty miles to Tamale. I dozed off and Pastor Salah talked to keep me awake and out of the trees. I dropped him off to sleep at the local pastor's house and I went on to the Lehmann's house to sleep; it was after midnight. Hal met me on the front porch saying how worried they had been, as they expected me much earlier, but that they had packed for furloughs before, so they understood. Finally, he said, "Never mind, you and the *kids* just come on home anytime." Of course, he made that statement because Naomi had arrived with meat from the three Saboba gift goats. I slept well, but awoke at 6 A.M. by habit.

Pauline Smith and Adeline Wichman arrived from Wale-wale soon after breakfast. Other people arrived from other towns all during the day, and that evening they had my fare-well party with Ghanaians and missionaries. First, we had a feast. There was enough Saboba goat meat in the stew for everyone. Complements were lavished during the evening. Ann and Becky, the British nurses from Nakpanduri Clinic, made up words and a tune to sing my life's story. Both have since exited this life, what a loss! I was so emotional about all the farewell efforts. The strong mutual element was that something specific made us feel we were supposed to be where we were. It was termed "a call from God." So we were happy and respected one another because of that *mutual element*. When all the people went back to their stations of work, I was left with deep nostalgia. I wept and slept little.

On Saturday, September 7, Pastor Salah and I drove to Kumasi. As we passed through a cocoa plantation, I stopped to get a cocoa pod for my nephew to use in show-and-tell at a San Diego school. Pastor Salah said, "Oh, don't go in there; they guard their crops with guns." I said, "If I see him, I'll ask." Pastor Salah stayed with pastors all the way and enjoyed visiting. In Kumasi, I stayed in the guesthouse of the Burdette Wiles' residence again. They asked me to take greetings to their son, Dick, in school so far away in the United States. On Tuesday, we drove through the beau-tiful Ashanti Forest to Takoradi. The Weidman family was still there. Their son, John, was also at school in the United States. Missionary Paul Weidman arranged my booking to America. On Saturday, September 14, I boarded a Norwegian ship, the *Tana*, of the Wilhelm's Lines. It was a freighter haul-ing bauxite, but there were a few beautiful rooms for passen-gers. The Weidman family and Pastor Salah were allowed to join me on the ship. Pastor Salah had never been on a ship this large. I was to spend the night on board and we would sail in the early hours of the morning. I did not see another passenger; I asked about it. I was the *only passenger*; I almost got off the ship! I said, "I cannot do this! No co-worker for over seven months! Now I am on a ship to cross the Atlantic Ocean alone!" Paul Weidman convinced me there was not another ship sailing to America soon. I don't remember how I said, "Good bye" to pastor or missionaries. *Alone again!*

The following are excerpts from my diary on my return trip to America:

September 17: Mostly I have slept since we left Africa; I am exhausted. I enjoy sitting on the deck at night. I need this rest before I face America! I eat at the Captain's table along with the Machinist Mate and his wife; she is the only other woman. She does not speak English, or I, Norwegian. The Captain speaks English. He asked what foods I got most hungry for in four years. I said, "Apples and homogenized milk." Both were on the table every meal! I write letters back to Ghana and listen to my Roberts Radio (from post-World War II England). It told of severe storms in the area. The Capitan asked how I knew and sent a steward to take down my radio aerial; it would interfere with the ships radio. Even without an aerial, I listened to C.M. Ward preaching from Bermuda.

September 19: The Captain announced tonight would be the *Captain's Party* for this crossing. He says the weather forecast is not good and we may not have a party if we wait. At the party, the Machinist Mate turned on the record player. It sounded like the wrong speed. He insisted that it was popular music in America; I did not believe him. It was *The Chipmunks!* One, who kept insisting I try sherry, gave up and ordered milk and cookies. I was delighted! The Third Mate had on a gold wedding band. That woman would be proud of him; he was the only one who seemed as out of place as I did. They played a record of *Norway, My Norway* and got sentimental. I hoped no one played *The Star-Spangled Banner.* I excused myself when I got full of milk and cookies.

September 20: I prayed for those aboard last night; it is obvious some need it as much as the Konkombas ever did. After supper, I sat on deck thinking until I had to hang onto rails getting to my cabin and it was impossible to sleep.

September 21: The ship is still tossing; I can hardly stay in my bunk. Facedown, I get sheet-burns. On my back, my head is bumped. I cannot dress for holding on. Surely, the Captain will alert us of danger. The drawers flew out of my dresser; I left them on the floor. They slid back and forth and were dangerous. At the only meal today, the Captain announced we had just gone between *two* hurricanes. The tablecloth was wet to hold it and the dishes on the tables. Chairs were tethered to the tables.

September 22: The Captain said, "One ship has sunk in the hurricanes. Our ship is being diverted to Newport News, Virginia, the nearest U.S. port. We still have one hurricane ahead and we might miss it by diverting. Our load of bauxite has shifted; we may not be able to ballast successfully if we are hit again." My family was to meet me in New York. I asked, "How will they know where I am?" We radioed Robert McGlasson in New York; he would manage to get me to Mizpah Lodge in New York. I also heard that *two ships, not one,* had sunk. One was a German sailing vessel with eight-four people and *no survivors.* Months later a Reader's Digest article said that one person was found clinging to debris. Two French ships collided; one sank.

September 23: I heard my first radio commercial in four years.

My diary ended abruptly as we reached America. I stepped off the ship into an area that had a glass-front counter with a cash register on top. I could not believe the candy bars, nuts, and gum-and I had no American money! I was jolted back to earth by my name being paged. The young driver, sent by Robert McGlassen to take me to Mizpah Lodge in the Bronx, had been through this before! How he ever got my freight rerouted from the ship to the right warehouse in New York, got me through customs and into his car that fast, I will never know! It was not the *dead slow and stop* of Africa and I had little to do with it! *Kidnapped again!*

Plebiscite over, British Togo joins the Gold Coast on March 7, 1957.
1. Naomi and Gretchen Lehmann at entrance to Tamale parade
ground. 2. Transportation. 3-5. Durbar to raise the Ghana flag. 7-9
His Excellency the Governor, General Sir Charles Arden Clark in
Tamale to bid farewell to Ghana. 10. Symbol of the new Ghana.

1-4. NGBI students, ceremonies and teachers (Thomases, Andersons, McCorkles, Lehmanns and Goodwins). 5-6. Trip to French Dahomey game reserve and hunting lodge with Phyllis Jones. She was a judge at a Saboba baby show, where she, the mother and baby all observe closely. 7. Torba (right), had a miracle in a bout of black-water fever 8. Wedding of Nakoja and Yanyi Gylima. 9. One of many of Hales; outstations I took over when they went to USA. 10. My first furlough via M/S Tana, Capt. R. Kolderich.

CHAPTER SEVEN

Once Every Night and
Twice on Sunday

PPARENTLY, THERE WAS NO speed limit on this thing
called a freeway with several vehicles going the same
direction! We were amongst them and all going *the
wrong way*! I had been driving on the left side of the road for
four years. The young driver bragged a bit about *frighten-
ing females fresh from the bush*. I trusted God did not save me
from a listing ship to let me die on a United States highway
this soon! I thought, "Every man, woman and child in America must own at least one automobile and no two the same
color." Pre-World War II automobiles were usually black or
navy blue.

So much for my family's plans to meet my ship! The
original date of arrival in New York was yet two days away.
At Mizpah House, I located my elusive family by phone;
they were as disappointed as I was. The first day back in
America, I took the subway to New York locations. I got my
freight forwarded to New Mexico. I renewed my driver's
license and bought a new Chevy. A Chevrolet dealer and I
phoned my dad and a New Mexico bank and got it financed.
It was declared *not ready for me* to drive yet. A letter, from

Rowena Vanzant and some ladies in New Mexico, was waiting at Robert McGlassen's New York office. The letter contained funds for new clothes for me. I saw nothing wrong
(yet) with the ones I had on!

Before I joined my family, I had time to visit for one
night with the Parker and Phyllis (Layton) Johnston family
in New Jersey. From there, I would drive to Helen Kopp's
home in Lancaster, Pennsylvania; I would meet my family
there. The Chevrolet dealer delivered my car. The lady in
charge of Mizpah handed me the keys. I had never driven in
New York City and had been driving on the left four years. I
asked for directions to the New Jersey Turnpike and left. As
I set out, there appeared a car in front of me and I prayed it
would go to the New Jersey Turnpike. If I followed another
vehicle, perhaps I would not be tempted to drift to the left. I
followed that car straight to the New Jersey Turnpike and all
humanity was safe! I could not get on the wrong side or go
the wrong way; traffic nudged me along.

The Johnston family was a welcome sight! Phyllis was
from New Mexico. She went through my suitcase and laughed
the whole time. She never let me forget the old clothes and
hats bought in England to mold in Africa for three years.
We went shopping with the New Mexico women's money.
We bought a suit and coat, as the cold weather was not far
away. Being fresh from the tropics, I was already freezing! I
was also relaxing; driving to Lancaster was a pleasure. The
meeting with my family and Helen was so emotional that it
is yet vague. My mother was with them; I had not a clue she
was coming! My joy was mixed with shock as I saw her with
the signs of aging. She probably noticed I had aged! I met
my niece, Roxanne, for the very first time. She was the doll I
had seen in photos and movies they had mailed to me. She
was shy and someone asked her, "Who is this?" She said,
"Auntie Who." They had been showing her my picture and
asking her, "Who is this?" To Roxanne, I have been *Auntie
Who* since that day!

We went back to New York City, parked our cars in a garage, and went sightseeing. My brother's movie camera and other items were stolen from his glove compartment. At a cafe, a waiter came and scattered things on the table looking for his tip. He hit a cream pitcher. It dumped into the lap of my new suit and ran down each side onto my new coat. The manager paid for having my clothing sent to the cleaners, but time was wasted. I thought about my father's song, "Saw a little box all painted red; I put my letter in it. Whoopee, gee, what they did to me, squirted water all over me. Dumb ol' root from a high grass town." Grass was really high in Africa, but I was not too impressed with civilization, either! Our family toured upper New York to Niagara Falls. The leaves were beautiful in October. Culture shock showed up in surprising ways, like being slow with the money. Hey, I once worked in a bank!

Mom and I headed west and left my brother and family to tour the eastern states as planned. We drove to Springfield, Missouri, where I reported to the Missions Department for debriefing. On Sunday morning, we went to church. As we were going up steep steps to the entrance, a tall young man in his late teens came bounding down two steps at a time calling, "Auntie Charlese!" He threw his arms around me and we were exuberant. My mother looked that young man up and down; she knew my nephews and this was *not* one of them! He was Dick Wiles; I had just left his parents and sister, Cheryl, in Kumasi. Dick introduced me to his friend, John Weidman. I had never met him, but his parents and sister, Faith, had just put me on the ship at Takoradi harbor. I was a link to their families and so pleased to be *Auntie.*

I reported to Noel Perkin, Secretary of World Missions; to Everett Phillips, Area Secretary for Africa; and to the Promotions Department. We met a nurse, Eloise Smith, who had Africa as her goal and was soon going for her midwifery training in England. At a place called Mission Village, we met many missionaries on furlough. We left Missouri and stayed overnight in Tulsa, Oklahoma with Darrel and Clairena, a young couple from the Sunday school class I taught in Albuquerque. They had a son, Warren; their daughter, Rheette, was a newborn. I tried to forget I was a midwife and just enjoy the new baby. Our next stop was Portales, inside eastern New Mexico, to visit Pastors Earl and Rowena Vanzant and family. It was as if I owed them personal thanks. They had promoted items we needed like a stove, a fridge, and a car. When the Vanzants promised to pray, they prayed! Their daughter, Velma (Vanzant) Owens voiced a bit of insecurity about bathing her new baby, Brenda. I remember telling her something like, "Hey, they don't break; they bounce." Then, like a seasoned British midwife, I soaped the baby all over, dipped her into warm, relaxing water, and toweled her as she wailed. Today, I would like to ask Velma, like the Ghanaians do, "And did you learn anything?" Perhaps I scared her to death! I told the Vanzants how hard it was to leave Saboba Clinic without a doctor, nurse or midwife. Ruby Johnson, in Kansas, was packing to go back to Saboba. However, she did not have her budget raised for the three years, so the Mission Board would not clear her to sail. The Vanzants made this known to their church members. Together they contacted Ruby Johnson and the Mission Board. People in the Portales church gave the amount she lacked. She was then left to find a co-worker, pack, get her visa, and go sooner than expected.

It was October when I walked into my parents' home in Belen. Dad was watching television. Wow, it was *color* by then! I was still resting at home when an invitation came from the women of Northwest and West Central Sections of New Mexico. I was to go for a homecoming welcome and shower in Albuquerque's Public Service Company (PNM) Hospitality Room. There were over one hundred women, some from as far away as Farmington. During the party there was a power outage; we were in the dark for a time. This was surprising, considering where we met. The ladies showered me with clothing and other personal items that I needed more than I knew. It was a bit of an emotional shock, as my mind was still functioning on the small-town Saboba level. My thoughts ran like, "Why are they treating me as if I have done something unusual? I only did what I felt God asked me to do." In fact, it rather frightened me. Before I slept that night, I prayed, "God don't let me get all my reward here; save some for heaven." Then I prayed the special prayer I usually close with, "Lord help me to do thy will and *all that you require of me.*" I meant it then; it scares me now!

I visited former friends in Albuquerque National Bank where I had worked and at St. Josephs Hospital School of Nursing. I visited a midwifery program in Santa Fe, sixty miles north. The icon of the American College of Nurse Midwifery has *New Mexico* on it; it has roots in this state. I met a Catholic Sister who taught at that school of midwifery; she gave me a tour. She had also worked in Ghana! We discussed two more midwifery programs, one in Kentucky, and one in a New York university. Ruby Johnson, who worked in Saboba, got her masters in midwifery from New York.

I was soon busy itinerating to share results I had seen in Africa and raise my required support for another three years. At first, the K.D. Comptons allowed me to stay rent-free in a small house behind their main house in the south valley of Albuquerque. Their five children were mostly gone from the nest. Then, Rev. and Mrs. Raymond Hudson, New Mexico District Superintendent, allowed me to stay in the third bedroom of their house in southeast Albuquerque. It was convenient, as we both had to travel a lot across New Mexico. Sometimes we could even travel together and save gasoline money. Once we fished in the Pecos River, near where I lived as a child. Once we joined a group of pastors to hunt in the Lincoln National Forest east of Alamogordo. The men went one way; Marie Hudson and I walked another direction. We saw no deer, so returned to camp to prepare a meal for the group. After we ate, I looked at the sun and decided I would walk one hour out and have an hour of light to return. I walked over some hills. Dark was descending faster than I expected, so I was *pickin'-'em-up-and-layin'-'em-down*, heading for the car! I saw a small deer across the canyon on the side of the hill ahead. I shot once and he rolled down the hill. I found him and tied my license to his ear with a hairpin. I dressed him just enough to removed some weight. Then I tied his four legs together with my headscarf and looped his feet over my shoulder; his head was dangling. When I noticed the license was not on his ear, I stopped to look for it. In the dusk, every rock looked like a white piece of paper. Then I was not sure where I had put my deer until I saw a white horse investigating it. I ran the horse away and retrieved my deer. A car horn honked in the distance and I saw a sawmill incinerator that I had passed earlier; I knew I was not lost. At the bottom of the last hill, I left the deer in an arroyo bed. I thought, "I am too tired; I will tell them I got no deer." The blood on my hands and dress would not let me do that. At the car, Rev. Hudson said they heard one shot and asked if I got a deer. I just held up my hands. He had not killed a deer, but had helped men bring in two, so he was tired! With no enthusiasm he asked, "Where is it?" Suddenly, I waxed impish and said, "I killed it over two hills that way," as I pointed. His response told me he was not too interested in going after it, so I pointed to the deer in the arroyo bed. The relief showed; he went and did a quick job of dressing it. The size was an advantage for us all, but he teased me about *killing a jackrabbit!* It had horns! Mrs. Hudson said they discussed whether I was lost. They decided, "No, she's been to Africa, she isn't lost." When they heard one shot only they said, "She would shoot again if she were lost; she has a deer!" They honked the horn anyway; it helped me. We tied Marie Hudson's license to the deer; it was the last day of the hunting season. In Cloudcroft, we went into a café to eat. Hunters cheered; my clothing announced my success. Back in Albuquerque, Rev. Hudson hung up the deer in the garage. The next morning he went out to cut it up and came back saying, "You know, that deer is not as small as I thought it was." I declared, "It is not nearly as big as I thought it was while carrying it!" The following week Rev. Hudson applied for a special permit to hunt in the Sandia Mountains nearby. He brought home a small deer and I insisted his was no bigger than my jackrabbit! Mine was already cut up; I knew he could prove nothing.

This was my first furlough and I was still within the age limit to be a Christ's Ambassador. That is what our church youth organization was called for many years and where Chi Alpha in universities originated. Melvin Sasse, DCAP (District C. A. President), asked me to speak at the annual youth convention in November 1957 at Silver City. With three years of living in the Northern Territories of the Gold Coast, I had lots to say. My main point was, "Every generation is responsible to get the message of Jesus Christ to their generation." New Mexico had three missionaries: Martha Roberts, Ellis Stone, and me. I felt a responsibility to inspire the youth of New Mexico. I concluded by giving them the message I promised U Na Febor Jayum, the Chief of Yankazia, that I would give. It was about Christ bringing light to his village as in Isaiah 9:2. I met a family by the name of Trewern in Silver City in 1953 as Helen Kopp and I itinerated. Jim Trewern, a son in that family, became the State Youth Director in New Mexico. He held various offices in New Mexico and Arizona. Then, I met a son of Jim and Jan Trewern, because he was a pastor in Sedona, Arizona. I spent summer vacations in the '80s and '90s with my Aunt Leonora at her Sedona condominium. Other sons of Jim and Jan became ministers in New Mexico and Texas. Again, I spoke in Silver City in the late 1980s. Jim's mother showed me an outline in her Bible of my 1957 message in Silver City and said she *remembered every word*. A compliment from a very special lady!

Letters started coming from Ghanaians and missionaries. One from Saboba was addressed to, "Madams Pencil and Cup." That may sound as near to Spencer and Kopp as the way I dealt with their names! A letter from our cook, Biyimba, said he and Makpa had a baby girl, Ruth, on October 29 and that, "She has been *donated* to God. I have been lonely as I watch over the empty Saboba mission house. Not that there are no persons with whom to speak, but that I have departed for a moment from one who took me as a son." Hal and Naomi Lehmann wrote, "Ruby Johnson is booked to sail December 12. We miss you terribly." Their workload had not decreased although it was vacation time at NGBI, at Kumbungu. They transported the seven Konkomba students on leave as far as Yendi. Market lorries were available north to their areas. The Lehmanns went south for a church dedication at Kpandai. Hal said Pastor Selah and Teacher Samson were going to help with printing the Konkomba songbook when he found time. Heavy schedules were par for most missionaries. In my reply to Hal and Naomi Lehmann's letter, I told them about my part-time job at Presbyterian Hospital. I requested to be rotated into every department as a refresher course before returning to Ghana. I did not explain fully, so the Lehmanns wrote back an admonition, "May I suggest that you itinerate and rest and *not* get a job! We don't want you weaned away by the sweet milk of a regular paycheck!"

A letter came from Phyllis Jones, the British lady who went to the game reserve with me. She said Government Officials Reginald and Barbara Wallace were now located in Tamale, so she would also be there. She said Dr. Ashworth visited from Yendi and had lunch with them about once a month. She ended with a great compliment, "You can have no idea what your friendship meant to me. I gathered great strength from you and always felt a new creature for the laughter that invariably followed our *most serious incidents!* Best wishes for the blessings of Christmas." In a Christmas 1957 letter from Dr. Ashworth, he said he had a chat with Dr. Faile of the Southern Baptist Mission, who was opening a hospital in Nalerigu, about sixteen miles from the Nak-panduri Assembly of God Clinic; they would need one more doctor. He added, "Since it was clearly the Lord's choice by which I came to West Africa, it seems likely that I should stay in this part of the world. No doubt the way will be clearly shown in due time. I pray your leave will be refreshing and blessed over Christmas. Go easy on the pinto beans!"

My brothers, sister, aunts, uncles, and their families on both sides came to my parents' home in Belen for a reunion and feast near Christmas. I was home for Christmas for the first time in four years, since 1952. After the holidays, my speaking schedule became heavy. There were few towns in New Mexico where I, or my family, had not lived. I did not need motels; I knew people. There were churches in most towns. The people in those churches supported me while I was in Africa. They wanted to know what I had done with my time and their money; I wanted to tell them. By speaking at churches almost every weeknight and twice on Sundays, and at banquets on Saturdays, I was able to go to even the smaller churches. It was difficult for out-of-state missionar-ies to do that because of travel costs. New Mexico churches were supporting my endeavor anyway, so if anyone could do it, I could. This included Indian churches and missions. At one time, *Once Every Night and Twice On Sunday* was going to be the name of my book *if I ever wrote one*. It certainly described my itinerary.

Letters continued to come. In January 1958 a letter from Gylima (my glory) Akonsi, said he was keeping the clinic open daily except Saturday and Sunday. He said, "Since your departure, we've had five snakebites. I put a blade in the flame for some time and cut where the snake bit, then sucked the blood. We had some prayers and I sent them home. Thank God, all got well." He reported that Akonsi, his father and the very first Konkomba Christian, was quite well but weak and old. He said his Mother Mawin and Aun-tie Majin were perfectly well. Finally, he wrote, "We have missed you and wished you were in our midst. Greetings from all people in Saboba; especially the church members and chiefs of Saboba and Toma. We hope you come again *one day.*" He told about the wedding of his daughter, Yanye, to Teacher Nakoja in Yendi. Gylima Akonsi was intelligent, capable, conscientious, and such fun to work with. This last letter from him will always be a treasure. Ruby started us all calling him "The PhD."

In the early spring of 1958, I went to San Diego, California to visit my sister, Mae. Dave, her Pearl Harbor survivor husband, was at sea. Mae and my two nephews, Jim and David, took me to Disney Land and Knott's Berry Farm for my first time. We visited New Mexico friends who had moved to California. Cecil and Lois (Bates) Holley and family were pastors in Fallbrook. Doyle and Lola (Bates) Wilson and daughter, Sharon lived in Anaheim.

Back in New Mexico, my once-every-night-and-twice-on-Sunday speaking continued through the Spring Conventions and up to New Mexico District Council in April. I met many people who had supported my efforts in Africa. I loved and enjoyed every minute with the people, but tried not to forget *the reason why*! I visited the Deming church where the Chambers family worshiped. After my presentation, I was told I would spend the night with them. That was where, five years before, Helen bit into the hot pepper thinking it was a pickle. Mrs. Chambers rode with me again to show the way. I remarked that the road had been paved since I was there. She said, "Oh, no! You were driving so fast the other time that I knew you would never manage a certain turn in the road, so I let you go straight onto a dirt road!"

In March 1958, Pastor Selah wrote from Saboba, "We now have our missionary, Miss Johnson. We were very happy to see her again. You tried your best to stay in Saboba, alone with the clinic. "I pung imung paa!" ("You tried yourself!") You showed that you loved Christ and wanted His work to go forward. I'm just sorry that I cannot see you now. Our

Lord bless you." Then I heard from Ruby soon after she got to Saboba. She was so grateful to the Vanzants and specific persons in the Portales church who helped with finances so she could pack instead of itinerate. She said, "This *perching in a different tree* every night, called itinerary, is *for the birds!*" She reported that Peggy Scott, from Florida, had joined her and was a lot of help, but not a nurse.

I felt my need of being able to speak and write the Konkomba language better. I tried to be as prepared as possible for what might help the people, wherever the mission put me. I wrote to Wycliff's Summer Institute of Linguistics (SIL) and found their session nearest to New Mexico was in June at the University of Oklahoma (OU) in Norman. Their objectives were to speak and write an unwritten language. I enrolled. That conflicted with the date for the *required* School of Missions (SOM) in Springfield, Missouri. Rev. and Mrs. Hudson planned to attend the School of Missions as New Mexico Officials. I asked to ride with them from OU to SOM and back again to Norman. Ozella Reed, who had worked with Ruby Johnson in Saboba, was weighing the possibility of returning to Africa, so she enrolled in language school; we were roommates. The Hudsons did come by Norman and I joined them to Springfield for the SOM. That is where I overheard a woman complimenting Melvin Hodges on his writing of articles and the Missions bible, *The Indigenous Church.* "They are so *simple,*" the woman said. He smiled and replied, "*Simple* is the only way I know to write."

On their return trip to New Mexico, the Hudsons dropped me off at OU, in Norman. Ozella came to the car and welcomed us with, "Oh, girl, classes have been going on two days and you are already *two weeks behind.*" The next day in class, I knew what she meant. That momentum was maintained for the whole summer course. Ozella called me Sherlock instead of Charlese. She said I was constantly searching for *phonemes and fricatives* with my spyglass. Well, weren't we all? We laughed the whole summer, but I had one more interruption. I would be in America during only one camp meeting time in New Mexico; I could not miss that! Camp meeting is for refueling. Neither could I miss much of SIL. I went by plane to New Mexico for camp meeting in July. While there, Rev. and Mrs. Statser said, "Charlese, a cousin of yours and her husband came to help us in children's work this summer in Espanola, New Mexico. Their name is Wederbrook." I did not put that name with what the Goodwins had said in Africa. I said, "None of my mother's relatives, so far as I know, are in my church denomination." On Missions Day at that 1958 camp, the NMDC Officials surprised me by raising money for a second bedroom at the Saboba house; the money was sent to Ruby's account as she was in Saboba at the time. I rushed back to OU at Norman.

After a very short, hot, humid summer, it was time for our final exam. An Indian from a tribe in Oklahoma was assigned to each of us as an informant for their language. We had a choice: at the end of two weeks, we may carry on a ten-minute conversation with our informant in their language while a SIL instructor observed; or we may present a written grammar of the informant's language. That included an alphabet, parts of speech, and sentence structure. Ozella chose to converse with her Cheyenne informant. I chose to write a Kiowa grammar. I learned about their greetings quickly; there were none! I asked, "What do you say to your friend if you meet her on a path?" The informant replied, "Nothing, unless you have news to tell her." *How different from the Konkombas* of Saboba, who consider greetings very important! After the first sessions with our two Indian informants, we discovered our dorm room was too small to tune out the tape recorder playing the other language we did not want to learn. I went uptown, rented a cheap hotel room, and put a "Do Not Disturb" sign on the door. There was a Kiowa alphabet in one corner, parts of speech in another corner, and syntaxes in another. My final grade was B.

Ozella did not go to Ghana. She married Vernon Hager

and they went to Liberia. As for me, language school was over and I was booked once-every-night-and-twice-on-Sunday in New Mexico. I planned to return to Ghana when the mission department said a nurse was needed. When it was time for youth convention in November, I realized I had been home a whole year, as I had been speaker soon after I arrived. The Foreign Mission Board had extended my furlough for language school. There was a problem, however; I had no co-worker, and I could not find one. Mission Officials in Missouri could not find a nurse or midwife who wanted to go to Africa. Helen Kopp's mother was still ill, so she could not go. Raymond Hudson, Missions Coordinator for New Mexico, wrote Ghana Field Officials that they did not want me to go back alone. A reply came from the Missionary Field Superintendent of Ghana, "We sort of put in a warning when Charlese left us here that she might have a reaction of extreme weariness to the *inactivity of a furlough*. In Saboba, she bore responsibilities that no one person should have been obliged to carry. And, being so very conscientious, she did more than anyone could possibly expect and did it thoroughly. The work that remained untouched all but crushed her. She not only had the responsibilities of the clinics and the spiritual care of the churches, but the terrific pressure of the unreached lost. Anyone weaker than she could not have borne the load. We can only thank God that He chose her and not another."

When I reached the southeast corner of New Mexico on my once-every-night-and-twice-on-Sunday routine, I first went to Jal. I met three married sisters with the maiden name of Henry. They were Pearl, Francis, and Rose. One had a dress shop in Jal. Rose and her rancher husband retired and moved to TorC, where he died. My Mom and Rose Ward became good friends in the TorC church. Then Rose married a former NMDC Superintendent, Rev. H.M. Fulfer, and moved to Mountainair where they retired. From Jal, I went to Artesia to speak in the church where Rev. and Mrs.

Howard McClendon were pastors. Wilma (Hunter) McClendon knew I was a nurse. She asked my advice about a lump she had found. It was no *lump*; it was a *mass*! I dared not voice my fears; I suggested she get a doctor's opinion. He scheduled surgery and a biopsy. The Hudsons came to support their long-time friends, the McClendons, and Wilma's mother. Wilma's father had recently died. The Hunters, McClendons, Hudsons, and I had all gone to school at SBI in Texas within the same decade. Wilma's younger sister, Tommy, was in my high school with me, while the rest were in Bible College. The Hudsons stayed through Wilma's illness although, as NMDC Officials, they were needed many places. On the day of the surgery and biopsy, I arrived late in the morning as I had made a mission presentation the evening before. When the doctor came from surgery with the results, Wilma's husband and mother were in deep shock! We all were. She had advanced cancer! She recovered from surgery, but the doctor allowed her to go home, only if she had an RN around the clock. I volunteered, as I had done for other ministers and their wives. I canceled some speaking engagements. I had helped the Watkins family in Albuquerque; I believe the minister and his wife were ill at the same time. Wilma McClendon took radiation and chemotherapy at Lovelace Medical Center in Albuquerque. I went with her into the treatment room. We put on heavy aprons. She voiced her concern by saying, "Hey, you are putting on aprons, but you are filling *my* body full of the stuff!" She had a point! Back in Artesia, the Hudsons stayed with the McClendons. When Wilma improved, I rescheduled meetings in Southeastern New Mexico and kept Artesia as my base. Wilma's mother rode with me to some meetings when I drove back to Artesia in the dark. A new church was being built across town. The new parsonage would not be ready for some time. Rev. McClendon bought a new house across the street from the new church. The Hudsons and I helped them pack and move. There was so much prayer for Wilma that I dared not verbalize my concern about the signs of deterioration. I felt her immediate family needed to be beside her at all times, so I went to Albuquerque to pack for my return to Africa. I was called back immediately for the funeral. What a sad day! I returned to Albuquerque, but the Hudsons stayed in Artesia a while longer. At the same time, the people in my home church in Albuquerque were experiencing a similar sad scenario. Grover and Betty Risner were our pastors. They, the church, and the family of Esther (Bazan) Martinez had been helping her fight cancer. Joe Martinez, her husband, was a deeply respected deacon in my home church. For reasons known only to God, Esther also died of cancer. The entire church mourned with Deacon Joe Martinez, Little Joe, David, and Kathie. Fred, Joe's brother, was in my high school graduating class at SBI; he had married Angie Bazan, Esther's sister.

I spent one more blessed Christmas with my family and friends. I did not allow myself to think about how many holidays I would be away again. In January 1959, I started taking immunizations at Lovelace Clinic for four more years in Ghana. As usual, I lost my hearing with the smallpox vaccine. I took shots for cholera, tetanus, and polio I and II. I continued touring almost once-every-night-and-twice-on-Sunday. I felt fortunate for the opportunities, but I was not getting much rest prior to my return to an African clinic where I would be on twenty-four-hour duty instantly for at least three years. In my New Mexico travels, my path crossed with, "Short and Sasse" touring the state. Melvin Sasse was NM Youth Director, and Kenneth Short, a Speed-the-Light Representative from Headquarters in Missouri. They toured during New Mexico Spring Conventions to raise money for missionary vehicles. That meant I would benefit from their tour if New Mexico's youth bought a car for my next tour in Africa. I bought a used 16mm movie camera from Rev. Short. It took beautiful African pictures for later furloughs.

When I had time to do so, I packed personal and household items in metal drums with lockable rims to ship to Ghana. Emery Swope and others on a New Mexico highway striping crew found and paid for that type of drum for me. I packed in drums all over Hudson's house and garage. What a mess! Sister Hudson said, "It would take *an artist* to get a house to look like this!"

At about the same time a preacher, who had a wife and was strictly joking, said, "Charlese, you would be married if you were not so *persnickety!*" A paradox again! Once the Hudsons came home earlier than I expected and I had the ironing board in the kitchen. I had not heard them drive up, but saw the doorknob between kitchen and garage move. I dialed 911! In walked the Hudsons. They almost fainted when they saw their lovely home. One time I thought I was doing them a favor by pulling crab grass out of their lawn. When they returned, they informed me I had dug up the grass they had been *praying* would survive. I think they survived in spite of me!

One Sunday morning I visited the Belen church and my parents to say my last farewells before flying back to Ghana. I visited Mom as she cooked the noon meal. Then she went to tend their store and help-'ur-self laundry so Dad could eat while I visited with him. They were both very busy in their store, so I left to prepare for a mission presentation that evening. For some reason, I knew the Hudsons would not be back that day, so I parked my car inside their garage. Later, I thought I heard kittens crying. I opened the kitchen door into the garage and the cry was indeed coming from inside their garage. "Oh," I thought, "they did not tell me they got a cat." At that moment, I saw a kitten. Then I saw two, three, and then four. I phoned my parents in Belen. When Mom answered the phone, I asked, "Mom, did you have baby kittens?" She said, "Yes, four of them." I said, "Well, I think they are now in the Hudson's garage. Shall I bring them home?" "No, find homes for them if you can," she said. I did not want the Hudsons to find them in their garage when they returned! I phoned a local radio station and explained. Four small kittens had ridden somewhere up inside my car thirty miles from Belen and none was harmed. He told the sad story over the radio and all the kittens were gone when the Hudsons returned.

One night I had one of those dreams that you feel you will never forget. At first, my co-worker and I were standing near several turnstiles. All at once, the turnstiles seemed to be churches. We were discussing which line to get in as some were rejecting more people than others. Finally, we settled on one and went through. I found myself on the other side of the turnstiles, alone. For some reason I looked up as that was where people seemed to be going. The whole ceiling was a layer of liquid that was almost ready to drip in places. It was blood! I left the ground and went through the blood. The scene changed. I was standing in a coffin with my grave clothes loosely around my feet. There was a large parade ground and many people like me were in caskets around the parade ground. It was like an African durbar; we were waiting for someone to greet us. In my dream, I knew who we were waiting for, Jesus! He was coming to welcome us. I saw Him coming and, as He came closer I thought, "I wonder if He will let me touch Him." We communicated by thought process. He smiled, and reached out His hand. The nail scar was there. I laid my hand in His! Again I thought, "This is more wonderful than I ever thought it could be." He smiled as though answering my thoughts and went on to greet the person in the next casket. The scene changed again. I was back on earth and two policemen were standing over me as if to protect me from bodily harm. As I awoke, I was saying aloud, "Two years; two more years." I told this dream to the Hudsons next morning at breakfast. We could not imagine why I had dreamed such a thing.

I wrote my farewell letter to family, friends, churches, and supporters in February. I told them that Nurse Lois Lemm would meet me in Accra, Ghana. She was to be on loan from the leprosy colony in Liberia where Nurse Steidle was located. Everett Phillips in the Missions Department and the Ghana missionaries were urging me to get back to Ghana. The British nurses at Nakpanduri were overdue for furlough and one was having problems with her eyes from oncho (falaria). For some time, we thought Franklin and Aneice McCorkle, from the Houston area, might be return-ing at the same time I did. I would not have to go alone. Their visa did not arrive in time. On Sunday afternoon, March 8, 1959, I was to fly Pan American back to Ghana. When I got to the tiny airport in Albuquerque, there were hundreds of people, not in the waiting room, but out on the tarmac a short way from my plane. There was a Ghana flag flying along with the American flag. It did not take long for me to recognize the people. They were from churches in Albuquerque and surrounding towns. Since it was Sunday, I could imagine they announced my time of departure from the pulpit and many people sacrificed their Sunday siesta. That was humbling! My pastors, Grover and Betty Risner and family, were there. Betty Risner pinned an orchid on my blouse; it was my *first ever*. Someone had an accordion and sang. The most emotional surprise was, however, that my entire immediate family was there--father, mother, my sister with her two sons from San Diego, my brother from Albu-querque with his wife and my niece, my youngest brother from Belen with his wife and my nephew. I was in shock, overwhelmed! When the time came to board, my dad and youngest brother carried my luggage, walked across the tar-mac, and went up the steps with me to the door of the plane. The flight attendant took my bags. I hugged my dad and brother and they went down the steps. I waved to the crowd and they waved and called to me until the flight attendant insisted I go inside. We waved through the window until the plane taxied out of sight. The flight attendant came to me immediately and asked, "What's with the flags, orchid, and crowd of people? By chance, do we have a celebrity or VIP?"

I said, "No, I'm a missionary nurse returning to Africa." She said no more and left.

I hate flying, especially takeoff and landing; it is just the best thing to do sometimes. I know the jokes like, "This is your automatic pilot; nothing can go wrong, can go wrong, can go wrong." That does not help! When the plane leveled to a cruising altitude, I decided to have my devotions and sleep. I turned to March 8 in my dated devotional book. It instructed me to read Jude 1:24, "Now unto Him who is able to *keep you from falling-*." I gave it to God and went to sleep. Chicago was fogged in and we were told we would land by radio. That dreaded automatic pilot kicked in! The landing was very rough. As I waited for my connecting flight, I wrote letters. I stopped in Lancaster, Pennsylvania to visit Helen Kopp and her family. She was not ready to return to Ghana. Her mother was still very ill; the family needed her. After three days, Helen took me to the train. She was allowed on the train up to a certain time. When the conductor called for all visitors to leave, she got off. The train did not leave, so she came back. The conductor saw her and said, "I told you to get off." She gave me a letter to deliver to the Mission Officials in Ghana and got off again. As the train moved down the track, the tears rolled quietly down my face as if I were in mourning. Phyllis and Parker Johnston met my train in New Branford, Connecticut. They had moved from New Jersey since I arrived from Ghana over a year ago. That evening, the community had a maple cook off. They made syrup and boiled some down to candy. I took candy for the missionary kids in Ghana.

On March 15, the Johnston's drove me to Idlewild Airport. I joined Pan American's flight 150 and it took off at 4:30 P.M. in snow. We flew east so we soon met the sun; it was a short night. Ten hours later, we made the only stop at Lisbon, Portugal. Ten more hours of flying south within Greenwich Mean Time took us across the Mediterranean Sea and the full length of the hot, bumpy Sahara Desert. As the plane began losing altitude to land, we crossed the Savannah where vegetation increased. Among the grass and first short trees, I could see Nakpanduri and Saboba Clinics, the Oti River, Tamale and NGBI at Kumbungu. What a thrill! I said to the flight attendant, "I can see where I lived for three years and where I will live another three years." She almost flung the words at me, "Well, home sweet home; you can have it!" I knew *people* there; she saw desolation. What a difference! There was the Volta River and the Ashanti Forest. We dropped down toward the Gulf of Guinea and landed at Accra, Ghana. It was 9:00 P.M., March 16, 1959. When they opened the door, we met a sauna of ninety degrees. My body could not adjust from snow on the runway to tropical heat in twenty hours of flying. For days my face, hands, and feet were swollen. Lois had not arrived from Liberia, but I was told she would come soon. *I was alone in Africa, AGAIN!*

CHAPTER EIGHT

Bimobas of Nakpanduri Area, 1959

I ARRIVED IN GHANA in time to attend a Mission Conference in Kumasi. There were twenty-one adults and six children present. It was like family again. Mel Harrell read the letter I brought from Helen Kopp; she could not come yet. When I opened my suitcase to get the maple candy for the missionary kids, black ants had eaten most and left holes in what remained! Missionaries arriving since the last conference were welcomed. That was the Ziemanns, McCorkles, Kesslers, Smiths, Elvis Davis, Peggy Scott, and I. Homer and Thelma Goodwin and Hal and Naomi Lehmann would soon be going to America on leave. Franklin McCorkle was elected the new Chairman of the Mission Executive Committee and Vivan Smith was the Secretary-Treasurer. Both lived at Walewale, sixty miles from Nakpanduri Clinic in northern Ghana; they would be my nearest neighbors. As usual, officials appointed me to the Auditing Committee. For the coming year, I was appointed to the Language Committee. I had just completed Wycliff's Summer Institute of Linguistics at the University of Oklahoma.

The British nurses, Ann and Becky, were going directly from this conference to England. They gave a report on the Nakpanduri Clinic and the Bimoba Tribal Section. The people spoke Mwor. The names of the villages were new to me: Bunkpurugu, Najong #1, Najong #2, Jimbari, Gbankoni, Bimbagu, Pakinatiik, and Jelik. I was interested in Ruby's report of the Saboba Section. The area was without a missionary for almost six months, until February. "Three Ghanaian workers left the area. The national pastor held the church together and although the Sunday school was almost without teachers, it had not entirely fallen by the wayside." My heart fell down; then she continued. "The Yankazia outstation church, sixteen miles from Saboba, is almost built. The congregation has outgrown the building before its completion. Nasoni church is complete. Bimbila and Kokonzoli Christians want to build churches." My heart felt better. I met Peggy, Ruby's co-worker, for the first time. They were going to Takoradi at the coast for some R & R after the meeting. I was also going back south to Takoradi after the conference for *two reasons.* Lois Lemm, a nurse but not a midwife, who had been working with Miss Florence Steidel in a Liberian leper colony, was arriving any day by ship. I had never met her. The second reason was that Missionary Eddie Ziemann was helping me buy a used VW Bug from R.T. Brisco, Ltd., an automotive company. That Wee Dubya was to stretch petrol money and to fit in with the larger Speed the Light Chevrolet provided by New Mexico's Youth Department for ambulance and hauling. The pale yellow 1959 Chevrolet Kingswood station wagon came. I took pictures as a crane lowered it off the ship. I discovered it had air conditioning and the rear window was electric; we were in luxury! Other missionaries also had air-cooled vehicles now.

While I waited for Lois in Takoradi, Edwin and Bernice Ziemann and their daughter, Patty, took Ruby, Peggy, and me to a beautiful beach at Dixcove on the Gulf of Guinea. The Ziemann's older teenage daughter, Marilyn, was in boarding school in Jos, Nigeria. Peggy and I did not go into the water. We walked the sandy beach and watched Ruby and Patty as they splashed in the Gulf. Edwin and Bernice had walked off westward after they admonished Patty strongly on how far from shore she could go. We had heard of flight attendants from airlines being drowned in the Gulf of Guinea because they were not aware of its powerful undertow. Suddenly, Peggy and I heard someone calling for help. It was first Patty and then Ruby also. Peggy said she could not swim well enough to save anyone. I did not know how to swim and was terrified of water over knee-deep. Patty's parents were out of sight down the beach. We had not seen another person since we arrived. As if by a miracle, a man and woman came walking toward us. They called something in French; we flung our arms, pointed, and called in English. The man ran like a deer and plunged into the water. He helped the two ashore. Ruby said she heard Patty call and went to help her. The only thing she could do was to keep them both from drowning. She was tired and about to give up when the man reached them. We saw a miracle instead of a disaster!

Nurse Lois Lemm arrived from Liberia. She did not know how long she could stay as Miss Steidel was not well. Although it was out of our way, we went to Accra to present ourselves to the American embassy, get our driver's licenses, and register both of us as nurses and me as a midwife. We drove the Wee Dubya and Chevrolet four hundred miles north to reach Tamale on April 15. I had been in Ghana *one whole month.* Hal and Naomi Lehmann and their daughter, Gretchen, were still at Tamale. They would soon go on furlough to America. I had received no mail since arriving, but we were getting closer to the post office in Gambaga. That is where we would receive our mail while in Nakpanduri. My shipment of freight from America might come any day. While we waited, we drove to Saboba. What a thrill to greet the Konkombas again! Greetings are so important to them. They always amazed me when they brought a sick baby at night. They would go through all the greetings. We answered, "Naa (Fine!)," to anything. When we asked what the problem was they might say, "My baby has a snakebite." I would have shouted, "Snakebite!" and tossed my baby to the first person I saw. We had just seen Peggy and Ruby at the coast, but it was great to see Ruby Johnson *with her Konkombas*. She had first introduced them to me in the United States by way of pictures years before. I was now seeing them together! I was an observer. When Pastor Salah came to greet us, he said, "I can't forget how the missionary stole the cocoa pod!" I told him I got it legally all the way to my nephew's show-and-tell in a San Diego school. We talked about his journey south and the big ship.

Ruby, Peggy, and hired workers were deep into building the much-needed second bedroom, new kitchen, and garage. Part of the money had come from the New Mexico District during summer camp. I was amazed how much the ladies had gotten done. Along with the Saboba Clinic, they had been checking on the Techimantia Clinic; no American nurse or midwife had been found. Ruby was hilarious, even when she didn't mean to be. Her comment on singles was, "This abnormal existence of two single ladies working together in the bush day and night! What with house, clinic, church, building projects, and travel, it is a miracle we get along as well as we do and the *good times still outweigh the bad*." True! Once when extremely exasperated at the unbelievable daily numbers they treated at the clinic, she said, "We have only enough time to be sure they are *warm and breathing!*" Clinics in America are quickly evolving to that!

Biyimba was an excellent cook by now. He had worked for many expatriate nurses throughout the years. That was his way of contributing to his people; it gave time for the nurses to care for the sick. Unbelievable, but we were in Saboba on April 17 when Ruby delivered another girl for Biyimba and his wife, Makpa. This one was Gretchen; their Ruthie was eighteen months old. (Gretchen had polio in early childhood; she limped, but coped well. I heard she went to a secondary school of music.)

We loaded my washing machine, ironing board, and

other items I had stored at Saboba since last term. As we worked, I told Ruby that the Las Cruces First Assembly, where Pastor James Brankle was, had deposited money in the Missions Department to put a metal roof on the Yankazia church. She said, "The Chief, Teacher Samson and the lay-people will be happy to hear that!" We were all dripping and sticky with sweat from loading the vehicle. The humidity was high between rains; we were miserable. Ruby suddenly retorted, "If I died and went to hell from Saboba, I would be forced to send back for a blanket." Gylima, whom Ruby and Ozella trained for the clinic once said, "If Madam Johnson died and was buried in Saboba and we stepped over her grave, she would rise and tell us something to do." Akonsi, Gylima's father had died while I was on furlough. This was one sad note, as he had made the way for the clinic to be in Saboba!

Lois and I returned to Tamale that afternoon. My freight still had not arrived by the eighteenth as expected. The Chevy station wagon had a broken shock absorber from our trip to Saboba; two hubcaps had flown off. The rear window was electric. It had dust in the contacts and did not roll up or down, and it cost extra. The radio cost extra and was not shortwave, so it said not a word. The doors did not fit; it rattled worse than my '55 Chevy when I sold it. Instead of miles, the speedometer was in kilometers; that cost extra. I decided that vehicle was meant for some French Country. Why didn't I think of a lemon when it was taken off the ship? It was pale yellow! We could have roofed another church with the money it wasted! I wrote this to Everett Phillips!

We shopped in Tamale for staples like flour and sugar. On Monday, April 20, we went on to Nakpanduri without our freight. As we passed through Walewale, we visited Vivan and Dorothy Smith and Franklin, Aneice, and Amonna Sue McCorkle. Amonna Sue had grown, but still had her African critters as pets. One monkey she called Bratinella would bite you! Both families shared some of their precious canned goods and two cereal dishes with spoons to tide us over until our freight arrived. Some tins were bulged and we asked them about it. They said, "Oh, just boil it longer; it will be all right." It was. Franklin, as Field Chairman, was almost apologetic about my not being able to return to Saboba, as he knew how hard it was for me to make the change. However, the Konkombas were Ruby's first love and she was there. Eventually this happened to all missionaries, and probably should. At the request of the Field Committee, Helen and I went to Techimantia in 1956. We were busy in Saboba, but we willingly helped. My policy was to go where the need was, so this time I was in Nakpanduri.

We stopped at Gambaga to get our mail and reached Nakpanduri about 3 P.M. Beginning at the market in the southwest part of town, the people lined the road calling their greetings. We stopped at the church in the middle of town to greet Pastor Musah and his wife. We greeted Nyankpen and Awuni at the clinic on the northeast edge of town and drove up a rocky road about a city block beyond the clinic to the rock house that would be home. There we met Allasan and Yamdouk, our house and yard helpers for the moment. I told Lois about the first time I had been inside that house. Helen and I had visited Vivan and Dorothy Smith when they ran the clinic in 1954. Vivan's gun had gone off inside the house and shot through the roof. Lois and I looked up and sure enough, you could see daylight through a small hole in the ceiling and on through the tin roof. The hole must have been in the hip of a corrugation; Allasan said it had never leaked. Nyankpen and Awuni, the clinic workers, walked up from the clinic to greet us. They took us to greet Nakpanduri Chief Selim and his elders. We saw a small boy, perhaps three years of age, standing very near to the chief. We were told he was Jatuat, the chief's youngest son. In the evening, Nyankpen's wife, Waniib, came to our house to greet us with an infant cradled on her back. Esther, a young girl about three years old, walked with her mother. We gave Esther a doll that she promptly put on her back in a cloth while Waniib watched. As they walked away, we noted the doll's feet, instead of the head, were sticking up out of the cloth. Waniib never said a word; we marveled at this wise mother.

Allason was our cook and house help. We planned the meals and he cooked them. He cleaned one room a day, so each week the whole house got the Sahara dust wiped off once. Kombet was our new yardman. He pumped and carried water from the cement cistern that collected water from the roof of our house during the rainy season. That was our only source of water for the whole year. Kombet went to the bush to collect wood for the cook stove and a campfire to heat wash water. He and Allason both helped me with the washing. Kombet kept the yard swept clean inside the firewall, a solid four-foot high mud fence about twenty to forty feet away from the house. It circled the houses completely and kept out some rock pythons and other snakes, but it also kept some inside once they got in. They would hunt for a drain hole at the bottom of the wall to escape through. A black spitting cobra, after our chickens, failed to escape before I shot him.

Everything in the Bimoba area was so new to us. I had visited when the Smiths were there and when Ann and Becky were there, but I had barely met a few others. My diary reads, "Lois loves it here. I will too, as soon as I can switch my mind from the Konkombas to the Bimobas." Thank God and the Walewale Smiths and McCorkles; we had food, two cereal bowls, and spoons. I always had my Boy Scout knife in my purse. When we emptied some tin cans, we kept them for drinking cups. We had one pan for boiling water and cooking; we even baked in that pan. Beds had been left, but no mosquito nets. I had left our beds in Saboba. When we paused for our afternoon rest, we felt the heat on our faces. We were told the pitch of this roof was wrong for putting grass on top of the tin as the Saboba house had for cooling purposes.

One day we drove forty miles north to Bawku in the Chevrolet to buy fuels. It was a town almost on the border between Ghana and French Upper Volta (Burkina Faso). The Bawku people were mostly of the Kusasi Tribe. That journey was a rare experience. Just north, as you left Nakpanduri, you turned a corner and suddenly saw nothing but space. In the far horizon, you could see an outline of the Bawku Mountain, forty miles away. The road tipped straight down the rocky Nakpanduri Escarpment. It was a part of a much longer range called the Gambaga Escarpment. The baboons climbed the steep rocky walls. As you descended, they sometimes threw small rocks at you or your vehicle. Flocks of gray parrots with red tails sometimes flew overhead and chattered down at you. The road was so steep that the government had roughly blacktopped it years ago, but only to the bottom where the road leveled off. Almost immediately, we crossed a bridge over a tsetse fly-infested river basin. This caused much oncho blindness. Several rivers merged under that escarpment. One went west contributing to the White Volta. An eastern branch went south to join the Oti River passing Saboba. At times one could see guinea fowl, wild pigs, antelope, or even elephants when the critters came for water. From the river to Bawku it was mostly flat farmland, but never dull. The people may be traveling or plowing by the use of oxen. We shot wild guinea fowl off limbs of the baobab trees. The villages we passed were different because some were Kusasi villages. The kind of pot that covered the very center of their round grass roofs identifies the specific tribe inside the house. We passed the empty mission bungalow just at the edge of Bawku. A man and wife with two sons were coming from America to live there. At the Swiss Basal Mission Bawku Hospital, we introduced ourselves to the Government Medical Officer, Dr. Lutz. We would operate the Nakpanduri Clinic as nurse practitioners. We could transport emergencies to the Bawku Hospital.

We opened our personal bank accounts and one for the

clinic. We located the Bawku Post Office and discovered that Postmaster Mensah had once been at the Yendi Post Office. When I was in the United States on furlough, he sent me first-day-issue-stamps of Ghana, like March 7. At the open market and some small shops, we bought a few items of food. We found we could sometimes trade our empty butane tanks for full ones without going one hundred twenty miles to Tamale. We learned we must have permits to buy petroleum products in fifty-five-gallon drums. *Kerosene* was for fridge and oil lamps, *petrol* for two vehicles, and diesel for a light plant. We went into a police station to get the permits. The man said, "You go to dis t'in' and turn. When you get to dis t'in', you will ask a man to direct you to dis t'in'. A man will give you dis t'in' and you bring it to me. I will sign dis t'in' and you can buy dis t'in'." I understood him. After a time of sleuthing, we took the items back to the man. He signed the permits. We bought our quota of fuels.

What a surprise when Think Twice arrived with the barrels I had packed in America-the very same driver had brought my freight to Saboba in 1954. He was the same jovial person, but he did not dash me a sixteen-inch pineapple as before. Unpacking started seriously. We were already getting extremely busy at the clinic. We were forced to unpack piecemeal. The rains came earlier at the harbors than up nearer to the desert, so everything inside my drums was either rusted or mildewed. Drums were not watertight. We had to wash everything before we could use it. The washing machine we brought from Saboba was useless. We hired a Bimoba youth to wash by hand. I stopped to deliver babies day or night and to check forty-seven women at the prenatal clinics on Tuesdays. Lois took the general outpatient clinic, as she was not a midwife. She treated fifty to one hundred outpatients daily, on Monday, Wednesday, and Friday. We kept the same clinic workers who were helping the previous nurses and they were super. They could even give the Gospel in the waiting room before clinic. Since we were new, they preferred that we speak, but we required an interpreter and time was valuable. In the first week of opening the clinic, the District Council Clerk and the East Mamprusi Member of Parliament came by to inquire of the condition of the clinic. We were happy that they were there and cared about the Bimobas.

On our first Sunday, April 26, Lois and I went to separate churches. She stayed for services in the local Nakpanduri church with Pastor Musah. I drove thirty miles east on a dusty two-rut road to four villages having churches. I am sure a Ghanaian went with me, as I never traveled alone. Perhaps it was Ngamtein, brother of our head clinic helper, as he was just home from Northern Ghana Bible Institute. First, we came to Najong #1. The building was mud walls with aluminum roof. The walls, inside and out, were whitewashed. The pulpit and benches were also mud. Samson, the lay pastor, smiled all the time and his enthusiasm was contagious. He did not speak English; my helper interpreted. I saw my need to learn the local Mwor. It was too early for a service at that church so we drove on two miles east and passed a tiny round mud church with a grass roof. It had a sign written on the mud wall, "Assembly of God, Najong #2." Elijah, a deacon, greeted us. We went five more miles to the Jelik church. Teacher Andrew had ridden his bicycle five miles to have church with the people. He spoke English so well and reminded me of Sammy Davis, Jr. On one side of the road was a long, narrow, mud hut. The walls were only about four feet high. The grass roof sagged low. The whole thing looked like it was threatening to collapse. The Christians informed me that was where the government personnel treated lepers on weekdays and where the Christians met for worship. Across the road was an unfinished new mud structure. The people were excited about their plans to go cut grass and roof it. The rainy season was near. I could not believe my eyes as churches in New Mexico had given me the money to put a few corrugated metal roofs on churches in Africa.

Since I did not know for sure where I would be, I had not suggested a specific town for the roofs. Here, inside a roof-less new church, I told them about the money for the roof. They were *not speechless* in their excitement. They said, "Isn't God amazing and wonderful? He knew we were building this church and He told people in America when to send the money for a roof." They had a praise meeting and I joined them.

From Jelik we went thirteen miles to what seemed the end of the road. It was the town of Bunkpurugu (roll the *r*). The pastor of this thriving church, complete with steeple and whitewash, was a young man, Elijah J. Namyela, of the Mamprusi Tribe. He was like a missionary to the Bimoba tribe and was considered an area leader. He had completed technical school before attending NGBI in Kumbungu. He and his wife, Karen, had two tiny daughters, Susanna and Priscilla. Suddenly I remembered the 1956 District Council in Tamale when, as a new missionary, I was awakened in the night by Hal Lehmann to deliver Susanna. (How could I, or anyone, look ahead and see that she would someday become a Member of Ghana's Parliament?) Now she had a little sister, Priscilla. When I saw the remote location of Bunkpurugu, I understood why Pastor Namyela had taken Karen with him to District Council, where she delivered. My Ghanaian inter-preter and I stayed in Bunkpurugu for services that Sunday morning. The building was full and the people alive. One man gave a word of prophecy. The pastor asked me to speak and as I finished, one lady accepted Jesus Christ as her Sacri-fice and Lord. After I ate some of Karen's good cooking, Pas-tor Namyela took me to greet a major Bimoba Chief, whose palace was in Bunkpurugu. Karen and I went to a meeting of women in the afternoon. Ngamtein and I traveled the thirty miles back to Nakpanduri after dark.

On our next trip together, Lois and I went southwest from Nakpanduri to the Gambaga Post Office to get our mail. We had been so anxious to get to Nakpanduri on our first trip that we had hardly noticed the towns we passed through. From Nakpanduri we first passed through Sakogo, a town where we would later teach a religious education class in a government school. Next, we reached Nalerigu, seventeen miles southwest of Nakpanduri. The Nayiri (roll the *r*), the Paramount Chief for Mamprusi and Bimoba Tribes, had his Palace there. A rather new Southern Baptist Hospital was there. We decided we would transport our emergencies to this hospital rather than Bawku, for two reasons. First, Bawku was twice as far away. Second, Dr. Frank Ashworth was here; we had worked with him in Yendi. While on leave in England, Dr. Ashworth had married a great lady, Ann, and she had come with him to Nalerigu. A sign on the south edge of Nalerigu directed travelers to a place where a part of a mud wall still stands. Milk and honey was used in place of water for building the wall that surrounded Nalerigu for protection from enemies. When forced laborers complained or died, they were put into the wall. They say, "The wall is to remind rulers how not to rule the people." About four miles on west from Nalerigu was Gambaga. We got our mail, registered as aliens, and licensed my gun. Homer Goodwin and Hal Lehmann had been keeping the license current on my 0.22. This time I brought a 0.410 shotgun to try for more than one bird at a time. It was still held in a government warehouse down south. The correct papers were being processed. A letter from Naomi Lehmann said a trailer for my vehicle and some large crates came to Tamale after Think Twice had delivered the barrels to us. We decided to get them next time we shopped in Tamale. Some shopping could be done in Walewale just thirty miles west of Gambaga but any serious shopping for food staples, lumber, cement, or corrugated tin roofing had to be done in Tamale. We returned to Nakpanduri tired and hungry.

The following Sunday Lois made the trip to Bunkpurugu and stopped at village churches on the way. I stayed to attend the church in Nakpanduri and got more acquainted with Pastor Musah and the local people. Again, the maturity of the Christians in this area impressed me. We were fortunate to have such a foundation to build on, but *palavers* were being brought to us already. That evening, we went eighteen miles to a village to help settle a dispute. Relatives were trying to force a young Christian man who felt called to preach to marry a woman who had been married previously. The opportunities and challenges were there.

At the end of one month, we drove the one hundred twenty miles to Tamale to shop and collect the trailer and other items that had come from America. The rains were coming so we got enough staples like sugar and canned milk to last at least two months. The other items that arrived were a wood stove, a metal box with seeds to plant, and a new washing machine. I had mentioned to Rev. Phillips that I had a washing machine in Ghana, but that it may not last much longer. He wisely ordered a new one. The trailer was too small for lumber, cement, fifty-five-gallon drums of petrol, and other items we were forced to haul. It looked like it belonged on the Wee Dubya that had no hitch. The Ghanaian helpers loaded the trailer. It was so heavy that it pulled down the back end of the big Chevy. It looked like a low rider at the back and a high rider at the front; we went to Nakpanduri that way. The engine got hot because we had to drive slowly. In villages, children ran out to greet us and froze in their tracks. Their calls of bature, akwaba, Na tuma, or some other greeting stopped in midair. They had not seen that one before!

In Walewale, we visited Vivan and Dorothy Smith. We told them we did not know how we would set up a wood stove, butane stove, and new washing machine as well as run the clinic, deliver babies at night, and go to churches on weekends. As usual, Dorothy said, "Vivan can do anything." We set a date for them to visit. We got to Nakpanduri before dark; no parts flew off the Chevy and the tiny trailerload was intact. That was three miracles! Someone said, "On Africa's roads, you do not drive miles-per-hour but miracles-per-hour." I wrote to Everett Phillips again. I complained about the *small* trailer as I had about the *wasteful* Chevrolet. I said, "When nurses are placed on remote stations and expected to do area work like men, then equipment should be equally sturdy for both." Letters I received about my appointment from both H.B. Garlock and Noel Perkin had included, "You are not going just as a nurse. You will use your nursing as a means to get the Good News of Christ to the people. That is why we require Bible College graduation and some experience in the Christian ministry before you leave America." I had done it all!

One day I took an eleven-year-old boy to Bawku Hospital. He had tetanus (lockjaw) and was admitted. Surprisingly, I found lumber and tin in Bawku. It cost more than in Tamale, but saved expensive gasoline and time. I had to be brave, stupid, or have a lot of faith. I hauled the lumber and tin *on top of* my wee trailer; it could not fit inside. The people of Sisi, just at the bottom of the escarpment, were making adobe bricks for a church. Rain on grass roofs allowed the mud walls to melt away sooner than with tin roofs. Hard work, even blood, went into building each church. I wrote Everett Phillips to send the money designated for roofs; it came exactly as designated. I sent fifty pounds to Ruby. It was designated for the Yankazia church roof before I knew where I would be stationed. A letter came from Ruby with thanks, "We shall use the money as directed for the roof; if any is left it will be used for windows. I will encourage the people to do the workmanship. The Chief of Yankazia has granted land. Pastor Samson Mankrom and I drove stakes to identify borders. The George Andersons are returning to Yendi soon. They were the first ones to take the Christian message to Yankazia. We hope the church will be ready for dedication by the time they arrive."

While I went to Bawku, Lois treated ninety people at a general clinic. I got home just in time to deliver a baby. The

Smiths came on a Wednesday for a nice visit. They spent the night and local Bimobas worked with Vivan to get equipment operating. We discovered the new wringer *did not fit* the new machine, but the old wringer did. Now, that is a problem in Africa! Parts of a fridge, wood stove, butane stove, and two washing machines covered our floor when two vehicles arrived. Franklin and Aneice McCorkle brought Papaw and Mimi Smitherman, the retired parents of Aneice. They were *out to Africa* on a lengthy visit. Don and Grace Jolley and two sons, fourteen and eight, were in the second vehicle. The younger son chattered. The older was quiet and said he missed friends and school activities. Since Franklin was Field Chairman, he was to introduce them to their new home. The two vehicles went on to Bawku. We would have American neighbors forty miles north.

The month of June was hot and sticky. Bimobas were saying it most surely was going to rain. I knew the rainy season was short so I was planting corn, beans, okra, radishes, tomatoes, chili, lettuce, and cucumbers. I was not prepared for all the animals. In Saboba, only people passed our house to and from the market. At Nakpanduri, we were at the edge of both town and bush. Rats, Rabbits, monkeys, goats, and baboons climbed over, went under, or through my garden fence; guinea fowl flew over. I hired children, as the Ghanaians did, to watch my crops in daylight. It was night when cows and elephants walked through.

Strangers (what Ghanaians called *visitors*) kept coming. Former missionaries had even built a stranger's room onto the storage room behind our main house. In Saboba, when we had visitors, we knew they were coming to see us; it was the end of the road. It was different in Nakpanduri; it was on the way to Bawku. If people chose to do so they could go through Bolgatanga, but usually they wanted to see the escarpment. The Landruses and two Swiss men ate breakfast with us one Sunday. One weekday, Joe and Eloise Judah came. She was a nurse, recruited for the Techimantia Clinic

that Helen and I had opened in 1955; it had taken this long to
find an American nurse. Later in the week, Hal and Naomi
came from Tamale for their last visit; they were leaving on
furlough. They brought two kittens and said they were from
Saboba. They brought our mail from Gambaga. In it were
pictures of my nephew, Darrald Ray, and his cat at my dad's
fifty-eighth birthday party. One day the Medical Officer of
the whole northern region came to visit the clinic.

On washdays, we helped with the washing because the
machine was new and dangerous until the Ghanaians used
it awhile. Eventually, someone got their hand in the wringer
in spite of warnings. At first we had to be present to hit
the release; they were so frightened. No one was ever seriously injured. Washdays gave us opportunity to be better
acquainted with the Ghanaians and to practice our Mwor
language skills. We had started lessons, and were already
greeting the people, "A jo ko poo" in the mornings. We all
had some good laughs when I tried to speak other than English. I was prone to use one word from each language I had
ever heard, *in the same sentence!* After I used one word each
from Lekpakpaln, Dagboni, Twi, and maybe Hausa and
Mwor, they would roar with laughter. I might even throw
in a word of Spanish, French, or English, whichever I could
think of at the moment. Finally, when they laughed I would
say, "But you knew what I meant." They would agree and
then explain what I should have said. *I was learning.* Even
while traveling on furlough in America, I would sing this
song as I drove along:

> *We shall reach Jerusalem (English)*
> *Ti Ga M'bue Uwumbor Do (Lekpakpaln)*
> *Ti Ni Pai Dzerusalem (Ngmampruli-Dagboni?)*
> *O! O! mbamowani, (Lekpakpaln)*
> *Ii, Yelmangni, ii (Ngmampruli-Dagboni?)*
> *Yo, mpara, yo (Twi?)*
> *Yes! (English)*

The Africans usually learned languages quickly. In fact, they learned anything quickly as their brains were not super saturated with mega-trivia from TV and every form of media. One morning after teaching a religious education class in Sakogo Primary School, I wrote in my diary, "Those kids are smart. I wish I could learn Bimoba as easily as they learn English. They answer questions about the Bible in English and I cannot do it in Mwor. My Mwor is progressing fairly well; I've only been here two months." I spoke in church within three months, but confess that I memorized some of it ahead of time. They did not laugh at me!

Kombet was not only our yardman, but also a good hunter. He used a muzzle-loader. He liked my *fast guns*. One morning before breakfast, Kombet called to us all excited. He said for me to get my gun and come; he had seen something for food. I grabbed my 0.22 rifle. We walked out through the bush. I knew it could be an antelope. Kombet would know my gun could not kill an elephant but we did see the markings of their skin on the ground where they had slept the night before. We walked and walked. Mercy, I had no idea he had to go this far to collect our wood! I began to wonder if we should have brought food or water. Finally, he slowed down and told me to be quiet. Then he pointed. There perched high in the crevice of a rocky cliff was an owl. I asked him if they ate those. He shook his head and said, "Oh, they make *sweet chop* (fine food)!" I shot it. Well, we brought home the bacon! I agreed he should have it all that time. On the way back to the house he said that every morning before I awoke there were guinea fowl and other small critters in my garden. I agreed for him to wake me when he saw them, but next time he would have to share, as I liked to eat guinea fowl. Then I wondered if that could be why my garden was not doing well. In spite of the critters, we soon ate green pinto beans and a few tender ears of corn. The Ghanaians allowed every ear and pod to mature for more food value. They teased us that we ate food soft and weak *like the monkeys*.

My new co-worker was due into the port city from England any day. I planned to take Lois Lemm down July 15. She needed to return to Liberia, her true assignment. I could take Lois down and bring the new nurse-midwife back north all in one trip. It was over four hundred miles, one way, of dusty dirt roads or potholed pavement. All four hubcaps usually ended up inside the Chevrolet Kingswood. They flew off; we stopped to find them. Since Lois was leaving soon, we took a day off and went to Bawku. We took pictures of Kusasi houses, ox carts pulling loads, and people going to market with high headloads. Mothers, with babies cradled on their backs, also had headloads. We ate a picnic lunch and took a nap under a Baobab tree. I was sunburned in the shade.

The next day, on the way to Gambaga to get our mail, we ran out of petrol near Nalerigu. Neither had thought of filling our car after the trip to Bawku. We walked to the Baptist Mission Hospital, where they sold us some of their hard-gotten liquid gold. In our mail were good pictures of my Speed-the-Light vehicle being unloaded from the ship by a tall crane at Takoradi harbor. There were pictures I had taken two months ago when we first got to Bimobaland. Some women, wearing only a cluster of leaves, were on their way to market. They came to general clinic, prenatal clinic, or to deliver their baby dressed that way. The cluster of leaves was attached in the back to a string of braided grass around the hips. The leaves usually hung down in the back but some had them in front and back. Sometimes the husband of these women came to the clinic to talk for her. She might seem totally mute! The husband would say, "She has been like this ever since she *came out of the hut.*" Our clinic helpers, Nyankpen and Awuni, said they were not letting their girls *go through the hut.* I did not understand about *the hut,* but was soon to learn! About a week after we ran out of gasoline, we were busy with a clinic in progress. A Baptist missionary from the hospital at Nalerigu came walking in. He had run out of gasoline near Nakpanduri as he was going to visit one of their churches. His bread, *cast upon the water,* had returned quickly; we sold him some petrol. On another journey, we met a Ghanaian. His huge truck had gotten hot and stalled. We gave him some water for his engine and months later, he found us with a flat tire. He helped us change it. We had never met since the first incident, yet we recognized each other and joked about being mutual helpers.

In the latter part of June, the rains got heavy as usual. It was my turn to go to outstations on a Sunday. That morning I drove east to Najong #1 for Sunday school and a church service. Then all the people from that church walked with me about a mile into the bush where a group gathered to worship asked us for a pastor. This broke my heart; I wanted to speak the word and a pastor would appear. We had a service with them and six accepted Christ as their Sacrifice and Lord. We walked back to Najong #1 and drove home. Lois and I ate lunch and rested. At 4 p.m., we drove north to Sisi. We helped about one hundred people with Sunday school and church under a brush arbor and trees. We had no trouble sleeping that night.

One Sunday I went to Bunkpurugu for services. There was a bridge out and the riverbanks were steep. I got across but was worried about coming back across later. After Sunday school and morning worship services, I stayed for an afternoon women's service. When I got back to that river, I met a truckload of men. They pushed my car up the steep side coming out of the riverbed. They told me that we were probably cut off from the churches out that road until the rains quit in October. In July, however, I wrote in my diary, "Lois and I drove out the southeast road today. She wanted to greet the people before she went back to Liberia. She let me off at Najong #1 and went on to Bunkpurugu. She drove fast, like Jehu in the Bible, but was not careless." At Najong #1, a baby had died and I had already been impressed to speak about our hope of the resurrection. It was a blessed service. Lois said she stopped for a short time in Jelik. Their church building was almost completed. They were working on the floor and whitewashing the walls. On the way back to Nakpanduri, we saw wild guinea fowl perched in trees. They flew before I could get close enough to shoot them with the 0.22 rifle. In the Konkomba area, I could shoot the partridges and guinea fowl off the yam hills. There were very few yam hills in the Nakpanduri area; the soil was too rocky. I wished for my shotgun that was still held in a government warehouse.

A letter from Homer and Thelma Goodwin said they were coming to see us. He was Principal of the Bible School at Kumbungu and they both taught classes. They came to check on Bible School students who were supposed to be busy getting practical experience in the villages. The Goodwins brought a tire for the Wee Dubya; we had been driving without a spare. They also brought the news that my new co-worker was forced to cancel her sailing date. She had been in the United Kingdom for the past fourteen months getting her midwifery training and had clinical time or something to make up. I had been looking forward to having another midwife; I would not have to get up at night for every delivery. The rest of July was an example; we had four deliveries in two days with only one being a normal case. As a result, there were two babies on the bottle and one that might have brain damage. The head of one baby was in a posterior position and took too long to come; we expected problems. A woman who had elephantiasis of the breast had no milk even though her breasts extended below her waist. The fourth woman was seven months pregnant, but arrived bleeding profusely. The placenta came first; a two pound, twelve-ounce baby followed. As soon as the baby was born, we were able to decrease the mother's blood loss to normal. The wee baby girl was very much alive and soon called for food. The father was there to learn the eyedropper method of feeding until the mother had milk. He fed and cared for the baby at the clinic and came for return visits with his wife and baby girl day after day. The baby lost four ounces after birth and then started gaining and developed well.

At our house, the problem surfaced that we were not collecting all the rain we could from our roof. Water that should have lasted us all through the dry season was being lost because guttering was not adequate. In our spare time, we were putting guttering under all the eaves of the house. I envied every little drop that escaped. What a job to get that corrugated tin formed into troughs. Our poor hands! Lois was still with me. Such a trooper; she was game for any project. She had already written to America and changed her address back to Liberia, but we drove to Gambaga for my mail anyway. On the way, we stopped at the Baptist Mission Hospital in Nalerigu and learned that Dr. Faile, an American, had lost his four-year-old son to snakebite within the past week. He had died within thirty minutes. How sad! I was in awe of the strength and grace they had available and utilized.

In the mail that day was a letter from home. Mom said she might come, if I were going to be left alone. She wrote that Calvin and his family enjoyed the homemade ice cream at her birthday celebration on July 25. Year after year in England and Africa, I became accustomed to being away from home for birthdays, anniversaries, holidays, and even funerals. I never allowed myself to get emotional or lonely for long. I was sure the Bible said, "Blessed is he that expecteth little, for he shall not be disappointed." Jude 2. (Jude has only one chapter.)

There was a telegram from Liberia to Lois Lemm. Miss Steidel was seriously ill and may need to be flown home to America. Lois must go back to Liberia immediately! As soon as we returned to Nakpanduri, I was called to the clinic to deliver a baby. It seemed to be a normal case so I observed her in labor as I wrote to Mom, "I'd love to have you come, but Dad may need you too. Find a place to pray for God's will. Don't decide when your mind is in a whirl." Nevertheless, I told her what shots she needed, how to get a three-month visitor's visa and a round trip ticket, which Ghana required whether sailing or flying. We could renew her visa in Ghana if she decided to stay longer. I said I could feed her while she was with me, but I could not pay her fare. I wondered who could get a visa faster, the midwife in England or Mom in the United States? I was hoping someone would come when Lois left because I was getting corn, beans, radishes, lettuce, cucumbers, and okra from my garden. The rains did not usually last long, so neither would my garden. I went to Gambaga often to hear from my future co-worker or my mom.

Lois left on Tuesday, August 18. This was difficult as she had been with me during the time we had been receiving reports of threats to the Christians. She was as willing to help the pastors and Christians as I was. In retrospect, she might have gone to Najong #2 with me if the telegram regarding Miss Steidel had not come. Lois was older than I was; her feet were not strong. I fear she might have been killed within a few days if she had remained. If I had tried to stay with Lois and protect her during the incident, then we both might have been killed within a week. That telegram saved her life and possibly mine. Also, the new midwife detained in England was so heavy that she could not possibly have run. She might have been killed, had she come on the first date we were given. God has control and He knew I would have a better chance alone to save myself.

When I took Lois to Tamale to leave for Liberia, the word was that my new co-worker should arrive by ship about September 1. I was planning to leave Nakpanduri about August 25 to go over four hundred miles to meet her at the coast. I was so happy that my permanent co-worker was coming that I wrote several letters on August 19. To Mom I wrote, "Are you on a jet plane coming to me? I have been praying for you and waiting for word. Some cult stole a lay pastor's daughter and took her into hiding. They have cut designs on her body. Lay pastor Samson, some pastors, officials, and others want to go tomorrow and get her. I hope we find her. Love, Charlese." That letter was *in my pocket* the next day when the people of Najong #2 beat two huge policemen, six other Ghanaians, and me. I had forgotten to mail the letter in Gambia, where the policemen joined us.

CHAPTER NINE

The War of Najong #2: Belittling the Devil Himself

WHEN NURSE LOIS LEMMA and I arrived in Nakpanduri in 1959, the pastors and other Bimobas started presenting palavers to be settled. One was about the fetish Kwonsi cult, who worshiped the water buffalo. They were trying to intimidate Christians with threats. People did say they feared for the lives of their children who did not want to be initiated into that cult. Initiation included being physical mutilation by cutting, and brainwashing so they had no will of their own. In particular, they feared for a young girl named Dindeuk. Other young people feared to eat with her; the food might be poisoned. They wanted me to go with them to the police immediately. I said, "You have neither poisoned food nor arrows to show to the police; it would be your word against theirs."

In the thirty miles between Nakpanduri and Bunkpurugu, there were other villages: Bimbagu, Najong #1, Najong #2, and Jelik. Off this main, two-rut dirt road and into the bush were other villages. A powerful fetish man lived in one. We drove to those remote villages with difficulty or walked part way to reach them. Some had struggling churches with lay pastors. They and former missionaries had done well, but Bible school prepared pastors were few. Samson Bimoba at Najong #1 was one of those valuable lay pastors. He had a niece named Dindeuk whom he had raised as a foster daughter along with his own two daughters, Eunice and Mary. He may have had other children. When Dindeuk was born, the headmen in Najong #2 bargained for her. In some places, chiefs and headmen bought girls with cows that were like money in the bank. A man may labor on a farm for years to pay for a wife born in another village, like Isaac in the Old Testament of the Bible. Different tribes had slightly different customs. They might trade a girl in their village for one born near the same time in another village. Dindeuk had been traded at birth. She would soon be of age to go to those who bargained for her at birth. During those years, Lay pastor Samson and his family, including Dindeuk, had become Christians. Samson informed the headmen of Najong #2 that, because of this, they were not to force her into their rites of Kwonsi fetish worship. Their custom was that the father of the girl must agree before they could put a girl through Kwonsi rites. The facts were that Kwonsi was about forcing freedom from the individual. If it results in death, the cult members do not inform the parents. One young man said his brother died beside him in the initiation; the body was put into an anthill where it was consumed. After the set period of three months, the parents came to get their sons. The cultists then told the parents, "Kwonsi took him." In other cases, the Kwonsi leaders say the initiate in the hut died of natural causes. These *natural causes* may be tetanus from a dirty knife, pneumonia from nudity, or some other illness that required medical aid. Initiates are not allowed out for medical help. The cult is associated with circumcision, cutting designs all over the body, and brainwashing to the point of insanity and even death. When such women came to the clinic to deliver their babies, husbands were forced to come along and speak for them. They were not in touch with reality and the husbands would say, "She has been like this since she came out of the hut." The Kwonsi is in direct opposition to individual freedom. This rather eliminates "old maids" in the tribes, but they may leave you to die if insanity develops from their treatment.

On August 16, I received a letter from Bunkpurugu Pastor E.J. Namyela about the situation. It read, "Samson, the pastor at Najong #1 has a daughter. She went to Najong #2 yesterday near her future husband's house in reply to their invitation. There were games and dances of celebration. In the midst of this, the Kwonsi followers grabbed her and forced her into the fetish hut about which *we have been telling you*. They have neither respected the wishes of Samson, the father, nor the girl. Her whole body has been covered with cuts; we want to take her to the hospital for treatment. Therefore, we aim to remove the girl from that hut with help from the police in Gambaga. We need your help with transportation to get the girl. We need urgent help from you now. Signed: Samson Bimoba and E. J. Namyela."

On August 19 Lay pastor Samson, Pastor Namyela, Pastor Musah, Pastor John Kombat, and Nyankpen Bimoba, our head clinic helper, came to my house. They asked me to type a letter to present to the District Commissioner of the East Mamprusi District at Gambaga. The paper read:

> We the Christians of the Bimoba Tribe request your kind protection in helping us against the custom of Kwonsi in our tribe. We do not agree for any woman, whether daughter or sister whom we agree to give or trade in marriage, to be put through this unhealthy and unnecessary custom. We hereby request help in obtaining Dindeuk in Najong #2, who is at present being held against her will and the will of her father. She became a Christian when one Rev. Musah Bimoba was pastor. We request THE PRESENCE OF POLICE TO GO WITH US to rescue THE GIRL. She was taken by deceit (kidnapped). Respectfully submitted.

The missive was thumb-printed or signed by eleven Ghanaian men: Musah, Nyankpen, Namyela, Fant, Fanam, Allason, Samson, David, John, Elijah, and Awuni. As an expatriate I did not sign, but I did witness a thumbprint and I was given a copy of the letter.

On August 20, we drove to Nalerigu; a copy of the petition was presented to the Nayiri, Paramount Chief of the Bimobas and Mamprusis. We asked his permission and advice in rescuing Lay pastor Samson's daughter, Dindeuk. The Chief said, "Those holding the hostage have gone against their own customs, since the father must agree for a girl to be put through the Kwonsi ritual." He agreed that we were right to proceed to Gambaga and present the petition to the police and district officials. He added that we had his permission to go get the girl. However, he warned that people had been unsuccessful in the past trying to curtail the operation of that cult and he had concern for us. He was a wise man, but the father of Dindeuk had already told us the dangers we faced.

We drove on a few more miles to Gambaga and gave a copy of the petition to the District Commissioner. He asked for a *more detailed petition* to be put in writing and delivered later. At the Gambaga Police Station, the written plea for help was given to the corporal. He was sympathetic and said he would have gone with us himself, since he felt the father was sincere and determined. However, his time was heavily scheduled and they had no transportation except bicycles. They agreed to send two huge policemen, if I would transport them to Najong #2. The nine who went in the three-seated Chevrolet Kingswood were: Samson, father of the girl; Nyankpen, my clinic helper, who eventually became a major chief of the Bimoba tribe; Pastor Musah of the Nakpanduri church; Pastor Namyela of the Bunkpurugu church, who later became the General Superintendent of the Ghana Assemblies of God for sixteen years; Pastor John Kombat of the Jimbari church; David, a Christian who was once a

Kwonsi member and whose brother died beside him in the initiation hut; and two huge Ghana policemen. I drove the Chevy.

In retracing our route from Gambaga back through Nalerigu, Sakogo, and Nakpanduri, we made no stops. Village people saw us pass with the two policemen. We drove on through Bimbagu, Najong #1, and stopped to pray before we entered Najong #2. We *committed ourselves* into the hands of God. We prayed for Dindeuk and the people in Najong #2. We were aware that we needed God's help. We reached the village of Najong #2 just after noon on a hot, humid August day. There I parked my station wagon off the main two-rut road into the edge of a cornfield. We were told to stay in a group along with the policemen. We walked, little more than a city block, up a pathway through the tall grain field. We passed typical, little round mud huts with grass roofs. They were quiet and looked peaceful. A person could not even imagine what torture existed for initiates in one of those huts just ahead. We reached a hut where we greeted the headman of the house and told him we had permission to come and get Samson's daughter, Dindeuk. He said the girl could not come out until the four months of rites were completed. In an instant, I saw the policemen dart around one side of the hut while the girl's father went around the other way. They had heard a rustling of the corn; Dindeuk was being rushed farther into the bush. When the men holding her saw the policemen, they dropped the girl and fled. The girl was brought around the house to where we were. We had her, but it was not to be that easy! The people believe that if the girl being initiated sees someone who does not belong to the cult that she will die. If we, who do not belong, see the initiate then we must die. She had seen us; we had seen her. Somebody must die! I saw and heard the women of the village give the shrill war cry using their hands and tongues to trill. Men came from every direction with a farm hoe, fence post, spear, or other weapons. I saw who struck the first blow! They began hitting the policemen and Samson, the father. I saw the Kwonsi men put Dindeuk back into the hut.

One policeman said to me, "Go turn the car around so we can leave." I left alone! All others were being beaten. I ran down the corn path toward the car. At some point in the tall corn, I strayed onto a pathway that would miss my car on the road by about one-fourth of a city block. As I ran, several screaming men with weapons overtook me. The tall corn protected me on each side, but they were beating me from behind. When one of them hit me on the top of my right shoulder and finally on the side of my head I felt I was going to fall, but I did not. My glasses flew off and I never saw them again. Suddenly two things came to mind. First, I was the only one who could drive a vehicle. If anyone was to escape, I must be able to drive. *The keys were still in my hand.* Second, a dream I had in America six months prior, came to me vividly. I had related the dream to the Hudson's next morning at breakfast. There was violence. Two policemen protected me, and as I awoke from sleep, I was saying aloud, "Two years, two more years." In the cornfield I said aloud, "I am not going to die; I have two more years of this term in Africa." Confidence and faith arose. It was obvious I could not stand up long under those strong African men beating me with fence posts. I turned around, raised my hands, and walked directly into the group. They seemed momentarily startled. As I faced them, I prayed aloud, "In Jesus name, I plead the power of the blood of Christ and the angels of God to come to my rescue." Instantly, a black man, whom I did not know, darted between the attackers and me. God had answered my prayer, that's all I knew. The man outstretched his arms over me and took many of the blows. That allowed me to make progress toward the main road, where I looked left and saw my car and a policeman; I walked that way. To my right was the little round mud church with a grass roof. A sign on it read, "Assembly of God, Najong #2." The beloved Deacon Elijah and family had built it; there were few Christians and they had no full-time pastor. The next thing I remember, a policeman was helping me into my vehicle, and a villager was pulling me out by the hair of my head. A policeman put me back into the vehicle; *that had happened in my earlier dream!* One man struck me in the face, breaking my nose and it bled freely as he forced the keys from my hand. The policeman got me inside and shut the car door. A man broke the window near me with a spear. The glass was shatterproof but its tiny particles sprayed into the blood on my face and clothing. A *second miracle* happened as a man appeared and wrestled the spear from that man. On the other side, the other policeman was putting Pastor Namyela and my clinic worker, Nyankpen, into the car with similar difficulty.

Pastor John Kombat and Dindeuk's father were already seated in the middle seat behind me. Villagers were prodding them through the back window with long poles. The dust had not allowed the rear electric window to operate properly. I reached under the dashboard and turned the knob; it worked! The *third miracle!* When the angry men saw the rear window going up by itself, they were frightened. They jerked their clubs out, turned, and ran into the field across the road. Sweat was pouring off us in the tropical heat, but it was dangerous to roll down a window. I had no key to turn on the air conditioning. Blood mixed with sweat inside the hot car produced a putrid odor. Perhaps the heat kept our blood flowing so we did not go into shock. With doors locked, we observed as people beat Deacon Elijah and his pregnant wife to the ground. When one moved, women called out and men came to beat them again. The pounding of fence posts on the car sounded like thunder. They tore off chrome strips. I discovered the mob calmed down a bit and did not beat the car so violently when I turned my head and leaned quietly on the headrest like I was dead, yet, I prayed and quoted scripture to encourage us all.

Finally, all but Pastor Musah, the two policemen, lay-man David, and the girl were in the car. The policemen were being beaten even as they rushed around to help us. Their caps and police sticks were taken from them. After what seemed like hours, a policeman came bringing my keys. I lowered the window just enough to let the keys drop to the inside floor. The policeman told me later that whoever took the keys from me had given them to the local Chief Masak. He had been holding them while the Christians were being beaten. He agreed to give them to the police if I would take the carload back into a remote area to be judged by their fetish man (witch doctor). The police directed me to back out onto the road, but headed the opposite direction from my house and the police station in Gambaga. This was a puzzle, but I obeyed. As soon as I backed out of the cornfield and onto the road, I decided to kill the motor so the people might think I was not afraid and they would calm down. The police might be able to get into the car. The policemen realized what I was doing and went to the back of the vehicle. I started to lower the tailgate window, so they could get into the third seat. The people stormed the car, grabbed the policemen, and started rocking the vehicle as if to turn it over. The policemen backed away, waved to me, and called, "Go, go!" The people had put tree limbs and logs across the road. I drove into the cornfield to avoid some. It was difficult to miss people on the road; each seemed to think he alone could stop this heavy vehicle. There were limbs across the end of a bridge to divert us to the fetish man's village. Had we gone there, *he would have ruled that we must die* for getting the girl out of the hut even for so short a time. I drove on top of the limbs and crossed the bridge.

We were free, but headed the wrong direction. We rolled down the windows to get fresh air and dilute the odor. The road behind us was the only way to the police station as far as I knew, but we could not go back through Najong! We went east to Bunkpurugu. I wondered whether we would ever get back west to Nakpanduri or the police station in Gambaga. In Bunkpurugu, we reported to the most powerful chief in that vicinity. I learned that Pastor Musah, who did not get into our car in Najong #2, was his nephew! He was rightfully concerned that no one knew where his nephew was. The chief and my passengers discussed an alternate route back to the police station. It would circle south of Najong #2 and eventually join the road we had traveled hours earlier. It was not far through the bush from Najong #2 at one point. If the people thought about it, they may send men there to intercept us. Also, that road was barely passable in the dry season; in the rains, it may not be usable at all. We decided to try. Pastor Namyela said, "Take me by to tell my wife good-bye as we may yet die." From the looks of my passengers, I knew they could be bleeding internally, so we stopped and Pastor Namyela went into the parsonage. His wife, Karen, followed him out and was crying as we drove away. We were off to the police station in Gambaga.

The road was true to its reputation. I could not recognize the faces of my passengers without my glasses, because I was so near-sighted. I missed the road and went into the bush more than once. Someone would call, "Madam, the road is this way!" The car fell into ditches just fitting the tires and killed the engine. Something seemed to be wrong with my right arm, so Pastor Namyela shifted gears. He had never driven a car before. We were all getting stiffer by the moment. We prayed for Dindeuk and the policemen who were left behind. We prayed for Pastor Musah and David, because we did not know where they were. Pastor John Kombat led us in a song:

My Lord is able, He's able, I know He's able!
I know my Lord is able to carry me through. (Repeat)
He heals the broken hearted; **HE SETS THE CAPTIVE FREE***!*
He healed my body and He saved my soul,
And he caused the blind to see.

My Lord is able, He's able; I know He's able.
I know my Lord is able to carry me through."

(Unknown)

We would start over and raise our voices each time we got to the words, *"HE SETS THE CAPTIVE FREE."* We were singing it for all involved, but especially for Dindeuk; she was yet a prisoner. That was our theme song from then on. Also as a diversion, we related humorous things and miracles that happened in Najong #2. The clinic helper, Nyankpen, had arthritis in his ankles and used a cane to walk. He said, "I threw my cane away and ran." He never used a cane again so long as I knew him! Pastor Namyela said, "We were all so quiet inside the car. We never said one word even as we watched people being beaten to the ground, except Madam Spencer; she prayed the whole time. In fact, *she never shut her mouth* one time!" Pastor John said, "I think those men who saw the window go up by itself are still running over the hills!" Only Lay pastor Samson was quiet; he was *speechless*. His daughter was still in Najong #2! I had not actually seen Pastor John Kombat's church at Jimbari, as I was quite new, but I knew it was on the road we were now traveling. I do not remember stopping to let him inform his wife, but I saw the church. I was relieved when we came to the fork in the road that put us on a familiar road again. The people of Najong #2 had *not cut off our escape route in two potential places.* Soon after that, we found David, the layman, walking down the road and we let him inside. He had been beaten, but was alive and we were grateful to God. It had rained somewhere, so the small river at Bimbagu was running. The bridge had been under construction for some time. I had received notice of an official opening. On the journey out to Najong #2 earlier that morning, we had gone around the bridge and passed through a relatively dry riverbed. Now, on our return, there was too much water to drive into. There were some preteen cowboys herding cows near the bridge.

We were all so stiff we could hardly move. Nyankpen called to them through the car window, "Go take the barricade down from that bridge!" The small boys, with eyes as round as saucers, cried, "Oh no! They will beat us!" We knew about that one! *Been there, done that!* Nyankpen stuck his arm out the window, flipped his hand so his fingers snapped and said, "We will beat you right now if you don't take it down." They took it down; we crossed.

When we drove into Nakpanduri, the roads were lined with people. They had gathered to go rescue us. They said, "We are ready to go burn the village of Najong #2." Nyankpen got up on the bumper of my car and said, "Do not go to Najong! This is God's palaver and He will solve it. We do not want revenge; we want Dindeuk. She is still there. If you go someone might be killed." They agreed not to go since they could see all but Dindeuk and the policemen were accounted for. We were told that Pastor Musah had come to Nakpanduri earlier on a bicycle and persuaded a road worker to drive him the twenty miles to Gambaga Police Station in a truck. We now knew Musah was safe, but his uncle in Bunkpurugu had no way of knowing. We were weak and dehydrated from having neither food nor water since morning. We passed the clinic and went up to my house, where Allason and Kombet served us bread and tea. Other clinic workers followed us to my house and all were in shock when they saw us, but thanking God that we were alive. We were in a hurry to get to the police station in Gambaga; two of their policemen were still in Najong! As I put petrol in the tank of my car, I felt that my back was injured. I quickly got my spare pair of glasses, a gown, and my devotion book with my Bible. We were off to Gambaga. What we did not know was that the Chief of Bunkpurugu had commandeered a market lorry and ordered it loaded with men to go to Najong #2 to find his nephew. When the truck got there, the village people came out with weapons to beat them so they drove on through. They were forced to pass over the new bridge at Bimbagu and as the cement was not yet dry, the heavy lorry damaged the bridge. In Nakpanduri, they also learned that Pastor Musah was safely ahead of them, but they continued toward the police station in Gambaga. Probably because I did now know their language yet, I did not know about that truck. We overtook it before we got to the Gambaga Police Station. The flaps of the truck were thrown up, and men leaned out and yelled. I thought we were in trouble again, until my passengers said, "No, No! The lorry is from the Bunkpurugu Chief to support us at the police station." It followed us on to Gambaga. Pastor Musah was already there. He said that when the first lick was struck, he dived into the cornfield as if it was water. He went to the nearest school, grabbed a bicycle belonging to a teacher, and raced to Nakpanduri. That's how the people in Nakpanduri knew we needed help. By the time we got to the police station, they were already taking steps to radio for reinforcement and transportation to go back to Najong #2. It might have been too late had we still been there, but at least they knew there was a problem. They were terribly concerned about their two missing policemen. After hearing our story, they sent the Bunkpurugu truck back to Najong #2. The corporal said to the driver, "See if you can get them to send the two policemen with you to the Bunkpurugu Chief's compound for the night." Much later, we learned they were successful. In Najong #2, they had put the two policemen in a three foot-high pig house and told them they were going to set the grass roof on fire. The policemen told them, "There are many policemen where we came from. If you burn us, you will be in bigger trouble than you are now; *no one has died yet.*"

I kept insisting to the Gambaga Police that I must go another thirty miles to Walewale to report to the McCorkles and Smiths; they were mission officials. The police said they would inform Rev. McCorkle, and insisted I take the injured back a few miles to the Baptist Hospital in Nalerigu. I knew they were right. Only that morning we had spoken to the Nayiri about the case. This would be the fourth time through that town in one day; it seemed like days! When I took emergencies to the Baptist Hospital, I usually drove over to Dr. Ashworth's home afterward to notify him. This time I went straight to his house. When he and his wife, Ann, came to the door I said, "Dr. Ashworth, this is my own blood this time." The three of us laughed and I told them what happened. The Ashworths let me stay in their spare bedroom. Dr. Ashworth took the injured Ghanaians to the hospital for examination and to sleep for the night. Ann Ashworth took my white uniform and put it to soak to get the blood out; that's all I had to wear. When the doctor returned to the house, he reported the men were severely bruised and may have small broken bones in hands, nose, or face, but no one was mortally wounded. Before sleeping, I read in my devotional book for August 20. It said, "If thou faint in the day of adversity, thy strength is small. Proverbs 24:10." Wow! I expected it to say, "Poor thing!" It went on, "He giveth power to the faint; and to them that have no might he increaseth strength. Isaiah 40:29." "My grace is sufficient for thee: for my strength is made perfect in weakness. II Corinthians 12:9" "He shall call upon me, and I will answer him: I will be with him in trouble: I will *deliver him*. Psalms 91:15" "The eternal God is thy refuge, and underneath are the everlasting arms: and He shall thrust out the enemy from before thee. Deuteronomy 33:27." I slept without a sleeping pill.

I did not know about further happenings that night in Najong #2 or at the Gambaga Police Station. I knew they said they would call for transportation and reinforcement by radio and go back to Najong #2. I learned they had informed Franklin McCorkle as promised. He came from Walewale the next morning, picked up the six injured men from the hospital, and followed the lorry carrying the reinforcement of nineteen policemen back to Najong #2. The injured men were to identify Dindeuk and those who had beaten us. They were gone all day. *How I prayed!* I did not want revenge. I was convinced they were wrong to take the girl against the father's will and her will. I knew they were wrong to beat us. My goals were still the same; I wanted to see Dindeuk out of there and the whole thing finished. During the day, a man from Ghana's CID (Investigation, like the FBI), came to the doctor's house. He sat and asked questions that sounded like he wanted to know whether the father or I, an expatriate, had initiated the trip to Najong #2. Of course, it had been the father and other Ghanaian men. The men even thought I was rather too hesitant to help them at first. However, I did know a kidnapping when I saw one!

About dusk, I heard singing, "He healed the broken hearted. HE SETS THE CAPTIVE FREE. My Lord is able- - -." I felt sure they had Dindeuk! Franklin McCorkle, the pastors, the girl, and her father came inside. What rejoicing! Dindeuk had a mask of horror on her face, but a smile flickered when she saw me. She told the men that there was a time when she thought I probably had been killed, especially when I was not in the car when the others returned. She was sent to the hospital and Dr. Ashworth went to examine and treat her. He said she had over one hundred knife cuts on her body, but was obviously happy to be free. She, the pastors, and all the men went back to their homes in a few days.

Franklin told me, "The two policemen who helped you have been brought to the Gambaga Police Station. He said that when reinforcement arrived in Najong #2, the people came out prepared to beat them. Instead, the nineteen policemen threw up the canvas flaps and began putting the cult members into the lorry. At least twenty-three people of Najong #2 were arrested. Some fled across the border to French country. Chief Masak was also arrested for possession of stolen property. He had parts of the policemen's fezzes (caps) in his pocket and the two injured policemen knew he also once had the keys to my Chevrolet. When the policeman asked the villagers where Dindeuk was, they said *they forgot.* He said two policemen *helped them remember* all the way to where they had hidden her. Pastor Namyela went with the two policemen to identify the girl and they retrieved her. Apparently, she was the first Bimoba girl or boy in the Nakpanduri area to have come out of the Kwonsi hut *alive* before the months of rites were completed. People came just to look at her; they could not believe she was still alive. They also looked at us; we were supposed to be dead!

After resting for two days, I wrote the first letter to tell my family that I had been beaten and a bit about what happened. How does one explain by letter to Americans about African customs? I told them I was in the home of a British doctor and his family at the Baptist Medical Center at Nalerigu, but *not* in the hospital. I said, "Don't worry. We have the support of chiefs, villagers, Ghana Government Police, and other Ghana Officials. I just feel sorry for the villagers who are now in trouble for doing this." Someone wrote that Dad was so angry that he might fly to Africa. I quickly wrote him *not* to come. The Ashworths and I played table games and had a very nice visit for almost a week. I had a headache, but never needed a sleeping pill. In fact, my new co-worker was to arrive in Accra from England on September 1. I fully planned to go over four hundred miles to the coast to meet her. It did not happen that way. On a later examination, Drs. Ashworth and Faile, both at the Baptist Hospital, found that my nose and right scapula (shoulder blade) were broken. My right shoulder and breast were jet black. My feet were black inside heavy nursing shoes. They suggested the headache might indicate a mild concussion. When we felt I was well enough to travel, Dr. Ashworth drove my car to Tamale. His wife, Ann, and I followed in their car. They stayed to eat the noon meal with Wheeler and Eileen Anderson and Alice, their daughter. They run the mission press; the Lehmanns had gone to America on furlough. People had a tendency to make the situation somber. On the other hand, this was the perfect time for Dr. Ashworth to tell the story of when Helen and I sent him a cartoon from The Saturday Evening Post. At the time we sent the cartoon, he was the responsible government doctor at Yendi to whom we answered and he had not responded. Soon after that, he went on leave, was married, and returned to the Baptist Mission Hospital. That allowed him the freedom to tell the story that day in Tamale for all to enjoy and diminish signs of gloom and doom!

While I was in Tamale, Franklin McCorkle came to show me a letter he had written to my family, friends, supporters, and Mission Headquarters in Missouri. He asked permission to get my address list. He asked Homer Goodwin, at NGBI in Kumbungu, to phone the American Ambassador in Accra to report the incident. There was a better phone link there than in Walewale. Franklin followed the phone call with one of the letters. It read in part, "I want to report a severe beating, which Miss Charlese Spencer, two policemen, and other men of the Bimoba tribe received by a wicked secret society as they were attempting to rescue a girl the cult had kidnapped. A girl is stripped of all clothing and her body carved. She is forced to eat large quantities of native mush until her stomach is extended and they pound on it. If she vomits, she is forced to eat the emesis. Sex with the girl is allowed, but a priority *order* exists. The initiates were forced to stand without sleep for days. When she can stand no longer, they tie her hands to a rafter. The local authorities are working to bring the wrongdoers to justice. The trial will probably start around September 1."

I received a letter from the Regional Commissioner in Tamale. It read:

It has been reported to me that you were involved in an incident in Najong #2. I am writing to express my great regret at this very unfortunate occurrence. I trust that you will soon be fully recovered, and (this) will not deter you from pursuing your valuable work in this region. Signed, —Regional Commissioner.

Because we received this correspondence and I was in

Tamale, Wheeler Anderson said we should pay a visit to the Regional Commissioner. He showed us correspondence he had received from the District Commissioner in Gambaga. It read:

RE: THE CUSTOM OF KWONSI: The attached petition comes from the Bimoba members of the Assembly of God Church, chiefs, officials and others in the Bimoba area, protesting the practice of the Bimoba primitive Kwonsi Custom. I suggest that the only effective means of stopping such a practice will be by an act of Parliament. (Making education for girls mandatory.) The custom involves confining human beings of either sex into unhealthy and wretched surroundings for three months for boys and four months for girls. The custom has been the cause of several deaths in the Bimoba area. (Copy to: A/G Church and others) Sig, District Commissioner.

He included the petition he had requested "with more information" from the Bimobas. It was two hand-written pages, written while I was in Nalerigu with the Ashworths. I received a copy, but *I did not even type it!* The authors and signers were Merchant J. P. Kont, Nakpanduri Chief Lari Selim, Clinic Orderly Nyankpen, and two ministers, Pastors Musah and Namyela. It read, in part:

An Appeal to Central Government: We the undersigned, representatives of Bimoba affairs in Local Government Services and others, beg to bring to the notice of the Central Government that the customary system which exists among the Bimoba tribe for untold years has brought many cruelties. This cruel custom is such that young men and women are confined in a room for three or four months, are marked all over the bodies with a sharp knife and a considerable amount of blood is wasted. Such people are known to be imprisoned and at times, they die of the wounds. In such cases if one dies, it is not made known to the parents. In three or four months when the parents arrive to get their child, they will then be informed of the death `by natural causes' or `Kwonsi took them.' (The natural causes can be tetanus from a dirty knife, anemia from blood loss, or pneumonia from nudity.) Nudity is another point in this system. Every year such deaths occur, but as no one attempts to make it a case (because of fear of death themselves), the performers have the advantage to persevere in destroying and endangering human life. Some of the signatures of this petition represent former members of this society. Unless the practice is abolished, more lives will be lost. Many women are forced to undergo this cruel treatment when they do not even want the husbands their parents force them to marry because of payment involved years before. When these women are forced against their will, the performers send for some herbalist who gives the woman herbs to spoil her mind. By drugging the women, they may forget their real love and marry these husbands without personal affection. At times, females become insane and the husband who forced them into the practice will then leave them to suffer and die. When the husbands do keep the insane women and they come to the clinic to deliver their babies or for some illness, the husband must come with her to speak to the nurses for her. The husband may say that her head has been spoiled since she came out of the hut. One such woman set a house on fire, in which seven men and six babies were totally burned to death. This, therefore, is a dangerous system and we beg the Central Government kindly assist to abolish this by law and save human life in Ghana. We are prepared to write details of secrets of this system if the Government will kindly put a sympathetic ear to this petition.

The Regional Commissioner in Tamale agreed with the

District Commissioner in Gambaga that the Ghana Parliament could not forbid the Kwonsi followers to practice their religion for consenting adults. He said, however, that it was wrong to put people there who were not willing to go for any reason. He agreed that to introduce a law in parliament making it mandatory for Ghanaian girls to go to school might be the way to go. The men would not be so apt to buy the girls when they were born if they discovered she had to go to school at a certain age. Any investment in the girl may be lost. Her father would know he might have to pay back all he got if he sold her. This did not exclude parents from decision-making about their child's marriage or education, but it did give the child or youth a vote. The act was apparently considered; I do not know what year or the exact outcome. As we talked with the Regional Commissioner in Tamale, he asked me how I was physically. I told him I was still having trouble driving my car and even writing a check, but it would right itself with time. He insisted I go to the General Hospital in Tamale and have a check-up with X-rays. I went and it confirmed Drs. Ashworth and Faile's diagnosis. They found a broken nose and a vertical fracture of the scapula (shoulder blade), from top to bottom. At the inner aspect of the right clavicle (where they meet in front) it was displaced an inch lower than the left. They x-rayed the cranium; it suggested a possible hairline fracture. No x-rays were taken of my back. I thought all I needed was rest. A doctor admitted me to the hospital for observation and bed rest anyway. The next day my fever spiked to over one hundred four degrees. I was treated for malaria. We requested a one-day pass to attend the first session of the Police Court involving those who beat their two policemen. The others who were beaten were asked to be witnesses; we made no charges. The doctors refused the requested pass. The court had been moved from Gambaga to Walewale, West Mamprusi District. Nakpanduri, Gambaga Police Station, and other villages involved were in East Mamprusi District; too many observers would have been a problem.

My new co-worker, Eloise Smith, arrived in Ghana while I was still in the hospital. Obviously, I did not drive to the coast to meet her ship as planned. She heard about the Najong incident and came north by plane. I slept most of the time I was in the hospital. While there, a strong vision or dream came to me. I say vision, as I knew I was in that hospital bed, but it was like a dream. Slightly above the bed appeared a metal gate. God, the Father, opened it. How do I know? In a vision, you just know. Someone came through the gate. He sat on the foot of my bed. I thought He was an angel until He spoke. It was Jesus! He quoted from The Revelation of Jesus to John in the Bible, "(2:v.7-21) . . . to him that overcometh I will *give*...; (v.11) ...he that overcometh shall *not be hurt* of . . . ; (v.26) he that overcometh will I *give power* . . . ; (3:5) . . . he that overcometh shall *be clothed* . . . ; (v.12) ...him that overcometh (I) will *make a pillar* . . . ; (v.21) . . . him that overcometh will I *grant to sit*...as I also overcame and am set down with my Father . . . ; (v.21;7) . . . he that overcometh shall *inherit. . . .* " He quoted the entire verses, but emphasized parts. It was like having a heavy meal. I felt fed and strengthened! Finally, He looked at me sternly and said, "There, you have it; *it's up to you* what you do with it!" He went back through the gate and God, the Father, shut the gate. I have told this at selective women's meetings and always ended with, "I wondered why He did that. I had no negative thoughts about what had happened or plans to blame God for any outcome, physically or otherwise." It was such a potentially positive situation for the Assemblies of God Mission. It suddenly is amazing to me that He visited me, in person, in a dream *before and after* the incident.

The most prized letter I received was dated September 4, from Noel Perkin, Executive Director of Foreign Missions Department in Springfield, Missouri; he held that position for thirty-three years. He wrote:

My main purpose in writing is because of the terrible ordeal which you recently went through. I do hope that you will not have suffered any lasting ill effect. Experiences of this kind are seldom suffered in these days. However, such events were not uncommon in the days of the early pioneers. I have just learned, from you and others, that you are recovering nicely. This is indeed good news and we want you to know that we appreciate your courage and determined action on behalf of one of the needy little lives of Africa. This, of course, is in addition to the thousands you have helped in so many ways. God bless you. We are proud of you and we will be praying for you.

Rev. Perkin said news of the Najong #2 incident was received *during the General Council* in San Antonio, Texas; they chose not to report it until they knew more. (I hope they had prayer-anonymously, of course!) He gave me a bit of news from the Council:

T.F. Zimmerman was elected General Superintendent of the worldwide Assemblies of God. He succeeded Ralph M. Riggs, who held that office six years. J. Philip Hogan was elected Executive Director of Foreign Missions. The number of Assistant Superintendents was increased to five to include that office. Signed, Noel Perkin.

Many people, to emphasize as many points, positive and negative, have used this incident. It is a credit to Samson, the girl's father, perhaps more than any other person. Without his steadfast determination and faith in God, her rescue would never have happened. However, there is no doubt who gets the credit, *God, Himself!* Without the police and the Speed-the-Light vehicle, the father may not have lived to get the girl. Without the father, neither the police, pastors, Franklin McCorkle, nor I would have known to try. Without reinforcement, Gambaga Police would not have gone to get the girl. Ghanaians said the rescue, "*Honored* the one true God, *embarrassed* those who kidnapped the girl, and *belittled* the devil himself."

Liberating Young People: 1. Site of Biboba churches and Najong #2, "C." 2. Pastor Samson and daughter. 3. Same ones during conflict. 4. Deacon at church. 5. Ten who were beaten, and girl. 6. Weapons and broken window. 7. Bungpurugu Chief who helped us. 8. My angels who saved me. 9. Mr. Missions retired, Rev. and Mrs. Noel Perkin receiving gift from missionaries and Ghanaian ministers.

Nakpanduri clinic. 1. General Clinic. 2. visit by dignitaries. 3. A family we helped. 4. Teaching and presenting the word before treatment. 5. Clinic helper, Nyankpen, and family. He became a major chief. 6. Another clinic worker, Awuni, and family. 7. Typical of a local woman the chiefs, official and Christian men were trying to elevate and liberate. 8. A cobra after my chickens. 9. Transportation.

CHAPTER TEN

It's Up to Me

ON SEPTEMBER 12, I got out of the hospital. My new co-worker, Eloise Smith, and I stayed two days in the Tamale rest house and ate with the Andersons. We shopped for food staples before going to Nakpanduri. I discovered I still could hardly sign a check, probably because of the broken scapula. Eloise drove, for the same reason. As we left Tamale, the Andersons came out to the car. Eileen said, "Drive carefully and we'll see you later." As we drove away Eloise complained, "What does she mean, drive carefully? I've been driving all my life." It surprised me, as it was a figure of speech in bidding farewell that I had heard all my life. We drove to Walewale, where we were to go eat a meal with Vivan and Dorothy Smith. At the table, Eloise repeated her opinion of Eileen's admonition to drive carefully. Then she patted me on the head and asked, "How do you like my little girl?" That went over with me about like the *safe driving* did with Eloise; this was my second tour in Africa and she was the novice. The Smiths glanced at me but said nothing. After lunch, we visited with Franklin, Aneice, Meme, Papaw, and Amonna Sue at the other mission house in Walewale. We drove thirty miles to Gambaga, got our stack of mail, and went to Nakpanduri. We were home at last!

236

Nyankpen, who had also been beaten, and the other Ghanaian clinic workers had continued helping people at the clinic as much as allowed. Eloise and I started delivering babies, tending regular outpatient clinics, holding child welfare clinics, and treating emergencies. Numbers treated were *higher than ever*. I was indeed happy that Eloise was there; she was a midwife as Helen was. I was not forced to attend deliveries night and day, in addition to the various daily clinics. One Friday, after treating one hundred thirty-three patients at the clinic, we drove to Bawku. I had my Remington 0.22 rifle with me at all times for rabbits. I did remove it from my car when we went to Najong; if they had seen a gun, they may have used it or their muzzle-loaders. My 0.410 shotgun had been released from a government warehouse; I took it along to kill guinea fowl. Eloise opened a personal bank account in Bawku. I needed to introduce her to Don and Grace Jolley, the American family in the Bawku Area. Their two sons were the age of my nephews Jim and Davy; one was even named Davy. We played basketball until I was exhausted.

Homer Goodwin and Franklin McCorkle came to Nakpanduri the first weekend after Eloise and I arrived. They took me sixteen miles to Najong #2 to greet Chief Masak; he was out on bail. He was the village chief who held the keys to my vehicle while the Christians were being beaten. Some forty-six from his village were still in prison. The number grew as those came back from wherever they hid when the reinforcement of policemen arrived in their village. We talked a long time with Chief Masak. We told him they were welcome to send their sick people for treatment and their women to deliver babies at the clinic; we would not seek revenge. We thanked him for having the grass roof put on the Najong #2 church after it was burned off that "day of infamy."

One day a newborn baby with tetanus was brought to the clinic from a village west of the Nakpanduri Clinic

(Najong was *east*). The baby died and the parents begged us to go with them to their village to have a Christian funeral. If they went alone, they would be forced to have a fetish priest do the ceremony. Their village was far into the bush where no vehicle could go. Eloise could not walk that far; she was a diabetic and termed medically obese. She was twice my weight, and I was not small. Nyankpen, said, "Madam, these are the only Christians in that village; we must help them." He went *without his cane* and carried the dead child; the parents were so sad. We drove the Wee Dubya as far as we could and parked it at the edge of the road. It was already getting dark. We heard dancing and drumming immediately. We had walked only a short way when we saw a village celebrating someone who had completed initiation into Kwonsi. Our path passed at the edge of that compound. None of our group said a word, but we walked rapidly for over an hour. The parents of the dead baby reported to their family. Then while many were digging a grave, we sang and read the Bible by torchlight. Then we had a service and committed the precious little one to God. We did not hurry; they seemed to need our presence. Nyankpen and I would be *the only two going back*. We did not talk about that or the village where the Kwonsi dancing was taking place. After the funeral, we walked over an hour back to the car. As we neared the celebrating village, we heard nothing, only our pounding hearts. The silence was overwhelming! Each time I put a foot down I said, "Jesus." Thoughts flashed through my mind, "How could they have been so noisy and finish before we did? Could they be waiting for us? They knew full well we were involved at Najong #2." Still we never said a word as we walked fast, but did not run, passed the compound where the drums had been so loud earlier. When we reached the road, the Wee Dubya seemed to be intact. That was small consolation; we knew anything could happen yet. As calmly as possible, we got inside, locked the doors, and sparked the engine. Only then did we look at each other and began thanking God for His protection. We had each had the same fears.

Among our letters collected that day at Gambaga was one from Ruby Johnson at Saboba. It was about the Yankazia church and dated August 20, the day of the Najong #2 incident. She could not have known about Najong at the time. It read, "Dear Charlese, Here are some pictures taken at Yankazia. Please send them to the New Mexico church that furnished the money for the roof. We are still building on the extra bedroom and new kitchen with money from the New Mexico District Council. The Foreman of Works at the police station let us have some sand for floors. If we have some sand left, they say we may use it for the Yankazia church floors. Now to get it hauled sixteen miles to Yankazia! I've been hauling when we don't have clinics on Saturdays. Ruby concluded her letter by saying that she hoped my new co-worker would arrive soon. She knew Lois, my temporary co-worker, was called back to Liberia. By the time we got her letter, she had written another. She knew about the Najong #2 situation and that Eloise had come.

Saboba Teacher Samson Mankrom was still pastor at Yankazia. The Yankazia Chief was Samson's uncle. Teacher Samson wrote, "Dear Madam, The Yankazia Church Membership wishes to thank you for the very benevolent incitation taken to raise funds to complete our church building. Kindly extend the appreciation of our membership to your members at home. Please assure them that while the church exists we shall never forget to mention our gratefulness in prayer before the Lord our God." A second letter from Teacher Samson Mankrom read, "It has been a profound grief among Christians and non-Christians within the Konkomba area to hear of the incident in which policemen, Bimoba pastors, you, and other Christians were beaten. Romans 10:15 came to us. We have thought it might be that the Lord put you in that particular village to be a symbol of destruction to that fetish and to save many souls who might have been ruined by Kwonsi in the future. *We wish you to take even more courage and boldness* in your mission. It has left us more refreshed in courage and determination to work for the Lord. News of the baseness of the people toward you did at first give us utter unrest. It even invoked in us past memories of our heathen days. We might have easily approached them who beat you and staged a bitter fight for your sake. However, such heathen ideas soon gave way to the Biblical examples. As Elijah did through the Lord destroy Baal, so have you morally and physically, through the Lord, *belittled the Kwonsi*. It is understood that the Lord is going to turn the Kwonsians to Him; He did it to Paul! And, Madam, who can tell, *a church building might spring even from the very ground* where the filthy Kwonsi room now stands or where Christians fell. Meanwhile, we hope our communication might be to you a token of inspiration of how much we love you in the Lord. We wish you a very speedy recovery from your wounds. To repeat our impressions, we say, how lovely it is to think that a true and noble Christian shrinks not even at the greatest of trials. Madam, enclosed is what the Lord Jesus has laid on our hearts to send you. We are, sincerely, The Yankazia Church Membership." (There was *money* enclosed! I was thoroughly convinced that U Na Fabor Jayum, Chief of Yankazia had a hand in this missive!)

A letter came from Raymond Brock, Division of Foreign Missions Promotions. He said he had seen my letter to Rev. Phillips and said, "You are to be congratulated for your heroic stand against the forces of evil. I would not be surprised if you do not see a great revival in the area. You have proven that your Christ is stronger than their juju." He wanted to use the situation with pictures as soon as possible. I started working on it. Another letter from him three weeks later contained a copy of a short item. Under "Evangel Deadline...Late News at Press Time," the news of Najong #2 was first mentioned in *The Pentecostal Evangel*, September 27, 1959. Other news in that deadline was that J.R. Flower resigned as Secretary. Howard S. Bush was elected an Assistant General Superintendent. Rev. Brock concluded his letter with, "I am still waiting for further information and pictures from you." I was working on it! Finally, I did get the item written and sent with pictures. Homer Goodwin and Franklin McCorkle sent along their best pictures with my item. A letter of thanks came from Rev. Brock. The material was to be in *The Pentecostal Evangel* dated November 29. At the end, Rev. Brock said, "Let me congratulate you for your humble portrayal of the situation. Surely yours is a testimony that should be read far and wide, a most outstanding missionary experience."

R.T. McGlasson, Foreign Missions Secretary since General Council in August, was special because he had seen us off in New York the very first time Helen and I sailed from the United States. He wrote, "We pray that God will not only restore you to health, but keep you safe. This is a story that should be told. We believe it is a great victory for His cause."

A "Summons to appear in court as a witness in Walewale on September 26," arrived. I was able to go this time, but would rather not as we were really too busy. On the date, all those beaten, and Dindeuk, went to Walewale to court in the nine-seat Chevrolet Kingswood; Eloise was driving. We came to the Gambaga escarpment, a very steep hill that appears rather suddenly. A truck was coming up the hill to meet Eloise. She stood her grounds and forced the trucker to drive on the right, like in America. One of the Africans said, "Madam, you are driving too fast." We were all shaken! Eloise became angry and asserted her ability again. I said, "Eloise, we are all still very nervous from the Najong experience. These are the very ones God saved by miracles. I cannot believe He now wants us to die on the Gambaga Escarpment." She seemed not to realize the seriousness of going slowly while learning Ghana road rules.

We were all dreading the court proceedings. They had

finally arrested forty-seven people from Najong #2. I was meeting them, face to face, for the first time since August 20. Some looked sad. Some looked as though they might like to try it again. It seemed the method of the court was to get at least two of us to identify the same man for doing the same thing. I had not been there during the first court date, but my identification must agree with those pointed out at that previous trial. The clinic worker, Nyankpen, told an incident where a man had an axe. The Kwonsi man held it high above his head to kill this clinic worker. Nyankpen said he only had time to say one word, "Jesus." The axe head fell off the handle onto the Kwonsi man's head. The judge demanded of Nyankpen, "Point to the man." When he did, the judge asked the Kwonsi man, "Did this happen to you?" He said it happened. In the midst of the court proceedings, a car passed through the throng of people forced to stand outside because of the small size of the building. The horn was honking long and loud blasts! The Judge of the Court demanded the driver be brought before him! It was Dorothy Smith, a Mission midwife on her way to deliver a baby. After a reprimand, she was allowed to proceed on her way. When I was called, I took the oath with my hand on the Bible. Others swore by their ancestors, the crocodile, a tree, stone, or the water buffalo. *Very interesting*! The judge demanded of me, "Walk near, and point to the man who was first asked to relinquish the girl." I recognized him easily. They asked, "Who hit the first blow of the whole incident?" Amazingly, I could still see his face. When I was asked who beat me in the cornfield and who protected me, I could not identify them. Others had already identified them. I was asked about my injuries. When I said my nose was broken, he said, "Walk near and point to the man who broke your nose." I have never forgotten his face either; he had one unusual eye. That was not to be the last of the court proceedings; I wished it were!

After court adjourned that day, the McCorkles and Meme

and Papaw Smitherman followed us from Walewale to the Gambaga Police Station. We wanted to get pictures of all Ghanaian policemen who had helped us. There I met the two men God used to help save my life in Najong #2 at the two times I would have been killed. They did a *good thing for their village* as no one died. They did a *good thing* for us; we did not die. *They were true angels!* Meme was happy to tell me that sometime while I was in the hospital, the two men had prayed the sinners' prayer with her. They had accepted the blood of God's Son as their Sacrifice. This was my first opportunity to talk with the two policemen who went with us to Najong #2 and to Corporal Atta Darko, in charge at Gambaga who sent them. I expressed my gratitude for the help. When I said to Corporal Darko that I felt badly to see the people of Najong #2 suffer and go to prison, he just replied, "You suffered." Then he repeated what he had said from the beginning that he wished he could have gone with us to Najong, but he had duties. He was so sure the girl's father, Samson, would not back down and he was correct; Samson stood strong. He said people had tried before and stopped because of fear. There was reason to fear, but not to surrender. Young men were sometimes assigned to kill fathers who defied the Kwonsi. We had previously been having services for prisoners in the Gambaga jail. We asked about that and the corporal assured us we could continue. While the men were waiting to be sent to prison, some who beat us were present when we told them of God's love by giving His Son, Jesus, as a blood sacrifice for them. Some may have heard that truth for the first time; perhaps some believed. The church in Najong #2 grew rapidly!

The two men of Najong #2 who helped save my life were the first to send their wives and families to the clinic. Soon other people in the village sent their sick to us. The women eventually came for prenatal clinic and to deliver their babies. (In future years, we had a small building in Najong #2 for a monthly well-baby clinic.) In spite of all this, word was still circulating that some had a bounty offered for anyone who could poison Dindeuk or any who went to Najong that day; we watched where and what we ate.

Both Eloise and I knew Murray and Marjorie Brown in Damongo. Their two children, Elaine and Murray Jr., were grown and in America. The family had been missionaries in French West Africa for many years. We decided to visit the Browns and ask them to come for a week of special meetings. We went in my personal Volkswagen to save gasoline and Eloise drove. Her Speed-the-Light vehicle was to arrive soon. I tried very hard not to say anything about her driving. On the way back to Nakpanduri, she was unable to negotiate a curve. The Volkswagen bug went out of control and literally spun like a top in the road, but did not turn over. Another miracle! I was so shook that I asked, "Eloise, what is it going to take to get you to slow down on these African roads?" She said, "Well, when my vehicle comes I'll drive like I want to." I said, "I don't want to die in your vehicle or mine!" We arrived home with no other mishap.

It was amazing the strength the Ghanaian pastors and lay Christians displayed before, during, and following the Najong incident. It was a testimony to the success of previous missionaries. We had visitors at clinic and house, officials and laypeople, Ghanaians and expatriates. Many asked the same questions, "How did you do this? How did the Bimoba Christians do this?" The Bimobas had a quick answer, "It was only with the help of God's Holy Spirit." Nyankpen and I were back to the normal clinic schedule. Pastors and laypeople who were beaten were back to their churches and usual work. The District Commissioner and the Member of Parliament for Eastern Mamprusi District came for a clinic visit. They found things functioning as usual in the area. One of the clinic workers whirled me around with my back to the visitors, and said, "Here is proof of the War of Najong #2. You can still see the stripes on her uniform." We all laughed, but that was the last time I wore the uniform. I stored my favorite uniform away. It is to remind me of all the miracles that took place. (Perhaps someday it will be in the NMDC archives along with a copy of this book.) Finally, the Commissioner said, "There is this little matter of the Bimbagu Bridge which was damaged in the process and will need repairs before the opening ceremony." That made me nervous until he added, "However, under the circumstances I would have done the same thing." The bridge was eventually repaired, dedicated, and opened for normal use.

In mid-October, the Browns did come for a week of special meetings; some marvelous events took place. People who did not usually come to church attended the special meetings. Some flatly said, "Lest we see the rescued girl with our eyes, we will not believe she is alive." Marjorie Brown had special meetings for the women before the evening church services. It was in a similar meeting of hers at Southwestern College in Texas that I decided to prepare for nursing as a single lady. Here we were, both in Africa and working together for such a short, but special time! Nakpanduri Chief Selim came to church. On Sunday morning, he had his three-year-old son, Jatuat, with him. After the service, I wanted a picture of them. The Chief stooped over and carefully buttoned his son's shirt so he would look good in the picture. I got the whole process on 16mm colored movie film. I prize that strip of film! (We eventually sent Paul Jatuat Selim to Bawku for nurses training and he became head nurse in charge of the Nakpanduri Clinic.)

The last court session was November 10. At that time, the Najong #2 people were sentenced. They had already been in jail over two months. Out of the forty-seven people arrested, twenty men and one woman were given prison sentences ranging from six months to one year. They each received a monetary fine of sixty to two hundred dollars. They could stay extra time in prison if they could not pay. I wanted to tell authorities to *release them*. Of course I did not; it was not my prerogative. Rather interesting that another letter from

Rev. Noel Perkin read, "You naturally feel for those who have been condemned to imprisonment for the violence inflicted on you and the Christians of the area. One would like to intervene, but this might make them feel free to inflict violence upon Christians or even policemen again. The government stood by the law. That means a lot. I wish we could get you out for a prolonged rest, but I can also see that, if for a time you could stay with the Christians, it may encourage them. God strengthen you, giving you grace. We are proud of you and thank God He has brought you through."

My dad did not come to Ghana. He finally wrote, "Why don't you come home until you get better? Then you could go back and *give them another round*." That was a temptation, but the Ghanaian Christians suffered, too. They had no place to get away to rest. I decided to stay and recuperate with them. We were working hard to get the Jelik church ready for dedication. Sisi and other villages were in building programs. In the process, I was gradually resenting Eloise. I saw the mistakes she was making as a new missionary and my attempts to help her were as ineffective as with the driving.

One morning I went to the bathroom to brush my teeth. Suddenly I had a mental block. I know where I was, but I didn't know where I was supposed to be, like my bedroom. The blocking only happened once, but when we told the doctor about the incident, he said that a blood clot might possibly be moving in my head. They tested my blood and found it to be full of malaria parasites. The critters can clump and act like a blood clot to block a blood vessel. Malaria was always devastating to me. After treatment, I was much better. However, Eloise never ceased to use that episode to say I should go home. I was feeling overwhelmed by her in every aspect of our life. For instance, the two cats Lehmanns brought to Lois Lemm and me months ago from Saboba were still with us. Eloise was not happy about the food our cook fed to the cats. She refused to leave any table scraps on her plate *or mine*. The amount of food she consumed destroyed my appetite; my weight was going down. I suggested we get a dog if she did not like cats. She quickly retorted, "Well, what can a dog do?" I said, "Cats kill snakes, dogs bark at strangers, but I never thought in terms of a pet having to do something in exchange for its food." I was defensive of her changing everything at house, clinic, and churches to be in immediate control. The Ghanaian helpers were reacting to it. I could predict negative consequence in many of her choices! When the cats got no food at home, they were forced to go to the bush to hunt. One cat disappeared. The yardman was hunting wood for us and found the other cat dead in a trap. I wondered if she was aware that someone new should not make changes that quickly. It was making me ill to assert constructive input; if I had been totally well, perhaps I could have coped with it. I have learned that the most difficult situation is a new missionary who does not admit cultural shock and wants to impose their choices before learning the *why* of local ways. This was the second overwhelming situation, and too close together. The Mission Committee was accustomed to my being able to cope with anything, so they seemed to think my reaction to Eloise were caused by Najong #2.

In November, there was a business meeting of all missionaries in Tamale. Eloise and I went. Three men from the United States headquarters came. They were Thomas Zimmerman and Burt Webb, the newly elected Superintendent and Assistant Superintendent of the Assemblies of God, and Everett Phillips, Secretary for the Africa Division of our foreign missions. Burt Webb had prayed the prayer of ordination over me at the New Mexico District Council some years before when he was guest speaker. Then, he just happened to be in Washington, D.C. as I was leaving America in March 1959 and he prayed for my success and *protection*; perhaps it saved my life. The only business I recall in the Tamale meeting was that they voted to close Techamentia Clinic. Helen and I, trying to cooperate, had grossly overworked two years earlier to open it. They finally found an American nurse for Techamentia. At that meeting, she clearly stated, "There is no opportunity in Techamentia." I never felt that way about any place on earth. I refused to allow the devil to pile on one more disappointment; I gave it to God.

The other thing I recalled about the Tamale meeting was how great it was to be a part of the missionary family and how nearly I came not being with them ever again. As usual, the British nurses lightened the situation with a comic song:

(A take-off from Old MacDonald Had a Farm)

Old Ev' Phillips has a field, eieio,
From desert heat, our homes unsealed, eieio.
'Tis a go-slow here and a no-no there,
With ai here and everywhere a xa-xa, (no, in other languages)
Dilemmas here and palavers there,
Here it's money, there it's funny,
Everywhere it's fun and money.
A station here and a station there,
Here a clinic, there a cynic,
Everywhere a clinic-cynic.
Old Ev' Phillips has a field, EIEIO!

—(RD & AS)

Following the meeting, I rode to Saboba with Ruby and Peggy. I needed to visit the Konkombas. As they say, "Lest we see you with our eyes, we continue to question your condition of health." I was forced to sell my Volkswagen so Eloise and I had only the Chevrolet, but she was expecting her vehicle soon. We really needed two vehicles in order to have child welfare clinics every eleven miles, yet have an ambulance available for general and maternity emergencies. While I went to Saboba, Eloise went to Nakpanduri in the Chevy to care for the clinics and came to get me the following weekend. That allowed her to see Saboba and meet the

Konkombas.

At Christmas time, after the Tamale meeting, all missionaries got a greeting from Rev. Zimmerman. A note with ours said, "It was wonderful to sit together in the Tamale conference in November. We still praise God for His protection of Sister Charlese during the recent testings." About the same time, I wrote home that I was feeling much better since receiving treatment against the malaria bug. Christmas cards and letters poured in from America with encouraging words from family and friends. Christmas was always such a blessed time in Africa! In the morning at the local church, there were so many people that they sat on the edge of the platform and altar, and others looked in windows. After the pastor's Christmas message, the local youth group presented the birth of Jesus in drama form. People were still coming when the service was over. Afterwards, we took seventeen young people to outstation churches where they repeated the drama. One was Najong #1, one mile from Najong #2, where a chief walked for seven miles in the bush to attend. Everywhere we went, the mass of people stood outside and watched through windows, as the churches were too small. Finally, Eloise and I went to Bawku and ate a late Christmas dinner with the Don Jolley family. They had been busy celebrating earlier with their church people, too. We drove back to Nakpanduri, grateful that the next day was Saturday.

A letter still dated in December came from Raymond Brock, Promotions Division. He sent me a copy of a letter that came from a teenage girl in California and had been used in *The Pentecostal Evangel*. It read, "I am writing concerning the article in the November 29 *Pentecostal Evangel*. I had an experience that started August 8. I awoke speaking in another language. I dropped to my knees. I cannot quite explain how I felt. Then on Thursday, two weeks after all this started, I do not know whether I was asleep or not, a vision or dream came before me. It was short." She saw conflict that involved a black man and a light-complected woman near some small huts. She said, "I prayed with a real burden that night; something I had never before experienced. I wrote of it on a piece of paper and put it in my diary. My parents heard me praying and thought I must be having a bad dream, so my dad called to me. About 1 P.M., the burden was so heavy I rode my bicycle to the church to pray; afterward I went to the parsonage and told my pastor about it. I would like to know more about the incident in Ghana told in the *Evangel*." Rev. Brock continued in a later letter, "I see that Brother Cunningham, Editor of the *Evangel*, has given additional space to the Najong incident, in an editorial to mention again of God's marvelous answer to prayer and to tell about the prison sentences of those who beat you." From that day at Najong #2, things have happened constantly that have proven God sovereign in His directives, control, and use of situations. I will tell about them as they happened along throughout the years. Already the Najong #2 people were bringing their babies to child welfare clinics and their sick people for treatment. The two men who helped save my life and accepted Christ after the incident were the first from Najong #2 to bring their wives to prenatal clinic.

About dusk on January 7, 1960, Homer and Thelma Goodwin arrived from the Bible school in Kumbungu. They had brought Eloise's vehicle. Thank God, we were back to two vehicles and her's was a beautiful Mercedes. The Goodwins, being from West Texas, were like relatives. They spent the night, went to churches with us on Sunday morning, and left after lunch. They had to teach at the Bible School on Monday. Now that Eloise had a car, I started thinking of going to the coast for a rest. It had to be after we completed and dedicated the Jelik church. The Sisi church and others were far from complete, but I had taken pictures and they were looking good! I had been back in Ghana less than a year and so much had happened!

On Saturday, January 23, we dedicated the new Jelik church, complete with whitewashed walls and a corrugated tin roof, thanks to New Mexico. We sent invitations to Ghanaian Officials, pastors, and missionaries. Franklin, Aneice, and Amonna Sue McCorkle and the Smithermans came from Walewale. Franklin McCorkle, being Field Chairman, was speaker and cut the dedication ribbon. It was a day of rejoicing. An offering was received for more benches. One man had no money, but put *his shirt* in the offering. I had never seen that before even in America. Revival Tabernacle in Albuquerque gave money for the roof on the Jelik church; their pastor was Rev. and Mrs. W.F. Watkins. I reported to a specific church each time a church was roofed and dedicated. There were young Bimobas in Bible School at Kumbungu preparing to return and pastor those churches.

The McCorkles allowed nine-year-old Amonna Sue to spend that night with us in Nakpanduri. The next morning, I dropped her off in Walewale as I left for that long planned rest at the coast. On the Yeji ferry, crossing the Volta River, a young man approached me. He said, "Madam, why are you driving your lorry alone?" I said, "Because they wouldn't agree to take it on the airplane." We both laughed. Actually, I brought my vehicle, as it needed more work done on it. Still the young man persisted, "You are an old woman (my hair was blond; I was in my thirties); you should have a driver." Obviously, he was looking for employment. That day I drove about two hundred fifty miles through the Ashanti Forest to Kumasi. I believe the missionary family was the Melvin Harrells. They had a son born just that morning at 9 A.M. One daughter, only thirteen, cooked dinner for the whole family that evening. I stayed only through Monday and drove two hundred miles almost to Accra on Tuesday, January 26. I visited a few days with the Reginald Wallace family, former British Government Agent in Yendi District. We refreshed old memories while more repairs were done on my car. Next, I moved into Accra to stay a few days with the Kesslers. Vangie and Annette were big schoolgirls. Benny, their young brother, went to the beach with me. I had to hold his hand carefully, as even a small wave on the rocks would knock him down. Pools of water were left in and among the rocks when the tide when out. In one rather deep hole in a rock, a small octopus was stranded. I took off one thong and touched him; he grabbed it. When I yanked hard to retrieve my shoe, he colored the water so we could not see him. I suspect he went out with the next tide.

From Accra, I drove west almost one hundred miles along the coastline, past Winneba, Saltpond, and Cape Coast to Takoradi. I was there the whole month of February. I wrote in my diary that I was staying with a very nice missionary family. It was Edwin and Bernice Ziemann and their teenage daughter, Patty. On visits in years past to that mission house, I had slept in sort of a dormitory on the ground floor. With Marilyn away at school, they gave me her upstairs bedroom. From my window, I could look over the top of the lush forest and see the ocean waves hitting the shore. I went to the ocean almost every day, alone or with the Ziemanns. My conscience hurt for being gone from my post so long. I made throw pillows for Bernice to keep myself busy so I would not think. She was kind and made me believe she liked them.

Eloise wrote that everything was fine and sent my mail. I wrote my thanks; there was no phone at clinic stations. If they were not deep in the bush, the government would have had medical facilities there. That very fact provided the great opportunity we nurses had to run clinics, build churches, and watch them fill up. One of my letters was from Helen Kopp. Her mother died January 18. I wrote her. Ruby Johnson would say, "Changing co-workers out here in the bush is *for the birds!*" Ruby was also right when she called it, "An abnormal existence in the bush!" Rev. Garlock said to Helen and me before we left America, "It is best to gain respect one for another before leaving America." I had so anticipated the coming of Eloise and now I was a *nurse without a clinic.* Up to that time, it was the most vulnerable time in my missionary life; I was not contributing.

The annual missionary conference was to begin March 9 in Takoradi. Bernice was to feed over forty-seven people for almost a week. She was so efficient, but I helped her some in planning meals. I wrote the other missionaries for her. She was telling them what to bring: linens, cots, paper napkins, and a batch of cookies. Helping her plan gave me something to do. The missionaries arrived for business and fellowship; and it was a grand time. Tallmadge and Marjorie Butler and their son, Stephen just four years old, arrived in their private plane for a visit from Kedougou, Senegal. His music was on the Beams of Mercy recording label. At the conference, he sang, *Follow Me* and dedicated it to me. Some of the words were, "Oh, Jesus if I die upon a foreign field some day, 'Twould be no more than love demands; no less could I repay. No greater love hath mortal man than for a friend to die. These are the words He gently spoke to me. If just a cup of water, I place within your hand, then just a cup of water is all that I demand. But if by death to living they can Thy glory see, I'll take my cross and follow close to thee." It was indeed touching; I never met that little family again.

Eloise Smith arrived from Nakpanduri in her new vehicle. The Field Committee talked with her. As expected, she said she would be happy to stay at Nakpanduri alone. I don't remember talking with her about it; it just felt like she successfully *threw me out*. Mom and I had met Eloise in Springfield on my furlough. I had looked forward to having her as a co-worker that far back. It takes time to adjust and we had no time. The fact that I was from the wild, wild, west and she was from the colonial east may have made a difference. Our philosophies were poles apart. The Mission Committee told me that I should go home for a rest and perhaps Helen and I might get to return to Saboba when Ruby's furlough was due at the end of that year. After the conference, Ruby Johnson rode north with me through the jungle to Kumasi. There we caught up with the McCorkles. The Jolleys were there in their new truck just off the ship. We trekked north in a group to Tamale, where Ruby had parked her vehicle and she went on to Saboba. The McCorkles dropped out of the caravan at Walewale; the Jolleys led me on to Nakpanduri and went on to Bawku. The money to fly across the ocean kept nagging at my mind. We could build churches with that money. In America, I would be wishing I were back in Ghana. I felt that going home was not the answer, but I *also feared to insist on having my way.* The heartache and headache continued in spite of the rest. As a nurse, I knew it could be stress. In letters I wrote home, "I do not feel that bad, so I do not want to go home to be pitied, petted, nursed, or felt sorry for." I had been in Africa a year and, as in my dream, I had two more years to the end of my term. In another dream I was told, "It is up to you." To me, *I had succumbed.* Only my packing and the sale of my lemon-colored station wagon was yet to be done. The vehicle was just a year old and easily sold. The money would be returned to Speed-the-Light to apply to my next vehicle. I packed my belongings and took a pickup load for the Andersons to store in Tamale *until I returned.* I wrote a letter to Corporal Atta Darko in Gambaga to give authority for Eloise Smith to sign for and receive any money coming to the clinic until the mission could officially change names of authority at the bank.

On March 28, I wrote to Jim Kessler in Accra to secure me a reservation to fly to America about April 15. A reply came:

> You leave April 18, 7 A.M. via Pan American Airways to Dakar, Lisbon, Boston, and New York. Rev. Phillips is on that same flight. I have paid your Ghana income tax so you can depart. Looking for you! Jim and Delta."
> In such a short time, the Bimoba people and I had gone through many experiences and tough times. Admiration and respect had certainly developed. It seems I was almost jerked from them and had little time even to bid farewell properly. On the plane, I cried solidly the first

few hours. It was more as if I was in mourning; the tears rolled even when I was not aware of them. I sincerely believed I was more sick-at-heart than body. With time, I learned it was both. Somewhere in our flight, Rev. Phillips went another direction on his necessary itinerary. I wrote him later, "It was kind of you to help me get started on that difficult journey home. Rev. Walegar, instead of Rev. McGlasson, met me in New York and helped me get transferred to TWA for the journey on to Albuquerque.

I was back in New Mexico and facing an unknown future. In spite of our rough beginnings, Eloise and I continued to communicate about the clinics down through the years.

CHAPTER ELEVEN

Repairs and Recuperation
BSN at UNM, 1962

T HE HUDSONS ALLOWED ME to move back into one bedroom of their home in Albuquerque. A barrage of correspondence took place with friends, mission headquarters in Missouri, and missionaries in Ghana. A public address system and tape recorder had long been missing. I had wondered why the items never arrived in Ghana. It seems the four cartons had been lost in the New York Neptune Warehouse by a freight transfer company. When we inquired until they were found, a *storage and handling fee* was paid by Speed-the-Light. I don't think I ever knew who used the equipment. Wheeler and Eilene Anderson were advising me about personal items sold in Tamale. My 1959 vehicle was unsold.

The *Missionette Memos* for April, May, and June 1960 chose George and Stella Flattery of Senegal and me of Ghana to feature in their devotional for young girls. I had written my part before the beating incident, but the editors of the publication added the story of rescuing Pastor Samson's daughter at the end. Physical examinations and tests scheduled solidly limited my travel and speaking. Friends and family living or pastoring from the east to the west coasts were asking to hear about the rescue, but I wanted to get well and back to *whatever* God sent me to do in Africa.

In June 1960, I was able to attend the School of Missions in Springfield, Missouri. The British nurses, Ann and Becky, were there from Nakpanduri Clinic. They were a novelty and made it interesting. We enjoyed visiting with missionaries from all over the world and had one recreational outing each year. That year we went to Branson, Missouri to watch the *Little Shepherd of the Hills* played on the hillsides. They actually burned the schoolhouse. One woman asked Rev. Hogan, Executive Director of Foreign Missions, "May we wear pantsuits to Branson?" He replied, "Some women will miss the Rapture because they will not know what to wear!"

Franklin McCorkle, Ghana Field Chairman, had sent two pieces of Kenti cloth from missionaries and Ghanaian Ministers to be presented to Rev. and Mrs. Noel Perkin on behalf of their retirement after thirty-three years. He was known as *Mr. Missions!* I presented the Kenti during the School of Missions and pictures were taken. As a novice in the presence of such great people, I was very nervous. Rev. Perkin sent me great pictures of the presentation and a copy of the thank-you letter he wrote to Ghana missionaries and ministers for the Kenti Cloth. He added, "I hope you are feeling better in health. We are proud of you and trust God's guidance in your future."

My parents sold their business and moved to Colorado. I felt almost too ill to go to the New Mexico family camp in July 1960. I weighed less than I had ever weighed as an adult. This would have been good, except for the reasons. I hesitated when I was asked to go to the platform to greet the people as a returning missionary. Rev. Robert Northrop came, took my arm, and escorted me to the platforms. That family was already admired and this kindness was forever etched on my mind. It was another necessary step, as I could do it alone from then on.

Dr. Overton, orthopedic surgeon at Lovelace Clinic, had decided on a trial of conservative treatment of my back rather than immediate surgery. I wrote to Rev. Phillips, "More than anything else I want to return to Africa, but I want to be completely well. While I am waiting, I will utilize my time by working toward a degree in the new nursing program at UNM." I enrolled in the fall semester, 1960. Part of the original entrance exam into my basic diploma program of nursing was taken at UNM in 1949, so they were aware of the extent of my former education. The mental block that occurred in Africa transferred to the education process. I went to a psychiatrist at Lovelace Clinic without telling anyone. He solved the problem in one visit. He said, "When a woman feels safe in her own home and the hot water heater explodes and burns her, she may develop this syndrome. You may not have believed, even without knowing it, that those people whom you loved would beat you. Each time blocking occurs, admit to yourself that they did beat you. This syndrome should then leave slowly as it came." I tried it; the blocking slowly left.

In one class, I was assigned to study a family with children. I chose the Lawrence and Nina Green family. He held an office in the NMDC in Albuquerque. They had three daughters: Lavenial Reveille, age sixteen and a junior at Highland High School; LoRee Chery, a middle girl like me, age twelve and in Jefferson Junior High School; NeVelda Sunny would soon be six and starting school. Sunny was so tiny, weighing sixty-four pounds. The family agreed to talk with me for the study. One evening, the Hudsons and I ate dinner with the Green family. Mrs. Hudson was placing the silverware. She put two forks at one place and to herself she said aloud, "Oh, Onie Marie, you are so stupid." Later as we were seated for dinner, Sunny said, "Oh, Aunt Onie, you are so stupid." Rev. Green flushed with embarrassment and exclaimed, "Sunny! That is a very bad word which we do not use." Sunny opened her mouth in awe as she looked at Mrs. Hudson who had *just used that word*. The incident about the forks was explained to Rev. Green. I was learning from the family that I chose to report on.

Dr. Overton said swimming would strengthen my back muscles against any injury or pain. I learned to swim at the YWCA. My brother, Calvin Lee, was still employed at Albuquerque National Bank. I spent Christmas 1960 with him and his family. His daughter, Roxanne, became my swimming buddy at the YWCA. She was still comfortable calling me Auntie Who.

A letter came from Eloise Smith. She had been the only nurse with the Bimobas for five months after I left. She said the British nurses, Ann and Becky, had returned from furlough for Nakpanduri Clinic. Ruby Johnson and Peggy Scott were soon to go on furlough from Saboba, so Eloise was moving to Saboba. She told me about a wreck she had with her beautiful Mercedes-Benz pulling my small trailer loaded with our furniture. She sustained minor injuries; I was so sorry! Helen Kopp's mother had died, so she went to Saboba Clinic in March 1961 to be with Eloise. She and Eloise wrote me quite often. Then Eloise left on furlough and Helen was alone for a matter of months; all nurses seemed to experience that eventually.

I had used the Hudson's '55 Studebaker so much that in February I bought it. The spring semester 1961 was heavy with regular college courses. I enrolled for anthropology, psychology, and three classes in sociology at the same time. Some required a book report each day on some point of view. Wow! I was that girl who never learned to read until I got glasses in the seventh grade! I never read a book completely through until I was a senior in high school. I quickly signed up with a tutor for a fast reading course; it improved my life to this very day! In a sociology class called *Formation of the Personality*, I discovered how many young students needed help to retain their faith in colleges. The instructor said, " —

stupid missionaries who go to foreign countries to change people and do not know the *scientific method of change.*" I could not sit still for that one! I raised my hand, identified myself as one of those *stupid ones*, but confessed that I did not go to Africa to change anyone. He asked me what I meant. I said that, historically, Jesus existed and that He said if He went away, the Holy Spirit would come and testify of Him. We go to teach people what the Word of God says about Jesus, and then the Holy Spirit does His job of drawing people to Christ. I insisted that I did not do the changing. I said that I believed he might influence the masses with his scientific method of brainwashing, but he could not change an individual if they chose not to be changed, *even unto death.* He replied, "I suppose you have been taught that all your life!" I replied, "I was not raised a Christian. My parents made and sold alcohol during Prohibition and my dad gambled. I never saw my parents inside a church until I was thirteen years old. I believe our whole family accepted Jesus, God's Son, as our means of salvation and became Christians within the same month." Students called, "Amen!" for me while others called, "Amen!" for the professor. One day, that professor met me on the campus and said, "I hope this class is not too much of a challenge for you." I replied, "On the contrary; an alternate viewpoint is necessary." He hurried on. In the next class he exclaimed, "These students! Some want a passing grade when they obviously aren't learning what is taught." I raised my hand and said, "I do understand, you are teaching a scientific method of brainwashing which neither gives place for faith in the supernatural nor considers the strength of a person's self-will, even unto death. I want my faith and plan to work hard to keep it." On the final day of the class he asked me directly, "Now, what do you think of your missionary efforts to change people?" I replied, "I still say we did not go there to change the people. One purpose of God's Holy Spirit is to do the changing. You continue to give no place for the supernatural (God)." He replied, "I do not have the capacity for such faith." I stated sincerely, "I am sorry! It also takes faith to believe God is *not* there." One student kept telling me, "He will fail you!" He did not; he said I proved that I understood by my disagreement. I have kept in touch with one student who went through that interesting semester with me. After graduation, she moved to Kansas, married, and had three children. My needed courses were completed. On July 18, 1961, I sat for the Graduate Record Exams and passed. I was given an evaluation that stated, "Possibly a photographic memory." My cousin, Robert, put that into perspective with, "Depends on what you do with that photograph!" My observation was, "I suspect a photographic memory could be a *precursor to hardening of the arteries.*" However, after my problem of blocking, this was quite a miracle! I completed in time to help as camp nurse in the Mountainair Summer Youth Camps. I went through graduation exercise later in 1962.

Becky and Ann wrote from Nakpanduri Clinic that Simon Dzato (pronounced *Jato*) Masak (a son of the Najong #2 chief who held my car keys in his hand while we were being beaten) and his wife, Eunice, from Najong #1 (a sister of the girl we rescued) got married and had a one-year-old daughter. Dzato's uncle's village had received a girl years ago and was to reciprocate with a girl later. The uncle wanted to promise Dzato's small daughter in exchange. Dzato was planning to go to Bible College and did not feel this was right. What if his daughter wanted to go to college in the future? They were asking for prayer for guidance. It sounded as if the results of the War of Najong #2 had made people aware that *they had a choice.* It was a victory that should be used when appropriate. They did not give their daughter in exchange; she grew up and went to college. Dzato, her father, graduated from two Bible Colleges to become the Principal of Northern Ghana Bible Institute at Kumbungu (NGBI). When Pastor Namyela wrote from Bunkpurugu, he told me about the problem involving Dzato and Eunice's daughter. Then he added, "God has given Karen and me a son, born March 10. We now have Susanna, Priscilla, and Gideon. Madam, we will be very happy when you can come back to Ghana; tell us when you will be coming."

I flew to Portland, Oregon on August 18 to the biennial General Council of the Assemblies of God. Rev. and Mrs. Hudson went by car. General Councils are awesome; we get to work on our objectives for being an organization. During that council, I met a lady who was married to the Southern California District Superintendent. Her maiden name was Florence Blossom. She told me, "I was a co-worker with Beulah Buckwalder, who died in Yendi. The Konkombas at Saboba shot an arrow into a British District Commissioner's shoulder; I helped to remove that arrow when he arrived in Yendi." Missionaries and Konkombas in Ghana had told me the same story! I rode back to New Mexico from Portland with the Hudsons. In Yellowstone National Park, the Hudsons were compelled to go fishing! They had caught some fish when a bear came by and said, "Thank you, I'll have those." Someone grabbed the fish and ran to put them in the trunk of the car. We barely got inside the car before the bear realized he could not get into the trunk and came to the car door. We left. We visited the Dinosaur National Monument in northern Utah and Colorado. We visited Colorado's Planetarium in Denver; then it was a straight run south to Albuquerque.

My back was paining fiercely when I returned from that trip. I had to wear a brace even as I continued my part-time job at Presbyterian Hospital; Dr. Overton was talking surgery. The Hudsons were very busy people; I chose not to be a burden if I had surgery. I moved to a small apartment on High Street. On November 11, at Battaan Memorial Methodist (Lovelace) Hospital, I had a laminectomy at the level of the fifth lumbar vertebra. My mother came from Colorado to be with me when I was discharged from the hospital. My father was still not well from a gastrectomy and they had a business to run, so Mom did not stay long. Then the Berna-lillo County Public Health Nurse, who helped me through that UNM course, visited me several times. The pain never went away. Dr. Overton said I could not return to Africa for one year after surgery, to be certain of the success. Rev. Phillips wrote that I should pass a psychological testing from a Dr. Montgomery in Dallas, Texas before my return to Africa. I made an appointment for the following April.

In December 1961, I was able to be with my sister and her family in San Diego for Christmas. I even scheduled three services for the first week in January 1962 with friends in nearby towns. Those were in Escondido, where Fred and Bonney Chambers lived; near El Cajon, where Stanley and Irene Davis lived; and in Anaheim, where Lola and Doyle Wilson lived. As usual, on my return to Albuquerque I had a stack of letters. Eloise Smith and Helen Kopp wanted to know about the success of the surgery. Hal and Naomi Lehmann had been with them for Christmas. The Saboba Clinic had "*only* twelve thousand nine hundred eleven patient visits in 1961."

I was very proud to learn that my brother, Calvin Lee, was the February 1962 Anniversary Honoree at Albuquerque National Bank. I had memories of working as a bookkeeper in that bank, from 1948 to 1949. I saved my money for my basic nurse's training. Calvin Lee had worked there fourteen years and had advanced to Head Teller and an officer with a title. Roxanne, his eight-year-old daughter, was still one of the joys of my life.

The Hudsons had moved into a new house on Quincy Street in Albuquerque. Since I was going to be traveling a lot, I gave up my apartment on High Street and they allowed me to use Quincy Street as my return address. I planned to return to Africa soon. The New Mexico District Council was held in Clovis the first week in April 1962. I had appointments to speak in church services and women's meetings in eastern New Mexico and western Texas while on my way to the required appointment with a Dallas psychiatrist. The results of that testing went directly to mission headquarters. Earl and Rowena Vanzant were the pastors in Portales; Kenneth and Patsy George and Tommy and Linda Crider were pastoring in West Texas towns. Homer and Thelma Goodwin were in Hereford. I spoke in all their churches. As I was setting up my equipment in Hereford, Thelma Goodwin and another lady approached me. Thelma said, "Charlese, I want you to meet this lady. Remember when we told you in Africa that you reminded us of someone? Well, this is the lady and *she is your mother's first cousin.*" I went home with Meta and her husband, Jack Wederbrook, and we talked family. She said her German grandfather spelled his name *Lehmann*; some part of his wife's family originated in Surrey County, England.

After the psychiatric testing, I spent time with my friend Martha Roberts Sherrick, who lived near Dallas. I had chauffeured her in New Mexico, before she went to India in 1947. We decided to attend chapel at SAGC, our old college. It was mission day, Wednesday April 25. We arrived a bit late and were rushing up the front steps when Elizabeth Galley, Director of their Missions Program, met us. (We students at SAGC had prayed for her when she was a prisoner of war in China in the 1940s.) On those school steps, she grabbed the huge yellow hat off my head and informed me I was late! She said she wrote to New Mexico to have me speak *that day.* I had left home before the invitation arrived! We walked swiftly down the aisle and directly to the platform, where I *started to sit down.* I was ushered directly to the podium, where I spoke to a full chapel. As a student, I would have fainted had I been asked to speak on that platform with *days of preparation.* Now the students were so easy to talk to and pulled from me what they wanted to know. I asked someone if they had cut down the size of the chapel. As a student, it had seemed huge; now it seemed so small! While there, we learned that Miss Florence Steidel, from the leper colony in

Liberia, had died. That was where Lois Lemm came from to help me in Nakpanduri, Ghana. Miss Lillian Trasher, of Egypt, had also died less than six months prior. When I planned to go to Africa as a teenager, I thought I might go to help Miss Trasher. She had an orphanage in Egypt and was called the "Nile Mother."

The money I was receiving was being sent to my account at mission headquarters for travel and equipment. I was scheduled for meetings all the way back to Albuquerque. At a fellowship meeting in Albuquerque in early May, the sectional ladies gave me a birthday shower. I told them my plans to return to Africa. I even made a quick trip to Montrose, Colorado to bid my parents farewell. I visited my Great Uncle Sam and Aunt Bessie Layman, who had a cabin in the Colorado Mountains. They actually lived in Texas, between Earth and Muleshoe.

In the first part of June, I went by train to the School of Missions in Springfield, Missouri. On the way, I visited with Betty Jo (Compton) Jones and family in Tulsa. She was a sister to Vernon Compton (my computer tutor while writing this book) and to Clairena (Compton) Redfearn in Alaska. At the School of Missions, Ruby Johnson and Peggy Scott said they were returning to Africa on the Barber Line on June 27. Ruby was going to help Helen at Saboba Clinic. Peggy was not a nurse; she was to help with Sunday school and youth projects. Ruby's visa did not arrive. Peggy sailed alone—the *story of our lives* as we juggled American, African, mission, ship, airline, and personal schedules.

While itinerating and at camp, I met other relatives. Bill and Gail Dunning were pastoring in Silver City. At family camp in Mountainair in the summer of 1962, I met Eddie Lee Layman and his wife, Frances, Gail (Layman) Dunning's father and mother. Eddie Lee was another of my mother's first cousins, the son of Uncle Gilmer of Hereford, Texas. Gale's parents simultaneously exclaimed that I looked like Eddie's sister, Meta Wederbrook. By that time, I had met Meta. I was amazed as that is exactly what Homer and Thelma Goodwin said when I met them in the Gold Coast of West Africa in 1955. In this process, I learned that Daniel Grubbs, a pastor in Deming, was married to Dorothy, another granddaughter of Uncle Gilmer in Hereford, Texas. In our lifetime, we knew very little about Mom's Layman family in West Texas. Now we were meeting them at the Assemblies of God camps and churches. Could even religious preference be a case for *"them powerful genes?"* Or is the world just shrinking because of modern transportation?

The approved Ghana *field money project* was the Bible Schools, in particular the Southern Ghana Bible College on the coast at Saltpond. Everett Phillips encouraged me to help. Letters came from Oliver and Peggy Swaim, who were living at Saltpond, and Jim and Delta Kessler, in the United States on furlough from Saltpond; they were explaining the needs: a dike to divert floodwater, an unfinished house for the second missionary family, scholarships for students, and lorry fare for students going to practice points. At the New Mexico family camp, an offering was designated to help meet the Saltpond needs. In August through November, I designated one thousand two hundred forty dollars for the unfinished mission house and seventy-two dollars for an earthen dam. I sent over eight hundred dollars to world missions; seventy percent of that could be designated for Saltpond. I kept seven hundred dollars for four months of travel to forty-three towns and for speaking sixty times. In San Jon, the pastor was Mrs. Hermond Ragland and in Logan, Mrs. Frank Norred, former Southwestern College friends. The R.G. Hutsells were in Texico, the Botelers in Lovington, and the Tillerys in Carlsbad. The Jenkins were pastoring in Artesia and the Newmans in Hobbs. They each sponsored a SGBI student for ten dollars per month.

The McClains were pastoring in Alamogordo and the Chaneys in Silver City. James and Jan Trewern were pastoring in Bayard, where I was November 7. Before the service,

I went on a neighborhood stroll with their only son at the time, Jay. He was showing me where certain people lived and telling me the names of their dogs. We sat on a cement wall to rest. The huge, almost-full moon appeared. I asked, "Jay, do you know the moon is made of green cheese?" I got busy and forgot to follow this up with his mother until years later. While standing in a cafeteria line behind Jan Trewern at a New Mexico camp, I told her what I had said to Jay. The words burst from her, "So you were the one who told him that!" She laughed, but said it took ages to convince him otherwise. Wow! As the Africans ask, "And did you learn anything?" I hope I did!

While Helen was in Saboba alone, she wrote that she spent a night in a tree, when a swelling river suddenly inundated her Jeep. She also related a famous dream: "I dreamed all missionaries on furlough were to attend a two week *School of Donkeys*, where they would be taught by DFM staff to ride and establish rapport with a donkey. Diplomas would be issued. It was decided that, WHEREAS, Ghana missionaries had more car expenses and WHEREAS Ghana is flush with donkeys, all who returned after 1963 would have to consider using a donkey for local work and cars only for trips of length and hauling. Any station desiring two vehicles must be happy with one car and one donkey. Allowance for the donkey's *hay and corn* would be five dollars monthly and a classification of *H & C* would appear on the monthly statement. This money would be raised on a *Ghana Donkey Day* in American churches, the second Sunday in October. Speed-the-Light would agree to purchase donkeys from the Ghana Government. The missionary could name his own donkey. Travel in excess of one hundred miles per month would be allowed two Quabo (pence) for each additional mile for extra hay and corn. There, coming up the Saboba road were dear Hal and Naomi Lehmann, their feet dragging against the heaving sides of two dedicated donkeys!" Hal Lehmann added a note, "The young shall see visions;

the old shall dream dreams. I am thankful God let Helen dream this rather than Phil Hogan! Better that this be simple prophecy than rigid policy!"

In northern New Mexico, snow was a constant problem. The Criders had moved to Milan, the Masons were at Los Alamos, and the Elliots in Aztec. I spent Thanksgiving Day, November 29, with the Dyers in Taos. I went to Indian Mission churches, every one that could fit a service into their schedule. Charles and Coralee Lee were in Shiprock. In November, I spoke twenty-one times in sixteen towns. Only a few times I unloaded a 16 mm movie projector alone; usually I had help. In Farmington, where the Stovers pastored, back pain and possible pneumonia made me cancel all appointments; I returned to my home in Albuquerque. Within days, Dr. Overton planned another laminectomy along with a spinal fusion. It was difficult for me to inform Rev. Phillips. This uncertainty was even depressing *me*! The Executive Committee in Ghana could not depend on me to replace nurses due for a furlough. Ruby and Helen wrote that, because of the roads in Africa, I might profit from a spinal fusion. They also said, "Thanks for seven hundred dollars from Mrs. Newbill for a cement cistern for the Saboba kitchen." It was from New Mexico!

Helen was the first to write me about the horrible fire at Tili, a village twenty-two miles out of Bawku. Bawku was forty miles north of Nakpanduri Clinic. (Sandra and the Homer Goodwin family wrote later in more detail.) A malfunctioning gasoline engine caused a fire and the death of Sidney Goodwin near Christmas time. He was the husband of Sandra and the father of Gwenda. He was the first son of Homer and Thelma Goodwin. The Goodwins have been special to me since about 1939. In 1962, Homer and Thelma were living in Kumasi, about three hundred miles south of Bawku where Sid, Sandy, and Gwenda would be stationed. Presbyter Abiwini Kusasi had planned, along with the Tili Na Ba (Chief), to honor the two Goodwin families at a great

Christmas rally. Sid had lived with his parents in Bawku as a child and so had grown up with the Africans. After the fire, Sidney was admitted to the Bawku Hospital. It was staffed with excellent Basil Mission (Swiss-German) doctors and nurses. Southern Baptist Hospital personnel from Nalerigu, sixty miles south, assisted. The American Embassy and President Nkrumah's private plane flew in blood plasma from Accra, the capitol city. This involved both the British Royal Air Force and Ghana Air Force personnel. A British burn pathologist, on loan to the Ghana Army, was found to have the same blood type as Sid's and he donated blood. Peggy Scott seemed to be their Girl Friday, transporting people and blood to and from the airport. With Helen and Ruby at Saboba Clinic and Ann and Becky at Nakpanduri Clinic, Sidney had the best special duty nurses. Wow! What a loss *on New Years Day*! Hal Lehmann and Franklin McCorkle assisted at the funeral. Sidney is buried in Bawku.

My house hunting became serious when Dr. Overton and others convinced me I should have a fusion. Before I went to Africa, I had sent my 1953 tax refund of seventy-nine dollars to my friends, John and Grace (Davis) Embry, in Sweetwater, Texas, for interest compounded for over nine years. It had reached the grand amount of six hundred sixty-five dollars. I sent for it. Neither John nor Grace answered. A banker sent the money with a note that said they were both in the hospital. I learned that John did not survive that illness. I looked at buildings for sale that included two or more apartments; I could live in one and rent the others for income to pay the mortgage payment. However, I settled on this little house on Hume Street, where I would take over a veteran's very low interest. The cost of taxes and insurance was included in the monthly payment of sixty-six dollars, so my monthly allowance from the mission was raised from seventy-eight dollars to one hundred three dollars. New Mexico people donated used furnishings. I am living in that same house and using most of that same furniture forty-five years later. I rented the house to make the payment when my work took me out of Albuquerque or the United States.

That spring and summer were busy as I went to the New Mexico Ministers' Institute, where Rev. Edgar Bethany, Jan Crouch's father, was the speaker. I was camp nurse at youth camps and attended the family camp where Rev. A. N. Trotter, the brother to Mrs. H.B. Garlock, was speaker. I missed my first School of Missions, in Springfield, since returning to America. When the money I raised in New Mexico went through the proper computers in the Missions Department and on to those needing it, I started receiving thank-you notes. Jim Kessler wrote from America and Oliver Swaim from Southern Ghana Bible College. Oliver said the protective dam was built and other projects were progressing. Eddie Ziemann was commuting seventy miles from Takoradi to teach, and the second residence was definitely needed in Saltpond before Jim and Delta Kessler returned in August. Eddie Ziemann was field chairman at the time and wrote that the Russians were engaged in geological survey (probably drilling for oil) around Saltpond and were driving the cost of housing out of sight. He requested more money for the second house in Saltpond than I had already sent from my itinerary. He begged my pardon and requested help to buy a new refrigerator for Takoradi as many of their conferences were held there. Everett Phillips wrote from Missouri that he was having the amount for the refrigerator taken out of my surplus support account, but if I did not agree to his actions, *he would itinerate and replace it.* Of course, he was joking, but I replied that he was welcome to itinerate in New Mexico! I not only agreed about the refrigerator, but I also asked permission of the New Mexico District Committee to send another sixteen hundred dollars for the second bungalow at Saltpond. I hesitated to send more as I might need the second surgery. Rev. Phillips responded immediately with, "The sixteen hundred dollars more will be like a gift from heaven to Oliver Swaim. Let me express appreciation to you for your very fine spirit."

While I was home repairing physically, Russian Communism became a strong influence in Ghana and the term *political correctness* (The "10 Commandments of Communism.")
was introduced. Pastor E.J. Namyela, one of those beaten in
Najong #2, was arrested and put in prison for *political incorrectness*. One Sunday in Bunkpurugu Church, he was preaching on Hebrews 9:27, "It is appointed unto man once to die,
but after that the judgment." He stated that everyone would
someday die, even their President. They were to believe
their president, their savior, O Sajafu, would never die. A
man in the congregation reported Pastor Namyela's statement to officials. Pastor was held in prison without a trial.
Later, when the political power changed, he was allowed a
trial. A judge said, "It is a known fact that we are all going to
die. Go home to your family!" The case was dismissed.

When I first heard the term *political correctness* used in
the United States, I was amazed that Americans had allowed
this communist term to be introduced in a free society. It is
an oxymoron! How can we have *freedom of speech* with *political incorrectness*? If the Ten Commandments were removed,
why would we want to replace them with another set of
rules that remove our so-called freedom? We never voted
on political correctness in America; it just appeared in the
American vocabulary as it did earlier in Africa. The Ten
Commandments do not change; in a society with two or
more political parties, the political *incorrectness* changes with
each party. There is no absolute. When he was free, Pastor
Namyela and his family moved from Bunkpurugu to pastor
the Toma Church at Saboba, the first church I ever helped to
build. It was one of the larger congregations in all of northern Ghana.

Back in New Mexico, I was working on my problems. I
tried to get a part-time job until it was time to have surgery,
but no hospital would hire me with my physical history.
Then someone directed me to a woman with terminal mela-

noma. Her husband was desperate, as his wife wanted to die at home, but the doctor would not let her go home without a registered nurse. The man was kind and put a cot near his wife's bed so I could rest when necessary. He even rolled her bed up and down when it was needed, so I did not have to bend. I supervised her care, medications, and food but did little actual physical care. When his wife died and I was off the job, he sent a lovely arrangement of flowers to my home. I never saw him again.

Dr. Overton knew that I had been in a car wreck as a teenager and had some back problems since that time. However, it had not stopped my education or employment down through the years. When they did the first surgery in 1961, he stated that since I had lived with the original back problems for so long that they would not disturb them, but would do a laminectomy to repair the more recent injury. That had not eliminated the problem, so they planned to do surgery that was more extensive. Finally, a myelogram was done to direct them in surgery on September 4, 1963. This included at least one more laminectomy, above or below the one done before. They chipped bone from the crest of the ilium (hip bone) and used it to fuse the bony spines from the fourth lumbar vertebra to the sacrum. When they finished the surgery, but had not yet sutured the incision, I was allowed to awaken on the operating table to see whether I could move my feet. The area burned as if red pepper had been poured into it. I could not move my right foot. They put me to sleep again, did more surgery, and sutured the incision after that. Dr. Overton was very concerned about the right foot all during my convalescence; full use never returned. As a student nurse in St. Joseph's Hospital I had surgically scrubbed, stood on a box, and helped Dr. Overton and his personal orthopedic nurse perform this very same procedure. He was considered the best! At those times, I declared emphatically, "I would die before I would allow anyone to do this to me!" The pain and lack of use of my right leg forced me to change my mind just twelve years later. For days during recovery in the hospital, I was given so much morphine that I learned exactly what a psychedelic trip was. Mine was a continuous kaleidoscope of colors in geometric designs projected on the ceiling. Pages turned continuously. I concluded that if I had a camera, I would take pictures and become an instant millionaire! In spite of the beauty, I did not like that mentally spaced-out feeling and begged for an aspirin; *I would not be a good dope addict!*

Before I was discharged from the hospital, I was put in a full body cast. They said this was because Dr. Overton was going to be out of the United States for a short time and he did not want anything to go amiss. I wondered if perhaps he thought I might start traveling, loading, and unloading 16 mm projectors if he did not tie me down. Whatever the reason, it was a rough three months in a full body cast and on a walker! Only my head, arms, and legs were left out. The half could not be told! No picture a person could imagine could equal the twenty-four hour torture! When I inhaled there seemed not to be enough room for my chest to expand; I dared not gain an ounce! When I exhaled and my chest got smaller, it sucked air down into the cast. When I inhaled, the air was blown out of the cast by my expanding chest. After *one week* the air exhausted from the cast and blown up into my face told me I needed a bath *badly!* Multiply that by *twelve weeks* and the putrid odor that came off rotting flesh! From the beginning, I got a stick, tied a washcloth onto it, and swabbed under the cast. I poured talcum powder into it all the way around. To occupy my time I got a job with the Albuquerque National Bank again, where I had worked before becoming a nurse. They gave me pages of phone numbers to call for marketing their branch bank on East Central Avenue and the newest one on Lomas. I explained services their bank and branch banks offered. All this was done while lying on my left side with papers and a telephone on my bed. I wrote fiction and non-fiction mission stories. John Garlock was Missions Editor at headquarters and said they paid one-half cent per word. He passed on what I wrote to potentially interested departments. Some stories were printed.

CHAPTER TWELVE

Teaching in Nursing Education

MOM AND DAD HAD moved back to New Mexico from Colorado some months before. When I had the second surgery, they moved into my house to help during my recovery. They bought a laundry and a house at Lomas and Ninth Street in Albuquerque. They started operating the laundry immediately, but did not move to their house completely until I could cook for myself. On TV, New Mexico's Governor Campbell had just reminded us that Thanksgiving Day was special as it marked three hundred years we had been giving thanks to the Almighty God for the freedoms in America. This was the scenario of my life on November 22, 1963, when the news flashed that John F. Kennedy, Jr., thirty-fifth President of the United States, had been slain by a sniper's bullet. It was a diversion from my circumstances for a time, but a sad one! I suspect there were few dry eyes in America, regardless of political preference. As the plot thickened, the killing of Kennedy's assassin and the funeral of President Kennedy totally engulfed the news. It occurred to me that freedom for the individual came with a steep price and could even vanish! When the shocking dust began to settle, we had a new President, Lyndon B. Johnson.

Christmas 1963 was a blur; I was still in the cast. I sent a Tammy Doll to Janie Dalton, a special little friend in England whom I delivered in London almost ten years before. In the New Year, she wrote a letter of thanks. She had a Dachshund called Dash. Her *mum* continued to inform me about Jane. I believe she became a secretary in the Houses of Parliament and later an editor of a newspaper.

The body cast was finally removed. I used a walker, as I had lost the muscle tone in all my body. With physical therapy, I improved slowly. Mom and Dad were slowly moving to their new address downtown. As soon as they left and I could drive, I responded to an ad in the *Albuquerque Journal* and got Miss Kitty, a calico kitten. I named her after Matt Dillon's girl friend on TV. It was something else alive in the house. My activity was limited and few people visit in larger towns. Karen Hughes came on some Saturdays, as she worked weekdays at Sears. We played Yahtzee and other table games. My UNM Public Health Nurse, who helped during prior surgery, phoned. She told me about a Civil Service position opening soon for a teacher at the Indian School of Practical Nursing here in Albuquerque. She said she was applying. She gave me an address and I sent for the application form, filled it out, and mailed it.

Eloise Smith sailed to Ghana on the *M.S. Corneville* on January 25, 1964. I could not believe her year of furlough was gone and here I sat. Devastating! She wrote in transit and mailed the letter from Monrovia, Liberia. She would be at Nakpanduri Clinic, where Nurse Ruth Anderson would soon join her from the northwestern United States. Ruth was a school nurse at CBI in Springfield, Missouri when Eloise was a student. Helen Kopp and Ruby Johnson were at Saboba Clinic. Helen wrote that her furlough was due in about three months. She said everyone wanted me to get well and come back, but that my things were rotting in the storehouse in Tamale. The stored items had been the last thing on my mind and I knew I must recuperate at least another year. I had come home for *six months* and it had turned into years! I wrote Wheeler and Eilene Anderson to sell, give, and throw away my belongings! A second letter from Helen followed on the heels of her first. She was in Pennsylvania; her father had a coronary occlusion. She admonished, "You be careful not to overdo; give your back a chance to fuse solidly." She said I had raised funds for projects when I should have been resting. She said, "I left Ruby in Saboba *alone.*"

In April, I rode with someone to attend the fiftieth anniversary of the Assemblies of God in Missouri. While there, Rev. Phillips told me that the Pan African Conference was to convene in September in Enugu, Nigeria. He asked if more of my surplus support funds could be used to assist some of the Ghana ministers to attend the conference. I talked with Rev. Hudson and other NMDC officials present and we decided on five hundred. I returned to New Mexico where I started working part-time at Battaan Memorial Methodist Hospital (Lovelace Medical Center). I worked as relief for every floor and department including the delivery room, where I assisted doctors instead of delivering the babies myself. The service of midwives was not yet accepted in America; in that, I was far ahead of my time. I lived to see midwives utilized in birthing units of hospitals, but never without a doctor available if necessary! I teased the doctors that the most serious complication in second stage of labor was the *strong arm of an intern on one end of forceps.* My rotation even included *night supervisor* of the whole hospital when the regular one had a day off or went on leave. My strength gradually increased and I was able to work sixty percent of a full-time job. I continued physical therapy and piano lessons, and spoke at a few banquets. I sold the Studebaker and bought the Hudson's 1964 Ford Galaxy when they bought a new car. It was the right move; my travels increased and the car was so comfortable and dependable. In a required monthly mission report, I included a visit to a Dr. Newfeld. He said that while lying in the cast without exercise, I had exacerbated an existing condition called endometriosis. They said it might take surgery to correct the situation. *What, surgery again?* When Rev. and Mrs. Phillips returned to the United States, he wrote me the sternest letter I had ever received from him regarding my return to Africa, "...decision by the Foreign Missions Committee...desire your full and complete recovery to health and at least one year of full-time nursing before we can consider your return to Africa." It hurt, but I knew they were right.

An invitation came from Mrs. Robert E. Goggin, District Director of the Women's Ministries of Oklahoma. She asked me to tell the rescue story on July 17, 1964 for the women's part of Missions Day at their District Council. I agreed and sent promotional items requested. I flew to Oklahoma City, where the Goggins met me and I lodged in a bedroom of their home. The night before I spoke, I took a pillow and a blanket from the bed and slept on the floor because of the pain in my back; I was forced to do this often. I discovered after I got to Oklahoma that the main speaker for Missions Day, after I spoke in the women's preliminary, was J. Phillip Hogan, Director of World Missions of the Assemblies of God, with other titles. His wife, Virginia, was with him. From the podium, he chided me for not being in Africa. Other officials had done it, but in a *kinder, gentler way*. For instance, at a General Council I saw Thomas Zimmerman, General Superintendent of the Assemblies of God. When we greeted, he laughed loudly and said, *for the entire world to hear,* "Charlese, am I following you, or are you following me?" We all knew he was asking, "Why aren't you in Africa, if you say God called you there?" That was their job; they must be good stewards of God's money, time, and message. The present speaker had been in meetings and knew I was trying to get physically better while contributing my time and thousands of dollars to missions anyway; he knew that. He had been in mission committees where some reacted to my many surgeries. I was not only angry; I was the one who was *hurting*. I believed God was the One to heal me and I wanted to be in Africa, but the pain was still there! As usual, I did not try to explain; I felt my problem was too small to consume the valuable time of top men.

After night shifts at Battaan Hospital, I got home about 8 A.M. and went straight to bed. One morning my phone jolted me awake from a deep sleep. It was my niece, Roxanne. She said, "Auntie, this is my tenth birthday. Miss Kitty should have her kittens on my birthday; I want to come over." I said, "Well, honey, I cannot tell Miss Kitty when to have her babies, but I will call you when she does." I went back to sleep. Later that day, I heard Miss Kitty cry outside my bedroom window; she had never done that before! She had a *private midwife* at the delivery of her three babies. I phoned Roxanne's mom, Evelyn, and they came over to help Miss Kitty brag. Sometimes at play, Roxanne was a bit rough on Miss Kitty. Once, she locked her in a closet. One day Miss Kitty dashed down my long hallway and flew into Roxanne's face as she sat on a sofa in my front room. I was horrified! Not a mark was left on Roxanne, but the cat's space gained respect.

At the end of August, there was an extra amount in my allowance check. My story, "Surrender of the Witch Doctor," had been published in the third quarter issue of the *Junior Teacher* Sunday school quarterly. I had sent in the story when I was in the full body cast. As the Africans say, "If you are carrying a pot of water on your head and the pot breaks, *take a bath!*" Since I could not go to Africa, I contributed in other ways. Letters from Africa encouraged me along the way. Ibrahama Namiten had been good to travel and interpret for me when I first got to Nakpanduri. He wrote that he was now pastoring at Najong. His wife had presented him with a baby girl. He sent greetings and news from his brother, Nyankpen, the head clinic orderly.

After the Pan-African Conference in Nigeria, several missionaries wrote declaring it a marvelous success. The total attendance, from many African countries, was two hundred twenty. Edwin went as Field Chairman, and twenty-two others from Ghana attended. No delegate came from Zaire, the former Congo. Missionary J.W. Tucker was killed in the Congo a short time before the conference. Back in Ghana, Edwin and Bernice Ziemann sent thanks for the financial help. The Wheeler Andersons wrote that the keys to my personal barrels arrived so they could empty them. What a job! They said the next General Council of Ghana would be held at Kumbungu on the Bible School campus and they might sell some of my *stuff* to pastors. Rev. Franklin McCorkle was the Principal and his wife, Aneice, was teaching. Ruby Johnson wrote in September that she was with the McCorkles in Kumbungu for some much needed rest. She said to be alone to treat nearly one hundred patients four days per week, be on call twenty-four hours a day to deliver babies, and take emergencies was *for the birds*! Those were Ruby's famous words; I termed it *inhumane*! Ruby had been in Saboba alone since Helen left and was on her way to the coast to meet Nurse Hilda Palenius, her next co-worker. Midwives were scarce in America and the many nurses did not want to leave a lucrative practice to go to Africa for an allowance of less than one hundred dollars per month. This eventually led to my determination to get Ghanaian young people trained in the medical field to help us. Ruby wrote, "Everyone would be glad to have you back, Charlese, especially the Konkombas!" My *heart fell down* when Ruby reported that one Konkomba pastor was *sacked* for adultery. She said, "We still have Pastor Namyela; he lives for God and is full of the Holy Spirit."

Rev. and Mrs. Phillips went from the conference in Nigeria to Accra for a meeting of the Mission Committee (made up of Ghana missionaries only) on October 17. Then they went four hundred miles north for the Ghana General Council, which included both missionaries and Ghanaians, held on Kumbungu Bible School Campus. The first *Constitution and By-laws of the General Council of the Assemblies of God of*

Ghana was adopted. From that point on, officers elected or appointed could be missionaries and Ghanaians. Rev. Lehmann was elected the first Superintendent and Rev. Gyanfoso, Assistant. For the rest of October, Rev. and Mrs. Phillips had a heavy itinerary to visit stations from Bawku and back to Accra, the capitol city, where they flew to America.

While this was going on in Ghana, my work in New Mexico was changing. I, not my Public Health Instructor who told me about the job, was hired to teach at the Albuquerque School of Practical Nursing under the Bureau of Indian Affairs (BIA). This BIA was under the Federal Department of Health, Education, and Welfare (HEW). I could not bear to write a letter to Rev. Phillips; I phoned him. I told him about the Civil Service position and that I could not take it while thinking I was going to return to Africa. *I resigned.* After I put it in writing, he wrote, "The brethren of the Foreign Missions Committee wish me to write of their sincere appreciation for your dedication to the work of God that took you to Ghana and has held you bound these years. We desire that the Lord will work out His very best plan for your life, and we will trust God together with you to that end. We will hold your account for a time until we can correspond with your District Superintendent. Your allowance will continue through January 1965. Keep me acquainted with your welfare and I will report it to the Committee." I said I wished my funds could be used *for a better house for the nurses in Saboba,* but that anything decided would be fine with me. In a few weeks, it was decided that the remaining two thousand dollars should go to the Southern Ghana project at Saltpond. That was my last link to the mission at that time! Even harder was the task of telling the Ghanaians and the people in America who showed the utmost confidence in me by faithful prayer and finances through the years. I told them in my Christmas letter. A letter of resignation went to the New Mexico District Council. They placed an item in the District News. Rev. R.H. Hudson, NMDC Superintendent, responded with a letter similar to the one I received from Rev. Phillips.

My beginning date at the Indian School of PN-HEW was November 23. I was hired to teach Obstetrics and Pediatrics at Fort Defiance-Window Rock. Temporarily, I was teaching Fundamentals of Nursing in Albuquerque, as that instructor was ill. I continued to work relief at Battaan Memorial (Lovelace) Hospital through January 2, so the night supervisor could have a leave. My two supervisors, at Battaan and at BIA, knew about this transition. Since my permanent job would be outside of Albuquerque, I spoke one last time for the ladies of the Pilots Club who had paid for my basic nursing course at St. Joseph Hospital years ago. They seemed so proud of their efforts to sponsor when they heard what I had been doing in Africa and that I was now going into nursing education. I kept in touch with them through Mildred Stamps, a member of the club who was employed by Albuquerque National Bank. Through a lady I met at Battaan Hospital, I spoke a last time to a ladies' group at Sandia Base, a U.S. Government facility.

January 1965 was transition month. Karen Hughes came to my house for a farewell lunch. I rented my house to a soldier and his wife from Sandia Base and they were to move in by the middle of February. My last shift at Battaan Hospital was January 22. I moved to Gallup, New Mexico on the January 29. No one had lived in the beautiful, new hospital residence complex where they assigned me a temporary apartment. The whole hospital was new. I was to teach Obstetric and Pediatric Theory to the Indian girls before they rotated to Fort Defiance-Window Rock Hospital on the New Mexico-Arizona border for hands-on clinical practice. I was very happy while teaching the Indian girls, but I wanted a life outside of the medical arena. My niece, Roxanne, was old enough to correspond with me. She wrote from Albuquerque, "Dear Auntie Who, We heard you had a bad flood in Gallup. I guess you weren't bothered by it, as you live on Hill Street. My dog, Potty, is doing well." That was our pet name for Spotty.

In Gallup, I met an interesting young nurse, Anna Olsen, who had accepted a Civil Service nursing placement at the Gallup Indian Hospital. She and her sister, Betty, had come from Long Island, New York. Their parents had come from Norway and built a three-story house on Long Island, where they raised thirteen children. Some of their family attended the Assembly of God in Bethpage, New York. I met Anna's sister, Betty, at a Gallup church where Rev. Adrian Harper and family pastored. I enjoyed Anna and Betty and their *cultural shock*. Anna and Betty went on excursions on their days off. They were also intrigued by the cowboy influence, and enjoyed a few encounters. My friendship with Anna, Betty, Marie, Ruth, and other members of that family remains today. Anna moved on to more education and employment at Stanford University Hospital in San Francisco. Betty has remained a friend to my whole Spencer family in New Mexico.

One day, Marjorie Lewis phoned from Albuquerque's BIA. The Fundamentals Instructor who had been ill was now having surgery. I was to commute thirty-five miles from Gallup to Fort Defiance Hospital to supervise students doing practical experience. BIA assigned a new automobile for my commuting; my Ford was parked. Driving from Gallup to Fort Defiance got tedious. One morning my car was straddling the middle white line as I read the manual. Well, I was flipping through to the jokes! One said, "There would be fewer motorist patients in the hospitals if there were more patient motorists on the roads." That was when I heard the siren and saw the flashing light of a reservation police car. The policeman asked, "Were you straddling the middle line?" I said, "Yes, I didn't want to run off the road." He asked, "Were you reading?" I said, "Yes, I get bored driving this same road every weekday so I was reading the new car manual." He asked, "Did you know you were driving fifteen miles over the speed limit?" I honestly did not know that; I thought I had been watching and told him so. He said, "You could hit animals; this is an open range. Have the speedometer of this new car tested for accuracy." He gave me a ticket that could cost me nearly one hundred dollars, but he was very kind. I was told which chief I should report to for payment. On my way back to Gallup that evening, I stopped by to pay the fine. The Chief told me they used the money to help disturbed Indian boys. He read me from the slip of paper, "I suggest leniency; this was a very polite motorist." Then he said, "It will not hurt you to help us with these boys so you will pay fifteen dollars." I paid! I thanked him very much, left, and stuck to the road rules.

A letter from Wheeler and Eilene Anderson in Tamale said, "It truly made me sad to open your personal things when you were not here. I think you should have someone with you when you open and unpack the two drums I am sending you. You may wonder why we are sending some things; we just had to use our best judgment. You said to give the basketball and net to a missionary child the right age. We gave it to *our own Kimball*; he was so pleased. When he comes from Jos, Nigeria on leave, he will use it. Benny Kessler and Bradley Driggers played with it when they were here, but they are a bit too small yet. The Tamale Church bought the bell and we kept brooms, paper products, and clothespins for the Tamale guesthouse. Wheeler bought the hacksaw, pliers, and steel rule. Bernice Ziemann needed an eggbeater in the worst way! I hope you have received your minutes of the conference at Kumbungu and saw that you were officially spoken of and thanked for money for Saltpond, Saboba, and travel to the conference in Nigeria. Eloise and Ruth from Nakpanduri, Sarah Cather from the Baptist Mission, Aneice and Franklin, Brahma who drives the lorry called Think Twice, even the Paul Chastagners and others from Upper Volta came by and bought some things. The Baptist Hospital in Nalerigu took the autoclave. Drs. Faile and Richardson said they tried it out before they paid for it. They had written an amount into their budget for an autoclave; they paid two hundred fifty cedes. The Executive Committee said you wanted that money to go to Saboba Clinic and they will honor your request. One day we had dinner with the Fosters and Diane Lay, the head nurse at Nalerigu. She said they were thrilled with the autoclave. In fact, they would be glad to have another one the same size!" Battaan Memorial Methodist (Lovelace) Hospital in Albuquerque had donated it. One day, as I ate a meal with Mark and Pauline Jernigan, I excitedly told them about the item. Mark, a plumber, went with me to where the autoclave was and showed me how to set it up workable. Louis and Lucille Davidson from First Church on North Second Street paid the freight to Africa. Eilene Anderson concluded her letter by saying they planned to transfer to Malawi for the balance of their term if the political situation allowed. I wondered why they were leaving Ghana. The two barrels of my personal items sent to me by the Andersons did come eventually.

Three months after launching my career in a new direction, I knew I was in physical trouble again. I phoned from Gallup to Dr. Newfeld, Gynecologist at Battaan Hospital, and made an appointment for April 6. Plans for surgery were set. That was the week of District Council in Albuquerque and I attended one night. The speaker was Rev. Zimmerman. He greeted me, but knew by then that I had resigned from the mission. He wished me well, but did not chide me about not being in Africa. I could not get leave to have surgery until May, when the other instructor was able to come back to teach the next rotation at Window Rock and Fort Defiance. Miss Kitty and I drove back to Gallup that night, as I must be at work the next morning. My cat stayed with my parents when I was in Albuquerque. If she thought I was ready to return to Gallup, she would sit on the hood of my car so I would not leave her behind. One weekend, Lou (Mae) and Dave Lynch, my sister and husband, came to Gallup from San Diego. They had come to show off my nephew, Kevin, who was a toddler. I told them to be careful with his being near Miss Kitty as she had not been around children and I had seen her fly at Roxanne. Dave, always quick with a reply, said, "And if she harms Kevin, I'll kill the (blasted) cat!" We got busy talking, when suddenly Dave directed my attention. There was Kevin and Miss Kitty; she was going around and round his legs, but being careful as if she knew he was a baby. Dave said, "So much for your vicious cat!"

As scheduled, I had surgery on May 10. It was impossible to explain how angry I was! It was necessary to stop the progress of endometriosis. I learned that bleeding into the abdominal cavity was painful. I drove from Gallup, parked my car in the parking lot at Battaan Hospital, and had surgery. I still knew most of the nurses. Flowers were delivered to my room one day. On the card attached was, "I, myself, welcome you to a new room for recovery. Love, Niece Roxanne." A week later, I put on my clothing, including high-heel-shoes, picked up my suitcase, and went to my car in the parking lot. After a spinal fusion, this had been like having a tooth pulled. I drove across town to the home of my brother, Calvin Lee, and his family on La Plata NW where my niece, Roxanne, did welcome me to a room and I rested a few days. Then I picked up Miss Kitty, who was staying with Mom and Dad, and we went back to my job in Gallup.

About the middle of June, I took three more days off to go to my nephew's high school graduation in San Diego. Jim Lynch, who sacrificed his famous wind-up record player to Africa, was now graduating from high school. He was my first! I drove to Phoenix, where I met Mom and Dad. Together, we drove to San Diego for the graduation and back to Phoenix. I drove back to Gallup by way of Payson, Arizona, where my aunt and uncle owned a cabin. I visited them over the weekend and was back to work on Monday in Gallup.

I was still receiving letters from missionaries and Africans. Helen Kopp wrote that she was sailing back to Ghana. Jim Kessler, as business manager, wrote from Saltpond,

"Helen did indeed arrive on June 5 to be with Hilda Palenius at Saboba Clinic." He expressed thanks for the last two thousand dollars to close out my account at Mission Headquarters. He reported that their daughters, Vangie and Annette, were home for holidays from school in Jos, Nigeria. Their son, Ben, had completed second grade in home schooling. The *Elder McCorkle*, as Ruby called Franklin, and his family, were leaving in July for furlough in the United States. Ruby Johnson was traveling with them.

I received another phone call from Miss Marjorie Lewis, my BIA employer. She said that Elizabeth Brock, Medical-Surgical Instructor in Gallup, was taking maternity leave, so she wanted me to teach that rotation. Theory lectures and clinical practice in Med-Surg took place in Gallup. For the months of June and July, I did not have to commute, so I returned the government car. It had been both challenging and rewarding to teach this same group of nursing students through their fundamentals, obstetrics, pediatrics, and med-surg. I was so happy in the hospital setting and when teaching the Indian girls. I was not comfortable, however, living in Gallup permanently. It was a deep feeling like, "If I can't go back to Africa, then I don't want something that remotely reminds me of it." I'm not sure what did, except that they called their headman *Chief*. The scenery around Gallup was beautiful; people could spend days seeing De Chelly and Chaco Canyons, the ice caves, red rock formations, sky city of Acoma, other Pueblos, ruins, and interests. Then there was Ship Rock farther north toward the *four corners*. I had lived in New Mexico all my early life and knew its enchantment. When Dad and Mom came for a visit, my Aunt Leonora and Uncle Nevin came from Phoenix at the same time. We went for a picnic among the red rocks and I discovered that the ants and gnats were as numerous as in Ghana's Ashanti jungle. My visiting family met Anna and Betty Olsen from Long Island for the first time. Their paths have crossed many times since.

I searched the nursing journals for teaching positions. One offer came from Taos; that would not help. When I received a reply to my inquiry from Miss Ilse C. Steg, Director of the Wesley School of Nursing in Wichita, Kansas, something clicked. It would be a step up from teaching practical nursing to a diploma program. In the mid-1960s, I would be following, *in reverse*, my Mother Spencer's journey from Kansas in the late 1880s to teach in New Mexico. She had come from a teacher's normal in Hays and ten years of teaching in Kansas. I would be going to Wichita, not Hays, but it was Kansas. At that time I did not know my grandfather had first migrated west to Dodge City and Medicine Lodge, Kansas in the late 1870s before going to Oklahoma and then coming on to New Mexico in 1880. When my grandparents met and married in New Mexico, they had Kansas and Oklahoma in common. I sent my application with required references to Wichita; they included Matron of South London Hospital in England, Instructor at UNM, and Director of Nursing at Battaan Hospital. I sent the name of Rev. Hudson at NMDC to represent my employment in Africa from 1953 to the mid 1960s. I do not know if all replied to Miss Steg, but the last two replied even to me. Miss Ahna Blake wrote, "We wish we could offer you a position and salary to keep you here at Battaan Memorial Hospital." It was a very nice complement. I had kept Marjorie Lewis informed about the status of my leaving ISPN-HEW. On July 7, I wrote Miss Ilse Steg that I could be in Wichita by August 15, 1965 for the start of a semester. She seemed pleased and replied by introducing me to part of their faculty, "Roberta (Bobbie) Thiry, Assistant Director; Helen Halstead, the Med-Surg-OB Coordinator; Joan Wells, the obstetrics instructor I would work with, who attended the Assembly of God."

My body threw me one last wallop before I left New Mexico. A lump the size of a walnut was removed from my right breast the last day of July. The doctor said it was possibly a combination of hormone changes caused by recent surgery and the black bruising that occurred when I was injured in Africa. A biopsy indicated no cancer; I was in and out of Battaan Hospital quickly and ready for the move. My house in Albuquerque was rented to the same military family. By now, they were looking forward to the birth of their first child. Miss Kitty rode all the way to Kansas with me as I pulled my piano and other belongings in a U-Haul trailer behind the Ford Galaxy. That was a far cry from the mode of transportation my grandfather and grandmother used to travel from Kansas and Oklahoma to New Mexico in the 1880s and 1890s. Ben was the wagon train boss; Sarah came by train with a steamer trunk. My friends, the Bonneys, have that trunk; it is so fragile by now.

In Wichita, I rented an apartment on Gilbert Street. It wasn't fancy, but space was more important to me. Even as I was unpacking, I had a houseguest. Loretta Lebsack had been a co-worker with Bonnie Roll in Nebraska Sunday School promotions. Now Bonnie was in Ghana as Peggy Scott's co-worker. I was sort of a link to Bonnie in Ghana; she was interested to know more about it. Also, Loretta and I had gone to Southwestern College in Texas at the same time. She said she might soon be married to a Nebraska rancher; that possibility become reality.

On the first day at my new employment, Miss Steg took me out to dinner to meet some Wesley instructors: Joan Wells, Katie Holl, and Helen Halstead with her husband, Norm. Katherine Holl, teacher of Med-Surg Nursing, had been a missionary in Africa; she was the faculty humorist. My new teaching job started on August 16, 1965. Joan and I shared an office since we would teach obstetrics together. She was comfortable to be with from the very first day. Her mother and stepfather, Helen and Woodie, had a cabin at a lake with a carved woodpecker on the outside wall beside the door. As time passed, the family included me on day trips.

In exactly two weeks, *I was a patient* in Wesley Medical Center. I had another huge lump in the right breast; same side as before! It was *not cancer*. I was grateful, but I have seen few people as angry as I was! After surgery, the doctor came to my room and said, "You have had nothing for pain and the incision was deep and extensive; there is no need to be stoic!" I did not explain: I was angry enough to be mute. He ordered an analgesic stat and at specific times. I was fed up at my body calling the shots! On the evening I spent in the hospital, Wichita experienced tornados. Betty Ann Lynch, a new instructor for pediatrics from Kansas City, came to visit me in the hospital. She said, "Did you know we are in the midst of tornados?" I asked how she knew. She said as she left her apartment to go to her car, she felt her feet were skimming the grass instead of walking on it. Inside her car, the warnings came on her radio. I asked why she went out in it! She said she had lived in Kansas all her life and *took tornados as they came*. My mother had told us about tornados she experienced as a child near Roswell, New Mexico. She said they blew wheat straw through a telephone pole and picked up a barn but left a small tub untouched on the ground. I was having second thoughts about my newfound Kansas home! When I was discharged, Katie Holl, the Med-Surg Instructor, insisted she transport me home from the hospital; someone brought my car later. I knew I did not need that pampering, but that kind of friendship continued with the Wesley Nursing Faculty.

Marjorie Lewis, my supervisor at ISPN-HEW in New Mexico, sent me a graduation program for the class I taught. I had rotated along with them and taught almost their entire course. She reported on their academic honors and rank in the class; they all passed their State Board exams. I felt I had given them my best. I was nostalgic that I did not see them graduate, but sent them congratulations.

It was mandatory that I be licensed with the Kansas State Board of Nursing to teach in Wichita. Miss Steg expected us to be active in Kansas nursing organizations and she usually held an office in one or more. She even expected us to be members of the American Nurses' Association, National League of Nursing as well as their Kansas branches. Since I kept up my membership in New Mexico and the American College of Nurse Midwifery, my annual dues were no small amount. Miss Steg sent instructors to represent Wesley School of Nursing at many state and national conventions and encouraged us to accept nominations for office. I accepted one. I became the secretary of a Kansas branch of an educational committee. Our activity report, as a Wesley Faculty Member, was due *monthly*. We reported on our time in class, the hospital units, committees, planning sessions, and even extra-curricular activities like civic presentations attended. I felt it added up to more than twenty-four hours per day and *loved every minute of it*!

In Kansas, I was on Ruby Johnson's home turf. She had even been a classmate in nurse's training with Miss Steg, my employer and Betty Ann Lynch, the newly hired Pediatric Instructor. I often saw Ruby at one of the churches in Kansas, as she itinerated to return to Ghana. It was interesting to watch another missionary present her plans. She went back to Ghana in November 1965 *without a co-worker*. Helen and Hilda were at Saboba. In January 1966, Helen Kopp wrote from Saboba that they had a ten-day revival effort with Stanley and Ethel McPherson. Many made a commitment to Christ. Among the thirteen filled with the Holy Spirit were Deacon Beso and his wife; Bilijo and their son Gewen; Belati's wife, Nabel; Beyimba from the Toma Chief's area; and others from the Saboba Chief's section near the clinic. In March, the news media reported that Ghana had a political coup, resulting in a change of government control. This is not an easy situation for expatriates! Missionaries are expected to be politically neutral, but can find themselves in harm's way!

Wesley School of Nursing was to have an evaluation for accreditation by the National League of Nursing in March 1966. This was new and terrified me! However, by the end of February, my faculty report said, "Completed work on Obstetrics Course Outline." Joan and I had done this above and beyond teaching the students in classroom and clinical supervision. We had made full use of the expertise of Helen Hallstead, our Coordinator, and Roberta (Bobby) Thiry, Assistant Director of the School. I was usually overly organized. Once Bobby asked me, "And when you get *that* organized, where do you go from there? It must not be sterile and finished; it must be fluid, changing, and improving." If her files looked like mine, she would be unable to function. If my desk looked like hers, I would have been useless and fired. The Thiry family had relatives in Albuquerque. The first Christmas I was at Wesley, Don, Roberta, and their children, Mark and Adriel, were injured in a horrible accident while returning from New Mexico.

I got involved in a small church about three blocks from my house. By doing that, I met another family in Kansas that has continued to be important in my life. They were also very good friends to Ruby Johnson. The family was Rev. Paul and Bernice Lowenberg; Sandi and Doug were their children. Sandi was in high school and very musical. Doug, in junior high was into sports. Paul Lowenberg was the Superintendent of Kansas District Council of the Assemblies of God. Bernice was the Director for the Women's Ministries for the State of Kansas. They traveled extensively inside the United States and out. The Lowenbergs knew I lived alone and that I knew very few people in Kansas. They started calling me to sleep at their house when they were to be away. Sandi and Doug would say, "Now, Charlese, you are not babysitting, you are our companion." They were really helping me! At times in summers at Wheatstate Camp, Mrs. Lowenberg, as Director of Kansas women's programs, seemed to be partly responsible to get camp ready. Sandi and Doug worked along side their mom; this impressed me so! I started going to help them when my job allowed. When anyone became weary, Mrs. Lowenberg would say, "Now, remember, you are doing this for Jesus!" Then that small, unusual laugh, as clear as a bell, would follow.

One day I got home from work at Wesley and met Miss Kitty's absence. Usually she came as soon as she saw my car arrive. Now, I ask myself, "What were you thinking to leave her out when you were not at home?" I would know *not* to do that now. Shortly thereafter, there was a knock at my door. Two children said, "Miss Kitty was hit by a car; she is in the street!" We had lived there such a short time; I did not know my neighbors knew her name. I started out to the street when a man and his wife from next door said, "Don't go there. We will get her for you." They put her in a small box and drove me out of town to a rolling, green hillside. We buried her under a beautiful tree. I cried as my heart hurt. My eleven-year-old niece, Roxanne, wrote me again, "So sorry about Miss Kitty! I am sending you a picture of her. I am not sure you have one. *Sincerely yours*."

The accreditation visit of examiners from the National League of Nursing to Wesley School of Nursing proceeded as planned in March. Diploma schools of nursing, which Wesley was, were being phased out. Nursing educators favored a degree in nursing, even if it was an associate degree (AD) with a particular school. Joan and I had to justify our obstetrics outline and lesson plans in person, as did all department instructors. Their only comment to us was, "Remember, you are not teaching a course in midwifery; these are *beginner nurses!*" Our students could probably have safely done an emergency delivery of a baby at the completion of our course! Wesley School of Nursing passed inspection and received approval to function as a valid diploma school. In April, an Obstetric, Gynecology, and Neonatal Nursing Conference was, very conveniently, held in Albuquerque. Joan Wells and I went to represent Wesley and learn what we could. We drove my car, as it was cheaper than two to fly. We stayed with my brother, Calvin Lee, on La Plata, so had no hotel fees to report; I had a visit with family. June 1966 was capping and graduation for Wesley students. I had been there ten months and it felt super to be a part of turning out needed nurses.

Helen wrote from Saboba that she was taking every delivery case, as opposed to taking every other one when there were two midwives in Saboba. I knew from experience that it was hard to be on call every hour of the day and night. General outpatient clinics and emergencies day and night could keep Hilda equally busy. We needed Ghanaian nurses and midwives to help the Americans and to fill in when Americans were on furlough. I decided to talk to mission officials and get permission to explore how to get Ghanaians trained to help at these specific times. Also, the churches were well established; they would become "indigenous." That is, the Ghanaians would pastor them. What about the clinics?

My nephew, James M. Lynch, donor of the wind-up record player, was a freshman at the University of California in San Diego, 1966. While there, Congressman Bob Wilson nominated him for appointment to the U.S. Naval Academy at Annapolis. Jim wrote me from the Academy in June, "I have a bruise everywhere there isn't enough muscle to cover the bone well. I think I will be very happy here if I can learn to do without food, sleep, and my three-year-old brother, Kevin." My vacation was two weeks in July, but not consecutive. I convinced Evelyn, Roxanne's mom, to allow my niece to stay with me for one of those weeks. I was finally enjoying my own nieces and nephews and their progress.

CHAPTER THIRTEEN

Teaching in Wichita:
Plans for Africa Again

UGUST 1966 WAS MY anniversary. I had been teaching
at Wesley School of Nursing a whole year; it seemed
like only days. The later months of 1966 fairly whirled
with activities of teaching and travel to nursing organization
activities. I bought a season ticket for Wichita Civic Music
and enjoyed attending with other instructors. Dino's Piano
Concert was most impressive; he seemed so young with this
mammoth talent. For Christmas 1966, I rode to Albuquerque
with the Thirys. On the day we were to return, a snowstorm
hit. We needed to report to work on time so we left on Route
66 in the snow, only to be stranded near the Texas border
and have to spend the night in a Tucumcari motel. The storm
plagued us all the way to Wichita.

In April 1967, I wrote Everett Phillips about the possibility of my returning to Africa. As the mission board had
demanded, I held a full-time job for at least a year with no
great problem. I also reported to Miss Steg, my boss, about
my plans. I was also tempted to stay and help turn out nurses
for America. Miss Steg tried to persuade me to do just that
by showing me positive things about Kansas. She had a visi-

tor from Germany, where she was born. She took him to a Registered White Charloi Cattle Ranch and invited me to go along. The owner drove us around the pasture in a luxury vehicle and called each animal by name. They had a number and were registered in his book. Another trip was to Medicine Lodge to see a portrayal of the wagon trains arriving from the east in the mid-1800s. I even got a raise in salary ahead of time. In spite of all this, I eventually submitted my resignation effective the end of 1967; it gave Miss Steg time to recruit.

Betty Olsen had gone back to Long Island sometime after I left Gallup, but we had continued to correspond. Anna, her sister, had gone for more education in nursing. Betty wrote me about how ill their mother was with cancer and she did die. Then Betty wrote to see if I had an extra bedroom and if I wanted someone to share my apartment. My answer was, "Yes, *to all of the above.*" In April 1967 Betty and her sister, Ruth, whom I had not met, arrived in Wichita. Betty found employment; Ruth returned to New York.

My parents came to Wichita in an RV July 1967. They were on their way to see Kurt, their newest grandchild, born in Seattle January 27. They had sold their business in Albuquerque, bought a ranch in Monticello and a home and business in Truth or Consequences, New Mexico (The former Hot Springs). They were taking a vacation before opening their new business. While they were with me, we spent time in my basement, as we had some of our most fierce tornado warnings. When I told my parents about a School of Mission's outing to Branson, Missouri; they decided to go there before continuing to Seattle. Betty and I joined them for that weekend. We watched *The Little Shepherd of the Hills* in an outdoor theater; the schoolhouse burned again. My vacation extended to the end of July, so I decided to accompany my parents to Seattle, see the new baby, and take a plane back to Kansas. A trip with my parents had been impossible since I was a young girl. We crossed the Badlands National

Park in South Dakota, and continued on to Mt. Rushmore. At Yellowstone National Park, we met family members for a small reunion. My handsome nephew, Darrald Ray, was nine. Vicki, my niece, was seven and such a doll. Dad, Mom, and I left the reunion early and drove through Montana to Waterton Glacier National Park. I mailed myself a card to Wichita from Canada. It said, "To remind you of how fortunate you are to share a wonderful trip like this with your parents." We rushed on to Seattle to see baby Kurt and the proud parents. After a quick trip to the top of the Seattle Needle, I had a plane to catch and a job waiting in Kansas! The grandparents remained to dote.

Ruby Johnson joined me in Kansas City one time when I was to speak at a mission convention. She was about to return to Africa. Pastor U.S. Grant had supported her efforts in Saboba for years. At that convention, she announced that I should "Raise money to replace the Saboba house *if the Missions Department expected young American nurses to go there.*" She and I had probably done more building and repair on and around the mud and rock house than anyone; she said we could not add-on any longer! A short time later, she wrote that she was having a few missionary meetings in Florida before leaving the United States in October 1967. She planned to study language in Tamale until one of the clinics needed a nurse. She did follow through with these plans. However, a letter dated soon after she arrived in Ghana said, "Ruby had a tumor removed at the Baptist Hospital in Nalerigu. On January 24, Dr. Faile delivered the results personally. Ruby is to go to the United States immediately for cancer treatment!" Helen, Hilda, and Rev. Namyela rushed from Saboba to Tamale to join in a rather sad farewell for Ruby. She flew to Kumasi the next morning, where Vernon and Maxine Driggers arranged her flight back to Miami, Florida. Ruby knew a doctor there who was excellent at cancer treatment. A letter from Bob Cobb, Mission Chairman in Ghana, said he heard I had received reappointment. Helen had been called

home to a sick father and had resigned from mission nursing. He wanted me there immediately. I had a job, no funds
raised for me or a house, and no co-worker. Hilda wrote that
she was closing the Saboba Clinic, sent me the inventory,
and said the keys would be with Herb Griffin in Tamale. She
planned to take midwifery in Scotland before returning to
Ghana, perhaps with Virginia Turner. I had just written Virginia Turner, a new nurse I'd met only in School of Missions
at Headquarters. She had never seen the Saboba house, but I
was writing all nurses. Then suddenly, Everett Phillips sent
out a letter from mission headquarters in Missouri about *our
terrible loss of Virginia*. She was driving to speak at a church
on Sunday morning when her car struck a bridge abutment.
Mercy, that was one day before I wrote her about the Saboba
house! No wonder I had no reply! Hilda replied, "I will send
what I can toward a new house for Saboba." I never heard
from Helen about the house; she had truly resigned and was
staying in the United States. Eloise, in the United States on
furlough, had left Ruth Anderson at the Nakpanduri Clinic
with a retired lady, so she would not be alone.

Even with cancer, Ruby's heart was still in Ghana and
she wrote me, "*When you get to Saboba and get your hat off,
let me know about building the new house. A man has promised
twelve hundred dollars toward the project!*" David Richards, her
Kansas District Missions Secretary, and his wife, once visited Saboba and declared the house *impossible to live in*. A
question posed by another visiting church official was, "Did
anyone from New Mexico ever come here and see what
you were living in?" One man encouraged me by saying he
would build it under the MAPS program. That meant he
would provide support for himself and his wife if I raised
the money for construction. Encouraging word came from
Edwin Ziemann, the new Mission Chairman in Ghana. He
reported that the Executive Committee decided the old house
in Saboba should be replaced, but strongly recommended
that the new permanent bedroom, built by Ruby with New

Mexico money, be included in any new plans. I wrote about the MAPS offer to Everett Phillips in Missouri and the new Mission Chairman in Ghana. Letters came from both saying that they agreed, but it would take at least ten thousand dollars and it *must be a Field Project*. Ruby reminded me that nurses had helped on Field Projects to build houses at other stations, why not have Saboba for the next *Field Project?* We nurses were not on committees; we were too busy. A committee was not likely to see the Saboba house for nurses as a priority for a Field Project. We nurses could raise funds; we only needed their permission. It took little math to multiply three thousand five hundred dollars times New Mexico, Kansas, and West Texas Districts! We could get the ten thousand dollars; it should not be difficult! I felt the chances were slim there would ever be a new house for the nurses regardless of how many times we raised the money, got offers to build through MAPS, or repaired the Saboba house. Saboba Clinic would close or be turned over to the Ghana Government when younger nurses could not be found or could not cope with what they found at Saboba. The church had been established by the clinics; it did not seem right to leave the remote tribe with no medical aid inside its borders. They were remote; that is why the opportunity opened to the mission.

Another shocker, on the heels of news about Ruby and Virginia, arrived in a letter from Phillip Hogan at Missions Headquarters. He informed us that the private plane carrying Tallmadge and Marjorie Butler and son Stephen, age eleven, disappeared in flight from Fort Lauderdale to the Bahamas (possible victims of the *Bermuda Triangle)*. They were on their way to Senegal, West Africa, for their third term. It struck me forcibly that the song Tallmadge sang and dedicated to me at the 1960 Mission Conference in Takoradi was *really for them.*

At the Kansas Wheatstate Camp Mission Service, I was asked to announce my re-appointment to Ghana, West

Africa. From there I started speaking almost every weekend. Everett Phillips, still with portfolio over mission efforts in Africa, informed Mission Secretaries Raymond Hudson in New Mexico and David Richards in Kansas. He alerted them, as well as the chairman in Ghana, that I was authorized to raise funds for my budget while holding my job. One day I was a guest to dinner with the Lowenbergs. Pastor and Mrs. Greisen and Pastor and Mrs. Lewis Hollis were also there. The Lowenbergs and I happily discussed my good news. Rev. Greisen handed me a dollar bill and said, "This is for seed; it will multiply and get you back to Africa." My first presentation after reappointment was in El Dorado, where the Benigas family pastored. The eldest Benigas daughter, Brenda, was planning a career in missions; she and Sandy Lowenberg were high school friends.

Director Ilse Steg informed me I must orient the person who was replacing me January 1968. Joan Wells and I were also to have the Obstetric Nursing Course Outline completed and ready for use by the new instructor in August 1968. We did these requirements, as well as the classroom and clinical teaching of obstetric students. I was driving to speak at churches on Wednesdays and Sundays. On December 31, 1967, I left my teaching job at Wesley School of Nursing in Wichita. I felt the loss in many ways.

In January 1968, I had no job, so I went to ten churches in six Kansas towns, five within Wichita. (Pastor W.R. Boyd, whom I met at Newton, became the Belen, New Mexico pastor later in the 1980s.) John Hollis was pastor at Seneca Assembly in Wichita and R.F. Hollis was at Caney. My last presentation in January was at Glad Tidings Assembly in Wichita for Pastor David Richards, State Missions Director. Ruby also spoke of him highly. After that, I drove to New Mexico to decide where to live.

The last week of January 1968, I left my car in New Mexico and flew to Wichita. Betty helped me move my furniture to TorC, New Mexico in a huge U-Haul. She was keeping the Wichita apartment for a while. I moved into a tiny rent-house on the back of my parents' property. We drove my car back to Kansas, where I was traveling to the far-flung borders of that state for the rest of February. That same month, Rev. and Mrs. Paul Lowenberg were speakers at a Ministers' Seminar in Louisiana. They met Rev. Mary (Gray) Waldon, Louisiana District Women's Director, a former New Mexico friend of mine. Her husband was Loyce Waldon, the Louisiana District Superintendent. They had invited the Lowenbergs, who held those same offices in Kansas, to be speakers. Mary wrote that my dear Mrs. Bernice Lowenberg gave me the highest recommendation. Since I was planning to return to Africa, Mary wanted me to speak at their women's meeting during the Louisiana District Council in June of 1968. I accepted and noted the date.

My February schedule started at Chanute, Kansas where I learned Pastor Owens' daughter was married to the son of Sectional Presbyter, O.W. Hollis. The McCleskeys, Pastors at Chetopa, had once pastored in West Texas, so they knew the Homer Goodwin missionary family to Ghana. The Pastor's wife at Cherryvale was a niece of Mary Watkins, an Albuquerque Pastor. Since my next meeting was not to be until Sunday, I drove back to Wichita to get my mail. John Hollis, DCAP and STL Representative, was keeping my mail at his Kansas District Council office. On Sunday, February 11, I drove north on the Kansas Turnpike to Topeka for two services. I spoke in a morning service at Faith Assembly for Presbyter O.W. Hollis. The Hollis name appeared so often in Kansas that I found myself speaking that name with respect! On Sunday evening, I spoke at First Assembly for Pastor Clare G. Rose. My Lowenberg friends had pastored that church when their new building went up. When Paul Lowenberg was voted in as Kansas District Superintendent, they moved to Wichita. Sandy and Doug, the Lowenberg children, told me so much about their *Aunt Ethel May in Topeka* that I could not possibly have stayed anywhere else.

Ethel May still wrote for the church bulletin. After I left, she wrote, "The missionary service last Sunday with Charlese had no dull moments. Not many American nurse-midwives want to go to Africa. Her proposed objective was to get African nurses and midwives trained to make the clinics indigenous, as opposed to closing them. It is hoped that Ruby Johnson will be able to return later and help to accomplish this."

In Pleasanton, the pastor was Bill Roberts. His brother, Jerry, was the DCAP (Youth Director) in New Mexico at the time. Jerry would be helping to provide my STL vehicle for Africa in the next few months. Pastor Rayborn and wife in LeRoy knew my friends Cecil and Lois (Bates) Holley and the Roy Stewarts, as both had pastored in Clovis, New Mexico, where the Rayborn's son was in the U.S. military. I stayed with a lady named Bates while I drove to meetings in Woodstown, Kensington, and Phillipsburg. I walked a mile a day and practiced piano. I was scheduled by Pastor Floyd Dennis to speak at the church on Woodston Campground; I had never been to that camp. I had only been to the Wheatstate Campground near Wichita. The Pleasant Grove pastor was named Rosenberg; they moved to Medicine Lodge after I spoke. The Anspaughs took the pastorate at Pleasant Grove and asked me back for the second service. On a Saturday afternoon, I spoke at a women's banquet in Hays. Ladies came from Kensington, Pleasant Grove, Hoisington, Phillipsburg, and other nearby towns. Yes, *I finally got to Hays*, where my Grandmother Sarah Adkins (Mother Spencer) had completed Teachers Normal. I did not realize it was so far from Wichita! In seventy-two years, the Teachers Normal had evolved into Fort Hays University. I had an interview with the Director of the College of Nursing. To teach there I must have a master's degree; Ruby Johnson was teaching Obstetrics. She had been in the Gold Coast from 1949 to 1952, before it was Ghana. I spoke in the Hays Assembly on Sunday. Mrs. Jenkins, the pastor's wife, was a daughter of the Rosenbergs who had just moved to Medicine Lodge. I recalled my grandmother mentioning Larned, Russell, and other towns near Hays where I spoke. In Great Bend, Pastor and Mrs. Botsford had two children named Tommy and Linda. The ladies of the church gave me a huge white orchid.

On Monday, I phoned my friend, Joan (Weimer) Wagner, who lived in Great Bend with her husband, Richard. Joan and I had remained friends since taking a class together at the University of New Mexico in 1961. The Wagners had one daughter, Lisa Jo. Their son, James Richard, was born on March 3 just after my visit. Later, they had one more girl, Kristle. On February 29, I drove back to Wichita to leave a forwarding address with John Hollis at the Kansas District Council. I also bade farewell to friends at Wesley Hospital School of Nursing and the Kansas churches.

I had written to Missions Director Raymond Hudson that Betty Olsen might quit her job and itinerate with me in New Mexico as I did for Martha Roberts years before. I would not have to travel alone and Betty could help set up equipment. He said it sounded like a good idea. Betty resigned her job, gave up the apartment, stored her things, and joined me to New Mexico. I planned to be back for Kansas District Council in May, if I were not in Africa. On our way toward West Texas, we paused to have a second service with the Rosenbergs in Medicine Lodge, Kansas. They had moved from Pleasant Grove and were complaining that Medicine Lodge was too far from their daughter in Hays. Both these towns had to do with my grandparents. My Grandmother Adkins-Spencer got her education as a teacher at Hays Teachers Normal, before it became a Kansas University. My Grandfather Spencer learned his sawmill trade in Medicine Lodge, Kansas. The two never met until both got to New Mexico Territory, in the wild, wild, West, for different reasons and by much different methods of travel. But that's another story!

Printed in the United States
94385LV00009B/123/A